Compound Cinematics:
Akira Kurosawa and I

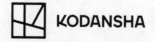

KODANSHA

Compound Cinematics: Akira Kurosawa and I

Shinobu Hashimoto

Translated by Lori Hitchcock Morimoto

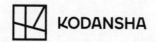 KODANSHA

Compound Cinematics: Akira Kurosawa and I
A VERTICAL Book

Translation: Lori Hitchcock Morimoto
Production: Risa Cho

FUKUGAN NO EIZO Watashi to Kurosawa Akira
by HASHIMOTO Shinobu

Copyright © 2006 HASHIMOTO Aya
All rights reserved.
Original Japanese edition published by Bungeishunju Ltd., Japan in 2006.
English translation rights reserved by Kodansha USA Publishing, LLC,
under the license granted by HASHIMOTO Aya, Japan
arranged with Bungeishunju Ltd., Japan

English language version produced by Kodansha USA Publishing, LLC, 2023

Previously published in hardcover in 2015

ISBN: 978-1-64729-322-2

Printed in the United States of America

First Paperback Edition

Kodansha USA Publishing, LLC
451 Park Avenue South
7th Floor
New York, NY 10016
www.kodansha.us

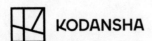

FOREWORD: "ONE BLOW"

A special foreword to Shinobu Hashimoto's *Compound Cinematics: Akira Kurosawa and I* by Masato Kato, Chairman, Writers Association of Japan

If the most famous Japanese filmmaker in the world is Akira Kurosawa, then the most well-known Japanese screenwriter is Shinobu Hashimoto.

Shinobu Hashimoto is a screenwriter among screenwriters, a towering summit in the Japanese film world.

When his memoir about his relationship with Akira Kurosawa was published as *Compound Cinematics: Akira Kurosawa and I*, it created a buzz amongst us cinema types for being a masterpiece.

The book offers a behind-the-scenes look at the peerless screenwriting team that supported the Kurosawa picture. It recounts in detail the roles played by Akira Kurosawa, Shinobu Hashimoto, Ryuzo Kikushima, and Hideo Oguni, first-class movie men, what their "repertoires" were, and how they constructed a screenplay.

In addition to being an entertaining work, grabbing the reader's heart and never letting go, it is an important document of film history.

The Hashimoto Screenplay's appeal can be summed up in one word: ferocity.

Even Hideo Oguni, his fellow scenarist on Team Kurosawa, conceded that Mr. Hashimoto wrote not just with his hand but with his elbow. Such was Mr. Hashimoto's authorial brawn, and no one could match the pressure he brought to bear on his pen-tip.

Meanwhile, Director Kurosawa said of the Hashimoto Screenplay that it was "covered in stakes," meaning bets. Discerning that his manuscripts were filled not just with words but with game chips, the director called Mr. Hashimoto, a famous fan of cycling races, "the gambler of cinema."

The Hashimoto Screenplay isn't the product of sheer brawn. It's composed according to his gambler's intuition and meticulous calculations.

Because his screenplays are both intricate and dynamic, their climaxes enfold overwhelming power. They go far beyond merely striking our hearts. With a destructive force a magnitude higher akin to a nuclear blast, they smash our hearts to pieces.

The screenwriter Shinobu Hashimoto wrote Akira Kurosawa's *Rashomon* in 1950 and made his film world debut at the age of thirty-two. As you know, it went on to win the Golden Bear Award at the Venice Film Festival—the first time a Japanese work fetched the grand prize in an international film festival.

In 1952, Mr. Hashimoto wrote *Ikiru*, and in 1954, *Seven Samurai*, participating in one Kurosawa picture after another. In just four years, no time at all, he stood at the summit of Japanese screenwriting. Following that, he took part in the collaborative scripting of Akira Kurosawa's *I Live in Fear* (1955), *Throne of Blood* (1957), *The Hidden Fortress* (1958), *The Bad Sleep Well* (1960), and *Dodes'ka-den* (1970).

The name Shinobu Hashimoto is most strongly associated with the screenplays of Kurosawa films, but he also supplied scenarios for many other filmmakers.

Tadashi Imai's *Darkness at Noon* (1956), Masaki Kobayashi's *Seppuku* (1962), Satsuo Yamamoto's *The Great White Tower* (1966), Kihachi Okamoto's *Japan's Longest Day* (1967), Yoshitaro Nomura's *Castle of Sand* (1974), Shiro Moritani's *The Village of the Eight Graves* (1977)—these masterpieces, each considered the representative work of eminent filmmakers, were all written by Shinobu Hashimoto.

It's fair to say that only Shinobu Hashimoto has such a brilliant oeuvre as a screenwriter. He is a solitary figure.

Mr. Hashimoto's road to cinema opened up when he met the director Mansaku Itami.

When asked by Itami, his screenwriting mentor, what stance an adaptation required, he responded:

> There's a cow…. I go to see it every day. In rain or shine… Standing in different spots, I watch it. And when I've discovered its weak spot, I open the gate and enter the pasture and with some sort of blunt object I fell it in one blow.

Then, using a sharp knife, he cuts the carotid artery and works with the blood that comes pouring out. What he needs isn't its shape or form, but only its fresh blood…

It was 1946, and young Hashimoto was only twenty-eight years old when he gave Mansaku Itami his take on the matter.

Twenty-eight years later, he took up the writing of the screenplay for *Castle of Sand* with Yoji Yamada.

Yoji Yamada felt that the original work was too complicated a story; perhaps it couldn't be turned into a film after all. Mr. Hashimoto showed him a passage in the novel that he'd underlined with a red pencil.

Those lines concerned an episode from the main character's past when he and his sickly father donned the clothing of pilgrims and wandered the country, begging.

This short description of a sad past was precisely the vulnerable spot in Seicho Matsumoto's original *Castle of Sand*. From there they spun the theme of "a man casting away his past for the sake of fame being avenged by that past."

Breaking the mold of a simple mystery movie, *Castle of Sand* grew into a magnificent human drama and an immortal masterpiece.

The original story was felled in one blow.

Another interesting bit is Yoshitaro Nomura's pronouncement that "For Mr. Kurosawa, Shinobu Hashimoto was a man he should never have encountered."

Director Nomura even asserts that Kurosawa would have been better off without the masterpieces *Rashomon*, *Ikiru*, and *Seven Samurai*. If it weren't for them, he argues, the director would have pursued entertainment and become the king of world cinema, an amalgam of Billy Wilder and William Wyler, since he had that sort of talent. Nomura shrewdly points out that the Hashimoto Screenplay ended up injecting ideas, philosophy, and social relevance into the Kurosawa film and that the burden hindered the director's pursuit of the pure entertainment appeal of cinema thereafter.

This was probably stated pedantically, but his words include a compliment that the bejeweled masterpieces *Rashomon*, *Ikiru*, and *Seven Samurai* could not have been born without Shinobu Hashimoto's talent. The Hashimoto Screenplay's composed air was what Director Nomura desired above all. To me, it comes across as a love letter: *Write them for me.*

The personalities of the movie men who appear in this book are all depicted clearly. Like characters appearing in a scenario, they are "fleshed out" well. You can feel his respect towards his comrades at arms in the brush of his pen. Thanks to that gentle brush tip, the work is a pleasure to read.

Prone to illness, Mr. Hashimoto went in and out of hospitals, but he made a full recovery upon completing this book. It sounds like a lie, but for many years his lifestyle had involved writing, and his condition must have returned to what it had been in those days.

I came into contact with a hale Mr. Hashimoto at a lecture at Waseda University and on the set of a special program filmed for NHK Hi-Vision (2008), and even now I cannot forget my pleasant surprise.

Restored to health, Mr. Hashimoto began work on a revision of his screenplay, *I Want to Be a Shellfish*. Broadcast in 1958, it had been his first television drama, and for the film version that followed the year after, he took up a megaphone to make his directorial debut.

The drama and film were hits and received high praise—but not from Director Kurosawa or Ryuzo Kikushima.

I surmise that Mr. Hashimoto saw fit to revise it in order to remove a thorn that remained lodged in his heart.

The rewritten screenplay uses the sea as a motif and focuses on the love of a married couple, substantially increasing the number of scenes. These include a razed Tokyo—hardly feasible back then before the advent of computer graphics technology. With details altered throughout the entire piece, it's a fairly major rewrite, a transformation that stands as a model for film remakes. The screenplay overcame half a century to return to the screen once again.

The remake of *I Want to Be a Shellfish* (2008) won an award based on fan voting in the 63rd Mainichi Film Concours, proving that Mr. Hashimoto was indeed an active screenwriter at more than ninety years of age.

It's a bravura feat worthy of a man who tirelessly wrestled the demon that is cinema and spectacularly brought it to its knees over and over again to bask in the adulation of audiences.

The epilogue contains the following sentences:

> Even if there won't be a second or third Akira Kurosawa, there's something I want willing souls to inherit and attempt in future years. And that's the collaborative scripting that Akira Kurosawa practiced.

As a screenwriter, I take the passage to heart. I wonder if it wasn't to tell us this that Mr. Hashimoto offered up the book.

With its many revelations, the work isn't just for us screenwriters but a must-read for film fans and aspiring cineastes.

I have a framed picture of the two of us on the wall of the room where I work, taken in the entryway of the Hashimoto residence where I had gone to interview him for a film magazine. Moreover, the copy of *Compound Cinematics* that I brazenly had him autograph for my daughter, who wrote her graduation thesis on Shinobu Hashimoto the screenwriter, is our heirloom. My whole family are Shinobu Hashimoto fans.

To date, Mr. Hashimoto has produced seventy-three cinematic screenplays (two of which were for foreign films).

I'm looking forward to the seventy-fourth.

This piece originally appeared in the Japanese pocket paperback reissue of FUKUGAN NO EIZO Watashi to Kurosawa Akira *(Bungeishunju, Tokyo). Copyright © 2015 by Masato Kato. All rights reserved. Translation by Lori Hitchcock Morimoto. Kodansha USA Publishing, LLC.*

COMPOUND CINEMATICS

AKIRA KUROSAWA AND I

PROLOGUE: TOKYO MARCH

Shall we to the cinema? Shall we tea?
Perhaps run away on the Odakyu?
Changing Shinjuku, that…

I was born and raised in the countryside in Hyogo Prefecture in the Kansai region.

My first awareness that a private rail line by the name of Odakyu existed in metropolitan Tokyo came not through my employment with the Japan National Railway (as JR was once known), but by way of the light, lively melody of a popular song from 1929 or 1930, "Tokyo March" (lyrics by Yaso Saijo, music by Shimpei Nakayama), each line of which was a conductor's announcement, an information board telling me of a Tokyo on which I had yet to set eyes.

But when I finally saw Tokyo with my own eyes more than ten years later, it wasn't the "Maru Building of love," "Urbane Asakusa," or "Changing Shinjuku" of the song's lyrics, but a desolate, burnt-out wasteland.

I enlisted for active duty with the Tottori army regiment in 1938, but tuberculosis resulted in my discharge and, after army and Red Cross hospitals and four years spent in a disabled veterans' rehabilitation facility, I eventually regained my freedom. I couldn't return to my job at the National Railway with such a blow to my body, however, and I became a salaryman at a munitions company and there welcomed the end of the war. Immediately afterwards, I was dispatched to Tokyo on business, and so it was that I set foot for the first time on the soil I had so yearned after.

My destination was the annex of Isetan Department Store in Shinjuku, where the Ministry of Munitions—similar to today's Ministry of Economy, Trade and Industry—was headquartered. The elevator was out of service, so I laboriously climbed the staircase to the sixth floor, stopping now and then on a landing to catch my breath, surveying the burnt ruins of Tokyo that stretched out under a clear blue sky as far as the eye could see. I found myself wondering if this Isetan might have been the department store of the "Tokyo March" lyrics: "Changing Shinjuku, that Musashino / moon shines over your department stores…"

Shortly thereafter, my company opened a branch office on Showa

Street near Okachimachi Station in Taito Ward that served as a foothold for all of my subsequent business trips.

There's a line in "Tokyo March" that goes, "Big Tokyo, cramped for lovers," and, indeed, even I had one acquaintance in Tokyo: Kiyoshi Saeki, a filmmaker at Shin-Toho. Mr. Saeki had been an assistant director under my screenwriting mentor, Mansaku Itami, and together they had departed Uzumasa, Kyoto's JO (a studio) to work at Toho in Tokyo. When Mr. Itami was invalided with tuberculosis a few years later, he went to work for Daiei to return to a familiar life in Kyoto, but Mr. Saeki remained at Toho and, when Shin-Toho was established, he was promoted to the position of director.

Mr. Saeki lived at Karasuyama in Setagaya Ward. Taking the Yamanote Line from Okachimachi to Kanda, the Chuo Line to Shinjuku, and transferring to the Keio Line for Chitose Karasuyama, or opting for the Yamanote Line to Shibuya, the Inogashira Line to Meidai-mae, and transferring from there to the Keio Line, I often visited him (those of us who were close to Mr. Itami called Mr. Saeki "Saeki-niisan" [big brother Saeki], while others referred to the rising filmmaker as "Saeki no anchan" ["bro" in the non-related sense]). And so it was that I spent a considerable amount of time riding the Keio and Inogashira Lines on my trips to and from Mr. Saeki's home but never once took the Odakyu.

It was early spring in 1949.

Over the houses along Showa Street growled the last winds of winter, the gusts blowing from the direction of Ueno awfully biting.

Wearing an overcoat and carrying a briefcase, I headed out from the Tokyo branch office of my company and took the outer loop of the Yamanote Line from Okachimachi. I got off at Shibuya and transferred to the Inogashira Line. Just before arriving at Shimokitazawa, along the intersecting line under the elevated bridge an outbound Odakyu train passed by like a stranger, its broad top leaving an impression on me.

Getting off at Shimokitazawa, and after much glancing about and the help of an information board, I descended to the Odakyu platform and waited to board the next outbound train. This was my first time on the Odakyu. I was headed for Komae, two stops after Seijo Gakuen, and the home of a Mr. Kurosawa, in Komae along the Odakyu…the film director Akira Kurosawa, on whom I was paying a call.

It had been decided that Mr. Kurosawa would film my script *Shiyu* ("Male and Female," later retitled *Rashomon*), and the producer, Mr. Sojiro Motoki, wanted me to meet Mr. Kurosawa. Today would be our first face-to-face, our first planning session.

What kind of person was Mr. Kurosawa? It wasn't as though I didn't have some sense that this might be a fateful meeting, but I wouldn't know until I met him. Either way, it didn't do to dwell on it, so I just turned my attention to the scenery racing past the window of the Odakyu train.

Vacant plot, crop patch, grove, house, house—the air raids hadn't left many scars along this route—crossing, station, shopping street, apartment building, vegetable field, harvested black rice field, house, house, vacant plot, crossing, another new apartment building... Endlessly sprawling out as far as I could see, house, house, house... A vague something was niggling at the back of my mind, gradually coming clear. Big Tokyo, cramped for lovers, urbane Asakusa... As I looked out at the scenery through the windows of the first Odakyu train I ever rode, a song that had been popular over twenty years earlier played over and over like a tape recording in the back of my mind. "Tokyo March."

> Shall we to the cinema? Shall we tea?
> Perhaps run away on the Odakyu?
> Changing Shinjuku, that Musashino...

CHAPTER ONE: THE BIRTH OF *RASHOMON*

The author at the time of his admission to the
Okayama Disabled Veterans' Rehabilitation Facility circa 1941.

My Comrade at the Disabled Veterans' Rehabilitation Facility

It was great luck surpassing coincidence, eventuality, or even inexorable
fate that brought Mansaku Itami-sensei and me together.

It was a hot day. Even now, I cannot forget the searing heat of that day.

The Okayama Disabled Veterans' Rehabilitation Facility was located in Hayashima, Tsukubo County in Okayama Prefecture, near where the Kojima Peninsula juts out into the Seto Inland Sea. It occupied forty-eight acres over a string of low mountains, and on this hilly terrain the hospital wards sat on red pine-covered rises on the east and west sides, with the main building between them, and open-air huts and the like on the west peak. As a tuberculosis sanatorium administered by the Ministry of Health and Welfare, it was open to navy and army officers and enlisted men who had become symptomatic during their military service.

The armed forces had grown like a blister during the war. Not knowing what to do about the many lung ailments developed in training exercises and tactical maneuvers and wishing to wash their hands of the consequences, the army and navy upgraded a Home Ministry division into the Ministry of Health and Welfare and aimed to construct one disabled veterans' rehabilitation facility per prefecture. The one in Okayama got going relatively early and hence served as a holding pen for the decommissioned and delisted hailing from the four prefectures of Okayama, Hyogo, Tottori, and Shimane.

Rather than getting sent there directly from a military hospital, I was first dispatched by the Japanese Red Cross to my home in Hyogo, and a week later and on my lonesome, I was admitted to the receiving facility in Ward No. 1 on the eastern hill. This was where all new patients were put on strict bed rest for a week while they underwent testing. There was no transfer of charts from the military hospitals, and instead a general diagnosis from scratch based on X-rays, sputum exams, fevers, and so on determined whether a patient would end up on the east or west hill.

The day I was admitted to the facility was hot, but the afternoon of the next day was even hotter.

The six-person room had three beds each along the eastern and western walls, and I occupied a middle one. Military rank had no meaning here, so if one of the beds by the window or corridor was free I'd have insisted, but five Matsue regiment guys had already colonized them and I had no choice but to settle for the empty middle bed.

There had been a light breeze before noon, the rustling of red pines both near and far riding it like the sound of waves through the cicadas' cascade. The wind blew in from the distant Seto Inland Sea.

Am I going to die here listening to these murmuring pines?

The breeze suddenly died in the afternoon, the fierce heat making the cicadas sound like an evening downpour, yet, under strict bed rest, I wasn't to move. The five from Matsue, perhaps forewarned about how things would be at the receiving facility, had all brought things to read, and passed the time perusing magazines or books, while I had brought nothing of the kind and could only stare up at the ceiling.

At some point I noticed someone moving on the corridor-side bed next to mine. When I looked over, a smallish fellow sitting up in his bed with a book in hand offered it to me saying, "If you like, you might read this." I responded to this unexpected kindness with a bob of my head and an "oh, thanks," and accepted a somewhat thick magazine with the words "Japanese Cinema" printed on the cover. I opened it, but finding no articles to my taste, flipped through the pages until I came upon a screenplay in the back. I read the first three or four pages, tilting my head in puzzlement, but continued on and asked the man when I was done, "This is a scenario...a film scenario?"

"It is," he answered.

"I'm surprised it's so simple... Really simple, isn't it?"

There was a curious expression on the small man's face.

"I feel like even I could write something of this level."

The small man, sitting cross-legged on his bed, gave me a wry smile. "No, no, they're not that easy to write."

"No, compared to this, even I could do better. Who's the greatest Japanese writer of these?"

The smallish man from 63rd Regiment, Matsue army hospital—Isuke Narita—looked a little flustered, and with a bewildered grimace that contorted his face he replied, "A person called Mansaku Itami."

"Mansaku Itami?" I parroted, somewhat argumentatively. "Then I'll write a scenario and send it to this Mansaku Itami."

However, just as Isuke Narita had said, scenarios weren't so easily written.

I wrote and sent to Mansaku Itami *The Mountain Soldier*, based on my experiences at the Disabled Veterans' Rehabilitation Facility, the year following the beginning of the Pacific War, after leaving for home without permission. In other words, it had taken me more than three years to complete one script. Even accounting for the disadvantage that miliary tuberculosis, deemed incurable, imposed on me, a scenario, the blueprint of a movie, wasn't something I could just pop out overnight and expect to show the world.

I didn't have any expectation of a response from Mr. Itami since, over the course of the preceding two or three years, I'd gained a vague under-standing of his person and standing as a director-scriptwriter. He was a giant on a cliff far above me, a great star nearly impossible to reach, whose slightest utterances exerted a great influence on the film industry. It was Itami who had predicted just from one screenplay, *A German at Daruma Temple*, that Akira Kurosawa, then a mere assistant director at Toei, would become a leading figure in the world of Japanese cinema, and focused un-usual attention and expectations on the man. He would likely ignore, or rather not even register, what I had written.

But Mr. Itami's response surprised me.

At first, I was so bewildered and excited that I couldn't comprehend what he had written. But on the second and third reading I was overcome with emotion. His remarkably polite, straightforward, and meticulous let-ter pinpointed weaknesses in my work and even offered specific guidance for what and how to revise.

By the time I had reread Mr. Itami's response three or four times in almost panicked excitement, my brimming delight and joy were uncon-tainable.

Isuke! I have to tell Isuke about this!

I telephoned the facility in Okayama, but Isuke Narita was not there. I was informed that a rehabilitation center had been built in Shimane Pre-fecture and, wishing to return home, he had left for Matsue a while back. During the year or two before my release I had been in an open-air hut, and as Isuke had been in Ward No. 1 we hadn't seen each other very often.

I called the Matsue Disabled Veterans' Rehabilitation Facility, but af-ter a short wait it wasn't Isuke who came to the phone, but the head nurse of the hospital ward, bearing gloomy news. Isuke's condition had wors-ened following his transfer from Okayama, and he had since passed away.

Sometimes the passage of thirty-two years can seem like just a moment.

The gray-haired man winding his way through a white copse of headstones in the dim twilight was Isuke Narita's apparently wealthy father. Isuke had had an older brother who had died on the battlefield, and now his father, small just as he had been, bereaved of two children, served as the chairman of the Shimane Prefecture association for families of the war dead.

The sun had set, but dusk lingered over the cemetery at a temple in Matsue. I had come to stand in prayer before one of the bristling gravestones, Isuke Narita's, brought here by his father on the occasion of location shooting for the film *Castle of Sand*.

I had always thought to visit Isuke's grave one day, but the intervening years had stipulated something like a condition. *Castle of Sand*, written not long after I'd embarked on my career as a scenarist, is mainly set in the Izumo area of the San'in region where Isuke had been born and raised. When the cameras began rolling at this nexus of associations would be the best time for a reunion, both for Isuke and for myself.

The studio shelved the project, however, and the long-awaited beginning did not come until 1974, when a friend and I established Hashimoto Pro and agreed to co-produce the work with Shochiku. It was twilight in early autumn, exactly thirty-two years after his death, when I bowed my head and clasped my hands at that temple in Matsue, still visible in the afterglow of dusk. I thanked my comrade Isuke Narita from the Disabled Veterans' Rehabilitation Facility for telling me about such a thing as the scenario and about Mansaku Itami, its preeminent practitioner and guiding light.

It might be said that at times thirty-two years occupy but a moment.

Mansaku Itami, master director and brilliant screenplay writer (1900-46).

My Lifelong Mentor, Mansaku Itami

Yes, that day had been hot, too.

The evening stillness of Seto is hard to bear, but the heat of the Kyoto Plain is also extreme. It sits thick and still, an unwavering heat.

Mr. Itami lay face up on his futon and I sat by his head. We were in an eight-mat room at the Itami residence in Ohno-cho, Koyama-kita in Kyoto's Kamigyo (now Kita) Ward. Near Mr. Itami's pillow was a screenplay, a pile of 400-character sheets of paper I'd sent him two weeks earlier.

Was it my seventh? No, eighth? A bad habit of mine. While writing I'd be in a fugue state releasing all that I'd dammed up, but once I was done and Mr. Itami had read and critiqued it, I would forget everything, the content and even title of what I'd penned fading from memory.

Sometimes, as in the case of *Saburo Toko* [the genesis of the film *I Want To Be a Shellfish*], he would be excited to revise and direct it himself once he got better. But he was displeased with the vast majority of them and would become irritated and angry with me, and in this way three years had passed since I'd first gained admittance to his residence by way of *The Mountain Soldier*. It was now 1946, a year after the end of the war and after noon amidst early August's unrelenting dry heat wave.

Mr. Itami craned his neck slightly. He reached out his right hand to touch the pile of papers. His fingers were long and thin. He brushed his hand over the first page of the pile of 400-character manuscript paper.

"It's very original."

"Yes."

"Such a long piece—you're lucky to be so healthy."

"Yes…"

I unfolded my crossed legs and sat formally on my knees. I always assumed the *seiza* position when I received comments or critique on my work.

But Mr. Itami removed his hand from the manuscript and once again looked up at the ceiling. He said nothing. I awaited his words in my formal position. Still he stared at the ceiling and did not speak. Silence reigned, a long one. Given the progression and ups and downs of his illness, perhaps he hadn't been able to read it in just a couple of weeks.

Not mentioning the work, I kept the conversation on my goings-on. "My wife and I had a baby about a month ago. A girl."

"The eldest daughter."

"Yes."

"What did you name her?"

"Aya, in one character. Aya Hashimoto."

"Aya…" Mr. Itami wrote the character for *Aya* in the air with his finger. "A good name. Good that you didn't add *ko* to it," he said, referring to the suffix meaning "child" appended to many female names.

Mr. Itami's wife, Kimiko, brought in the tea with a smile. "How nice to have a young lady in the family. Since the first was a son, now you have a boy and a girl, don't you."

"Yes."

I bowed my head and took a sip of the tea. Mr. Itami didn't rise and continued to look up at the ceiling. His eyes seemed to be focused on something far away.

"Hashimoto, you always write originals. Do adaptations turn you off?"

"No, not particularly... I just happened to have a lot of original ideas that I wanted to put on paper. If it was something interesting, I'd like to try an adaptation."

"If you were to, what stance do you think you need to take?"

Though I still sat in the formal position, for a second I crossed my arms. Mr. Itami had done the *The Rickshaw Man*'s screenplay, considered the top masterpiece pre- or post-war. The original story by Shunsaku Iwashita, an employee of the Yahata Iron Works in Kyushu, had been nominated for the Naoki Prize.

I knew quite well the process and care with which Mr. Itami engaged the original, a bit of which he chronicled in his book, *Seiga Zakki* [Random Thoughts Lying Prone]. In short, the theme mustn't become knotty. Condense it into the briefest possible self-contained story—in the case of *The Rickshaw Man*, into a complete, readily comprehensible "film about the *odd* love of *a certain rickshaw driver* for a widow." His assertions regarding theme provoked debate amongst scenario writers and became the most critical point in subsequent adaptations. But I didn't bring this up.

"There's a cow."

"A...cow?"

"It's in something like a fenced pasture, so there's no way out."

Mr. Itami was looking at me with a curious expression.

"I go see it every day. In rain or shine... Standing in different spots, I watch it. And when I've discovered its weak spot, I open the gate and enter the pasture and with some sort of blunt object I fell it in one blow."

"..."

"If I fail to finish it, the cow will become violent and out of control. I have to fell it with a single blow. Then, with a sharp blade I cut its carotid artery, drain its blood into a bucket, and bring the blood home and get down to work. The shape and form of the original don't matter, all I want is steaming blood."

Mr. Itami turned his eyes from me and looked up at the ceiling. His gaze was sharp. He said nothing. Glaring at a fixed point on the ceiling, he let a suffocating silence stretch on, then eventually said in a subdued voice, "It's probably as you say... In fact, such a bold method will be quicker and the success rate might actually be higher for a writer who sets out to do an adaptation... But, Hashimoto." Mr. Itami turned his eyes on me, a hint of something tender, like loving kindness, beginning to suffuse the harsh gaze. "In this world there are originals you don't kill, with which you have to commit double suicide."

I learned of Mr. Itami's death about forty days later in the obituary column of the newspaper. He passed away on September 21st at age 47.

For a moment my mind went blank; in the next, I grew so dizzy I thought I might collapse. Shocked beyond words, I went outside.

My hometown is a village in the mountains in the Chugoku range a little west of central Hyogo Prefecture, and a river runs just outside the house. The Ichikawa flows from the Chugoku watershed out to the Seto Inland Sea, gathering valley streams along the way. Crossing a bridge, I got onto the field flanking the river.

Before the war, a natural pine forest had run alongside the flowing water, and I had often snuck in as a child to cry out of sight, scolded by my mother or father. During the war, every last tree had been chopped down to make pine oil, and the austere landscape, laid bare, was a pity to behold.

Perhaps I had regressed to my earliest years numbed by the sudden shock; I entered that pine-less pine forest like a somnambulist. Yet I remained strangely aware. On the expanse of stones, the wasteland stretched out along the bank, I stood out to anyone looking from the bridge or on either side of the river. Crouching down or hiding my face was out. I might walk aimlessly, no, just standing still would do; at that distance no one would hear me, no matter how loud I was.

Unable to hold back any longer, I cried. Standing on the bank of the Ichikawa, reminiscent of the shores of a netherworld under the clear autumn sky, I raised my voice and cried. It was the first time in my life I had cried so loudly.

The day was warm, an early hint of spring.

It was now the following year and towards the end of January, a perfectly sunny day, a gift from the gods, the wind blowing down from the northern mountains stilling like it had just been a bad dream.

I had taken time off from company work. Running the bases in a match against a trading partner during the Nishi-Harima District Corporate

Baseball Autumn Tournament, I had suffered a disk herniation upon trying to reach home on an infield grounder, crashing into the catcher and falling. The pain worsened with the onset of winter and the biting seasonal winds and became unbearable after New Year's Day in the serious cold. Hoping to take it easy for four or five days, I asked for some time off and was lazing at a *kotatsu*, a traditional warmer, at home in broad daylight.

I grew bored of the book I was reading and abandoned it. Looking up, I saw that the sunlit *shoji* screen to the outdoor corridor looked almost blindingly bright.

I wonder if it's warmer out?

When I crawled out of the *kotatsu*, opened the *shoji*, and stepped onto the corridor, the sun-drenched backyard was like a greenhouse. A black wooden fence ran along the boundary with our neighbor's house, and in front of a stack of firewood for the winter sat a folding chair.

Going back in the room, I put on a baseball cap, bundled the sleeping baby up on my back, and took a cushion and clipboard. Then I stepped out to the backyard, where I laid the cushion on the folding chair, sat down, and placed the clipboard on my crossed legs.

The open corridor would be pleasant, but the best spot in the way of a greenhouse was right in the middle of the backyard.

That precious clipboard on my lap made for a convenient portable office.

A slab of plywood slightly bigger than A4, it had a clip to secure sheets of paper, on which I wrote sideways. I wasn't in the habit of tackling manuscript paper firsthand; rather, I drafted on multipurpose paper on the clipboard and transcribed the results on manuscript paper. I had written every work of mine since *The Mountain Soldier* on that clipboard. It showed its true worth when I was in transit.

It took me about fifty minutes to commute by train to my company office in Himeji, and those fifty minutes on the train in the morning, and the fifty minutes in the evening, were when I wrote, with the clipboard out and on my bag. In the morning, my station was second from the terminus so using my mobile office was easy, but in the evenings, when I couldn't sit for all the passengers, I had to take my clipboard out while standing, rest it on my bag, and hug the bag with my free arm in order to write.

There are no weekends or holidays at a wartime munitions company. Even if I had one or two days off during the month, I also needed to transcribe my drafts on manuscript paper, so I still needed to do my writing on my commute to and from work, in a train carriage. The seven or eight screenplays that Mr. Itami read for me were all completed thus. In other words, as long as you have the drive to write, you can make the time and space for it anywhere.

I looked over the first page on the clipboard. It was a list of the titles of stories I'd skimmed burrowing in the *kotatsu*.

"Rashomon" "Potato Gruel" "Hell Screen" "Kesa and Morito" "The Bandit" "Yonosuke's Story" "In a Grove" "The Princess of Rokunomiya"

All of them were short stories from *The Complete Works of Ryunosuke Akutagawa*.

The day before, I had planned to let my boss know that I'd be taking some time off, but as he was out of the office, I instead gave a message to his secretary and left, heading not towards the station but to a bookstore in town, where I purchased a volume. *The Complete Works of Ryunosuke Akutagawa*.

I hadn't really intended to buy any Akutagawa. I'd only thought to have something to read while I was off work and purchased it without forethought. By the time I reached Himeji Station, though, Ryunosuke Akutagawa was tugging at my mind. Perhaps because it was earlier than my usual rush-hour commute, the Bantan Line from Himeji to Wadayama had few riders. I was able to sit comfortably so I started to take the book out of my bag, but a thought stopped my hand. I recalled puzzlement about Akutagawa crossing the back of my mind a couple of times before.

Soseki Natsume's output had been adapted to film. Ogai Mori had been adapted too. Yet, there was not a single film of a Ryunosuke Akutagawa story. As the three greatest literary luminaries since the Meiji period they were all famous, so why?

I remember reading a comparison of the works of Natsume, Mori, and Akutagawa in a magazine during the war. The essay argued that Akutagawa had written his works on talent alone, that he'd become a writer straight out of university and had no experience of life, and that his stories had a certain flightiness born of mere talent. The impression imparted was that his works didn't compare with those of the earlier two writers, but I thought this ridiculous and wrong-headed.

A work's quality is the author's personality, and liking it or not a matter of taste. In today's terms, it would be like applying such a standard to judging the relative merits of mystery writer Seicho Matsumoto, a former newspaper reporter with ample experience of society, and Yukio Mishima, an established author pretty much fresh out of school, and is so stupid as to be pointless.

Moreover, while they may have been adapted, Natsume's *Botchan* and Mori's *The Abe Clan* were their representative works, and I couldn't help but think that it was mere happenstance that none of Akutagawa's had ever been filmed.

The Bantan Line departing Himeji traveled north past the settlement of Nishi-Harima along the Ichikawa.

Sunset came early in mid-winter, and the mountain peaks out the left-hand windows were a black cluster, while out the opposite windows the lights of faraway hamlets swelled for a moment and flickered as they flowed past. A cold, wintry breeze seemed to have picked up, a norther come over the Chugoku range and blowing south through the valleys.

And amidst the monotonous creaking of the train, Mr. Itami's voice revived in my ears.

There are originals you don't kill, with which you have to commit double suicide.

I sat a little upright in my seat. Those words, Mr. Itami's parting lesson so to speak, made my heart ache with such inconsolable poignance that I could hardly bear it.

His death had dealt me a severe shock. I had ceased thinking, my desire to create disrupted, and had cast off writing, my avenue to scenarios lost, and for nearly half a year I'd been chewing on sand.

I madly wanted to write. I wanted to return to those heady days when I was challenged, and possessed. If there was any way out of my dreary reality, a chance for scenarios to breathe again, then, given Mr. Itami's parting lesson, it would have to be via an adaptation.

But—but. Among all the fiction I had read, whether Natsume or Mori, there was none I could die with. Akutagawa was the same; those works of his I'd read in the past didn't quite compel me to take such a dive, and indeed, no matter how hard I scoured them, hoping for such an encounter felt misguided.

Yet, in any case, with so many stories there had to be one, at least one, that could be made into a movie.

There on the northbound Bantan Line train, I began to read *The Complete Works of Ryunosuke Akutagawa*. I skipped over stories I had read before and went on to the next. I kept reading after I got home and in the morning after I had awoken. After breakfast, I crawled under the *kotatsu* and read on, making note of the titles of stories that seemed ready for a film.

Eventually, however, I was just skimming, and having skipped over parts, I began to feel bored, then tired; seven or eight tenths through the book I clicked my tongue, fed up.

No point reading any more... Nothing left but to consider the ones I've checked out.

And so it was that I sat reviewing my memo of titles on a clipboard on my lap, legs crossed on a folding chair in a backyard as bright and warm as a greenhouse, a baseball cap on my head and a sleeping baby on my back.

"Rashomon" "Potato Gruel" "Hell Screen" "Kesa and Morito"... "The Bandit" "Yonosuke's Story" "In a Grove" "The Princess of Rokunomiya"...etc.

I only glanced over the titles though, removing the page and sending it to the back of the stack on my clipboard. On the bared sheet of straw paper now reflecting the light, all of a sudden I wrote in pencil:

(F · 1)
O The road from Yamashina to Sekiyama
A samurai couple is traveling. The husband, Takehiro Kanazawa, serving the Wakasa provincial government, wears a sword, has a bow out, and pulls along a horse. Mounted is a woman with a veiled hat—but its netting blows up in the wind and reveals a beautiful oval face: wife Masago.

The scenario I had suddenly started writing was "In a Grove."

There was no room for a comparative examination of all the different works. I had sniffed out the lifeblood of each as I read, and the list of titles was little more than a reference. "The Bandit" lent itself best to a visual treatment, and "Kesa and Morito" was easy too. But both of them were rather lifeless, their blood pale and lukewarm and ordinary. I wanted the sheen of dark red blood but had encountered nothing of the kind.

Actually, though not dark red, there was one story that was dusky. Its blood oddly murky with a raw stench on top, its sturdy frame promising backbone, practically the only one that might serve...no, in fact, that could even make for new, heretofore unseen Japanese cinema, a terribly absurdist *jidaigeki* (period drama).

Since I know which one, I might as well just start writing.

Chronicled in the *Konjaku Monogatari* (Anthology of Tales from the Past), "In a Grove" is a roughly thousand-year-old, Heian-era version of weekly magazine fodder but is woven through with a strangely vivid realism.

A cruel fate awaits the traveling samurai and his wife, Takehiro Kanazawa and Masago: the bandit Tajomaru comes on stage. With just one glance at Masago's beautiful face, he is driven to violate her and sets a trap for husband Takehiro.

The bandit ransacks a tomb on the opposite hill and sorts out mirrors and swords. Any items the couple fancies, he offers to part with. Greed lives in us all. Standing shoulder to shoulder with Tajomaru to discuss the matter, Takehiro takes the horse's reins and leaves the post road to enter a mountain path.

The two men leave Masago on her horse on the path and head into a grove, beyond which lies a clearing dotted with bamboo and surrounded by cedar trees. Suddenly, Tajomaru springs at Takehiro and pushes him down, tying him up and lashing him to the base of a cedar.

Tajomaru hurries back through the grove and tells Masago, "Something's wrong with your husband, he may have taken ill. Come quickly!" Masago hastily dismounts and follows Tajomaru through the grove and into the clearing. As soon as she sees her husband, she pulls a blade from the breast of her kimono and flies at Tajomaru, and the two of them fight. Accustomed to such rows, however, Tajomaru seizes Masago and knocks the blade away. Without her weapon, there's nothing she can do.

And before her restrained husband's eyes, Tajomaru begins to violate Masago.

The scenario didn't just go smoothly, it galloped, and the day ended.

The second day also hinted at spring.

I exchanged the baseball cap for a straw hat. It had a wide brim all around, so no matter how the sun traveled from east to west, no direct light would shine on my clipboard.

The work was a continuation of the day before's, but events took an unexpected turn.

The day after the samurai couple meets with misfortune, a woodcutter who has discovered the cruelly murdered Takehiro Kanazawa is giving his testimony to the judicial chief. A traveling monk who passed the couple by on the post road from Sekiyama to Yamashina the previous day does the same.

The next witness, Masago's mother who lives in the capital, confirms that Takehiro was a samurai with the Wakasa government and tirelessly pleads that they search for her daughter, who has gone missing without a trace. And then Tajomaru, arrested at Awataguchi, where he got dead drunk and fell off a horse he'd stolen, comes onto the white sand with both hands tied. Yet, he is utterly unrepentant.

A scoundrel who has committed many robberies and murders, Tajomaru will doubtless be beheaded or hung.

"I'm the famous Tajomaru... I wouldn't lie now," he begins confessing to the incident in an unexpectedly dispassionate tone.

After taking the woman, Tajomaru filched the man's sword and bow and made to flee the grove. "Wait!" Masago called out sharply. "M-My..." Haltingly, she implored—no, demanded, "My disgrace has been witnessed by two men, and I am so ashamed I could die. It would be better to die. Please! Just one of you! I'll spend the rest of my life with the one who's left standing!"

Tajomaru shows some emotion there on the court's white sand. "I shivered. I've raped lots of women and they all seemed the same to me, but this one was different. I wanted to kill the man and make her my wife."

Tajomaru tore his gaze from the woman who'd entranced him and looked upon the man at the base of the cedar tree.

"But I am Tajomaru and didn't want to act like a coward."

Approaching Takehiro, he drew and cut the rope. From a crouch Takehiro unsheathed his sword in an arc and slashed at Tajomaru, and their fight began.

It was as a battle between two raptors, one bearing down the other only for the other to rally in response and bear down upon the first. On and on they dueled, until at last they crashed headlong into each other and stopped moving.

Tajomaru's sword had pierced Takehiro's left chest. When the bandit withdrew the blade, Takehiro slowly crumbled to the ground, face up.

Tajomaru turned around, panting, and was astonished. Masago was gone. Perhaps she had run away during the fighting, and was nowhere to be seen.

Livid, Tajomaru flew into the grove, but no Masago. He pushed farther into the grove after her, running around and out onto the path like a wild beast. Awaiting its masters, the couple's horse lazily munched on the grass along the path. Tajomaru looked left and right, but Masago was nowhere.

"Damn it! She's run off!"

With nothing for it, Tajomaru went back into the grove to where he'd been and shouldered Takehiro's sword and bow. He made to leave but stopped to look at the corpse.

"You gave me a run for my money... You really were skilled."

On the commission's white sand Tajomaru bares his white teeth. "Listen well to this part... It took me twenty-five or so passes to bring him down. In this wide world, only he lasted for more than twenty... That excellent swordsman," the bandit says, triumphant with pride, "was killed by none other than me, Tajomaru!"

Meanwhile, Masago, who fled the grove in anguish and confusion, wanders the capital aimlessly and comes upon the statue of the three-faced and thousand-armed Kannon within Kiyomizu Temple, and there desperately confesses, "Once the bandit took me, he looked on my husband and me with scorn. Filching my husband's sword and bow and quiver, he made himself scarce... Beyond the grove now were just me and my husband, tied to the base of the cedar."

The third day was mild too.

They say there are four warm days for three cold ones, but it was rare for this kind of good weather to continue for so long. Since I was making progress on the work, I was grateful for it. Once again, with the baby strapped on my back, my straw hat on my head, I forged ahead on the seat in the back garden.

Having violated Masago, Tajomaru fled with Takehiro's sword and bow, and the scenario now concerned the unfortunate couple left behind in the grove.

—Masago sighed, righted her attire, and cast a glance at Takehiro. Still tied to the cedar's base, he was staring at a point in mid-air. Masago hesitated once, twice, and then called to him in a low rasp: "Dear..." But Takehiro did not answer. His unbudging demeanor signaled clear rejection of her. "Dear..." she tentatively called once more. But Takehiro still didn't respond.

"Dear..." Takehiro finally looked at her, and Masago's entire body began to tremble at the cold glint, the fathomless contempt in his eyes.

Masago shudders in front of the Kannon statue at Kiyomizu Temple. "Anger or sorrow would have been fine. But his eyes were cold and unforgiving, rejecting me."

—On the fallen leaves of the grove, Masago could barely contain her mixed feelings of sadness, shame, and vexation. But with difficulty, she thought better of it and said once again, "Dear... Forgive me, please, forgive me!"

But Takehiro didn't even budge.

Unable to take it any longer, Masago sidled up to her husband and appealed to him with a determined look, "Please, dear! Forgive me!" Takehiro met Masago's eyes. Still his expression remained unchanged. The cold, or cool, glint in his eyes betrayed thorough scorn.

"No matter what, he will not forgive me. We have ceased to be husband and wife. There's nothing left for me but to die... I will die, if I must! But f-first!" Masago could not forgive her husband, who only showed coldhearted contempt for her. "But f-first!"

Rushing to pick up her blade, which lay glittering atop fallen bamboo leaves, Masago held it at her side, ran toward her husband, and buried it in his chest as if in a trance. Almost at the same time she reflexively jumped away and tumbled back onto the bamboo grass.

Having prostrated herself before the Senju Kannon, Masago slowly rises. "A little while later, when I came to my senses... My husband had bled profusely from his chest and was no longer breathing."

Perhaps wishing him some ease, Masago cut the rope with her blade, and Takehiro's body slumped sideways at the base of the cedar.

"Now it's my turn." With a backhanded grip Masago brought the dagger to her throat, but could not thrust. She tried again and again to stab herself. She simply could not do it, the tip of the blade only shaking more each time. Impulsively she flung it away and ran into the grove behind her. She wandered like a somnambulist.

"I want to die." "I want to die." "But I can't die."

Exiting the bamboo grove, Masago staggered down the mountain path. When she arrived at the bank of a river, her body wavered. She leaned forward. But she could not jump in. Later she stood on the shore of a deep lake. Repeatedly battling her reluctance, she writhed in agony. But she simply could not die.

The inner shrine at Kiyomizu Temple—on her face at the statue's knees, Masago laments with abandon. "I was taken by a bandit, and moreover turned on my husband... I have killed my husband, my husband! What, what is such a woman to do?"

On the white sand of the commission, Takehiro, murdered by Tajomaru or perhaps by Masago, testifies through a medium clad in soiled white robes. The voice is Takehiro's, a mournful sound from beyond the grave: "The bandit didn't leave even after taking my wife and started consoling her with sweet words."

—Tajomaru nestled close to Masago and put his hand on her shoulder as though to comfort her.

Masago remained sitting on the fallen bamboo leaves, her eyes cast downwards.

"I don't have to tell you... Now that you've been with another man, things will never be the same between you and your husband, right?"

"..."

"As for me, I did this monstrous thing because I found you endearing." Masago's pale face flushed with color.

At the commission, the possessed medium writhes with jealousy where she stands. "I...I had never seen my wife look so beautiful!" The medium's face is distorted in despair. "No, I wanted to tell her, 'Don't listen to him! He's a big liar, he'll just sell you off somewhere.' But if I spoke, he would kill me with one blow."

—Behind the grove Tajomaru continued to woo Masago. "From the moment I first saw you, my desire for you drove me wild. No matter what atrocity I needed to commit, I had to make you my wife... That's why I did this terrible thing... So come, with me."

Masago lifted her beautiful, flushed face and stared into space. "Then... take me where you will."

At the base of the cedar, Takehiro's face twisted with shock and rage.

At the commission, the possessed medium wears an irate expression as she conveys Takehiro's wrath at Masago's words. "Where you will, where you will, where you will... But what came next was worse! What came next was so much worse!"

Masago stood up, reached out toward Tajomaru's outstretched hand, and held his sleeve as if to leave together. She glanced at the cedar tree.

Tajomaru smiled wryly. "We can't let him get in our way, let's leave him like this... Somebody will no doubt find him today or tomorrow."

Masago shook her head violently. "No, that's not it. Please kill him."

Tajomaru looked taken aback, while Takehiro's face froze in horror.

"I can't rest knowing he's somewhere out in the world. Kill him, please, kill him!"

Her eyes and brow angled up, she was the ultimate picture of severe beauty—and there was a flash of the demoness too.

Without warning Tajomaru kicked Masago away, crossed his arms, and for a moment held his breath. Then he slowly walked towards Takehiro and brought his face close to the samurai's. "Hey... now I want to kill that woman."

Not daring to breathe, Takehiro looked at Tajomaru.

"But I want to hear what you think. Nod if you want her dead, shake your head if you don't. So...does the woman die?"

At the commission, the possessed medium's face is stiff and solemn. "When I heard those words, I thought I could forgive everything he had done."

Takehiro and Tajomaru stared at one another, eyes bloodshot with murderous intent. A tense, breathless silence. Takehiro, ready to nod, spied movement across his field of vision and unlocked his gaze. Tajomaru whipped around to see Masago turning and running into the bamboo grove. The bandit hollered and chased after her, diving into the grove, but Takehiro could no longer see Masago—and Tajomaru, too, faded in and out of sight until the samurai lost him too.

At the commission, the possessed medium says mournfully, "I waited. I waited for so long… Faint from the flow of time… Then, from between the bamboos emerged a figure."

But only Tajomaru appeared from the grove, with no sign of Masago. "I don't see her. She must be possessed by a fey creature to flee that fast… I went out as far as the path, but though the palomino was still there, I couldn't find her anywhere."

Still tied up, Takehiro bowed his head in defeat.

Approaching the cedar's base, Tajomaru took away Takehiro's sword and bow and arrows, balanced their weight, and quickly drew and cut the rope that tied Tajomaru.

"By the way, I'm taking the palomino too."

Tajomaru left, and Takehiro was now alone beyond the grove. He remained still for a time but eventually clambered up to his feet. It was almost sunset and the grove was awfully quiet. No breeze rustled the bamboo leaves, and not a single bird chirped.

"How quiet. Not a single noise… How could that—wait, I hear somebody crying. Someone… No, I'm the one who's crying."

He looked around to find the setting sun reflecting off Masago's dagger lying atop bamboo grass.

Without hesitation, Takehiro took the blade in hand and plunged it into his left breast. "No pain. There's something cold and hard in my chest, a stench rises…but no pain to speak of…"

Hemorrhaging an immense amount of blood from his left breast, Takehiro began to wobble a bit.

"But my surroundings were growing dim… The grove faded before my eyes…and into the gradually thickening darkness." At the commission—the body of the possessed medium is teetering. "Dark… I can't see anything. I, myself, my own chest…stabbed my left chest… Deep, dark, into the depths of darkness…unending….unending…"

Unable to hold out anymore, the medium collapses on the white sand.

When I finished the scenario, I looked up and around.

At some point the sun had become obscured by clouds. It was dim and terribly cold, and white specs were sprinkling down. Snow! It was snowing.

I hadn't noticed at all. I remembered the warmth of the shining sun from when I had settled in to work after lunch. I'd become engrossed and was completely unaware of the sudden change in the weather. Both my straw hat and the baby sling covered in white stuff, I'd crossed the finishing line looking like a misshapen snowman.

In any case, I'd written this scenario over the course of three days— two and a half days of early spring sunshine, and a couple of hours of snow.

When I later transcribed my draft onto half-sheets (200-character manuscript paper), it worked out to ninety-three pages. That would be between forty and forty-five minutes of film. It seemed most straightforward to name this awfully short scenario after the original story (whose title alludes in turn to the saying "The truth lies in a grove," meaning that it is obscure), but that felt too straightforward. Since it was a story about men and women, male and female, I entitled it *Shiyu* (Male and Female).

How blue the sky, and how high.

It wasn't a plain blue, nor deep blue or aubergine. Perhaps azure or ultramarine; I had no words to express it.

As for how high, it was in contrast with points of reference. In wide-open places, the sky looks wide, but not high. But before it in splendid contrast was a row of great red pines whose trunks and branches soared aloft, from between which the sky loomed high.

I was standing before Ninnaji Temple in Kyoto's Rakusai District, a bit away from the great temple gates, in the corner of a square covered in gravel.

The observance of the anniversary of Mr. Itami's death took place on September 21, 1947, a year after his passing, at the Ninnaji Temple in Omuro, Ukyo Ward, Kyoto.

I arrived at the temple about forty minutes before the ceremony. Reluctant to pass the time in a waiting room full of people I didn't know, and since it was a beautiful autumn day, I instead wandered the grounds, not passing through the great gate, and looking up at the sky I'd halted in a corner of a gravel-covered square.

I continued to look up at the sky. Precisely because I'm not in the habit of keeping a diary, never even making note of customary events, and have little memory of when exactly the most important turning points in my life took place, the color and height of the sky that day seemed to me a transcendental presence that would remain burned in my eyes and memory.

I looked at my watch again. There were still about twenty minutes until the ceremony.

Since this was the first anniversary, perhaps Mr. Itami's apprentices might come. As far as I knew, he'd had very few. Indeed, though it was hard to believe, for scenarios I was the only one. I had originally assumed that geniuses and prodigies crowded under him, but during the three years I spent visiting his residence, I came to realize that I was the only one who might be considered an apprentice scenarist. I have no idea why that should have been the case.

For example, take Seiichiro Eida, a contemporary of mine. At first, like me, he brought in a screenplay, but Mr. Itami gave it a once-over and told him, "You have no talent for writing, give up. You're a good talker, though. Japan will soon lose the war, and we will adopt the American way of filmmaking. American films have producers, an important role. Quit writing and become a producer."

Eida faithfully followed his advice and set out to become a producer, but I cannot imagine that Mr. Itami gave similar feedback to everyone who came knocking on his door. All I can think is that, because Mr. Itami's criticism didn't mince words, people with some idea of their own level and competence must have hesitated and refrained from showing their work to him. Perhaps fewer souls than I imagine knocked on his door, but in any case, I don't really know why.

The point is that he had only one disciple, and I only one master— maybe it was some sort of fate.

The anniversary ceremony began with a priest's recitation of sutras in the main building of Ninnaji Temple.

Once the sutras were completed we were shown to another room, where three or four celebrated friends and acquaintances, including Chiezo Kataoka and Hiroshi Inagaki, shared their memories and reminiscences, and the event concluded. When I stood to leave, I heard Mr. Itami's wife calling to me from behind.

"Mr. Hashimoto! Don't go straight to Kyoto Station, drop by at our house in Koyama!"

When I arrived at the Itami residence in Koyama, Kamigyo Ward, there were several ceremony attendees gathered there. Apparently they didn't live in Kyoto and had come from Tokyo. When she saw me, Mrs.

Itami said, "Ah, Mr. Hashimoto…" and to an older man standing next to her: "Saeki-niichan, that's Mr. Hashimoto. The one whose scripts my husband minded."

I had heard the name before and bobbed my head. Mr. Saeki also smiled and returned my greeting, and Mrs. Itami continued, "Now that my husband is gone, take his place and read Mr. Hashimoto's drafts and lend him an ear and what not. All right?"

Flustered, I bowed my head, and Mr. Saeki, also a little flustered, said, "By your leave" and lowered his head. All thanks to Mrs. Itami's rather heavy-handed introduction, that was how I met Big Brother Saeki.

From that time on, whenever I was in Tokyo on business, I dropped by at the Saeki residence in Chitose Karasuyama.

Then one day—on a sunny veranda at his home, I joined Eida and some friends he brought with him and sat chatting about movies with our big brother. As we discussed the direction of period pieces subsequent to the lifting of the GHQ (MacArthur's General Headquarters) ban and the direction they ought to take, the conversation turned to recent Kurosawa works.

When the name came up, our host said, "I'm quite friendly with Kurosawa."

Everyone turned to look at him.

"We rented at the same place the whole time we were assistant directors at Toei."

"In that case, *niichan*," I said, looking straight at Mr. Saeki, not having had an inkling of their relationship, "could you have Mr. Kurosawa read all the scripts I've left with you?"

Big Brother Kiyoshi Saeki's reply was perfectly casual and simple: "Yeah, sure thing."

I don't know how much time passed following our conversation, but when I came home from work one day more than half a year and less than a full year later, my wife handed me a postcard that had arrived from Tokyo. The sender was Sojiro Motoki, a producer with the Film Art Association, and the message was simple and to the point:

> Greetings. We have decided that your work, *Shiyu*, is to be filmed by Akira Kurosawa as his next feature. To this end, you will need to meet with Kurosawa, and we ask that you come to Tokyo at your earliest convenience. Please let us know of your availability.

Forgive the brevity of this message.

Sincerely...

I glanced at the postcard and set it down on the table.

My wife stared blankly at me. The postcard had been delivered while I was at work, so she had already read its contents. She had been looking forward to witnessing unparalleled excitement—would I jump up in happiness or raise both arms in a "banzai"?—but that was all she got.

She turned away and began preparing dinner.

I didn't mean to ignore my wife's feelings. In the back of my mind, the sky had risen. Azure or ultramarine, it was the one I had seen at Ninnaji Temple. Farther yet beyond the end of that sky, far, far away—was Mr. Itami. He seemed somehow relieved.

Given the state of his illness he had anticipated not just his death but its aftermath and had worried about me. At one point, he'd tried to brave his illness and take me to Daiei Studio. His wife and I had managed to talk him out of it. He had even introduced me to Mr. Daisuke Ito in hopes that a master director who had taken his country by storm would look after me after his demise.

But evidently he had changed his mind. If Mr. Ito would have done, a simple request to look after me if the worst came to pass would have sufficed. If Mr. Itami had decided not to do this, it was because in the end he thought that due to significant differences in approach Daisuke Ito and Shinobu Hashimoto were not a good match.

Mr. Itami finally settled on a former assistant director, Kiyoshi Saeki, now a director in his own right. He would do—lives in Tokyo, where the film world is wider than in Kyoto; has a big heart, and likes to look after people; has a good reputation, and connections.

"If I die, ask Saeki to look after Hashimoto."

That was why his wife had made her move. The funeral would have been a good time, but for some reason that fellow Hashimoto didn't show up. If she sent advance notice, though, he would certainly attend the first anniversary. Kiyoshi Saeki would too. She'd introduce them then.

Born to a family of elders who had served the Matsuyama fiefdom in Shikoku, Mrs. Itami had a dignified beauty and strength, but she was an easygoing person at heart who didn't meddle in other people's business, let alone force their hands. The briskness with which she maneuvered at the anniversary to hook me up with Big Brother Saeki had to be due to an explicit directive on Mr. Itami's part—it had all been willed by him.

And Mr. Itami himself appeared relieved.

Saeki had been the right one. My only disciple now has prospects at last. But to think that he'd be partnering with that rare talent Akira Kurosawa, whom I discovered through a script of his...

Actually, Mansaku Itami stroked his mustache and grinned.

"My Hashimoto... The man that you'll encounter someday, no, that you must encounter—Akira Kurosawa is the one."

CHAPTER TWO:
THE MAN CALLED AKIRA KUROSAWA

Akira Kurosawa in 1948, around the time the author first met him.

Rashomon

I had little prior knowledge of Akira Kurosawa.

His screenplay *A German at Daruma Temple,* published in *Eiga Hyo-ron* [Film Criticism] during the war, had received extravagant praise from

Mr. Itami. I saw the first film he directed, *Sanshiro Sugata*, but not *The Most Beautiful*, *Sanshiro Sugata Part II*, or *The Men Who Tread on the Tiger's Tail*. After the war, *No Regrets for Our Youth* was well regarded, but I missed it. Nonetheless, I was astounded by his subsequent films, *One Wonderful Sunday* and *Drunken Angel*. Their worlds of image and sound—these films indicated that a creator's talent and sensibility could reveal cinema's hidden, limitless fertility. As Mr. Itami had once predicted, Kurosawa was the new standard-bearer of Japanese cinema and might become its reigning figure before long.

I had little prior knowledge of him, but the impression he left was thus intense.

But there was something that bothered me a little—no, greatly.

(A list of screenplay writers as seen through the eyes of a writer)

Year	Title	Screenplay writer
1943	*Sanshiro Sugata*	Akira Kurosawa
1944	*The Most Beautiful*	Akira Kurosawa
1945	*Sanshiro Sugata Part II*	Akira Kurosawa
1945	*The Men Who Tread on the Tiger's Tail*	Akira Kurosawa
1946	*No Regrets for Our Youth*	Eijiro Hisaita
1947	*One Wonderful Sunday*	Keinosuke Uegusa
1948	*Drunken Angel*	Keinosuke Uegusa Akira Kurosawa
1949	*The Quiet Duel*	Akira Kurosawa Senkichi Taniguchi
1949	*Stray Dog*	Akira Kurosawa Ryuzo Kikushima
1950	*Scandal*	Akira Kurosawa Ryuzo Kikushima

From his first film, *Sanshiro Sugata*, to *The Men Who Tread on the Tiger's Tail*, he had penned all his screenplays himself; however, his postwar films, after 1946, were all co-written with another screenwriter. *No Regrets for Our Youth*'s Eijiro Hisaita and *One Wonderful Sunday*'s Keinosuke Uegusa each had solo credits, but according to Big Brother Saeki, they were actually co-written screenplays for which Kurosawa forwent credit. In other words, all his postwar films were co-scripted, and the world of collaboration where multiple writers partner or relay to script was unfamiliar to me.

Mr. Kurosawa's house was near Komae Station on the Odakyu Line.

I followed the directions the producer, Sojiro Motoki, had given me. The imposing residence sitting on nearly a thousand square meters of land turned out to be only five or six minutes from the station.

I rang the doorbell and was greeted by a small, white-haired man entering into old age. This was Mrs. Kurosawa's father, who lived with them. When I gave him my name, he said, "Please come in…" and showed me to a drawing room up a half-flight of stairs from the hallway. It was ten mats—no, larger than that, a Japanese-style sitting room steeped in elegance, its ceiling panels and beams made of the finest wood.

Mr. Kurosawa appeared right away. He was astoundingly tall. I especially remember his graceful, deeply-chiseled features and the red sweater he wore. I was thirty-one, and since he was eight years older than me he would have been thirty-nine, and in his hand he held my handwritten draft of *Shiyu*. Once we were seated across from each other, he pushed my draft forward and began to speak.

"This *Shiyu* you've written, it's a bit short, isn't it?"

"In that case, what if I included 'Rashomon'?"

"Rashomon?" Mr. Kurosawa cocked his head. It was a momentary blank like an air pocket, but the tense silence didn't last very long. "Well then, can you add 'Rashomon' to this and rewrite it?"

"Yes, I'll do that."

Our first meeting ended so simply that it didn't feel complete. We spoke for only one or two minutes, and then I put my manuscript in my bag, and both Mr. Kurosawa and his wife Kiyoko showed me out when I left.

As I left their residence, however, my regret and shame began.

Why had I said that? Put "In a Grove" and "Rashomon" together?

I had blurted out something that I hadn't even thought of before, that hadn't even been in the back of my mind.

By the time I returned to Komae Station and boarded the train, regret left me quaking with unease. Off the top of the head as it may have been, how would one ever combine "In a Grove" with "Rashomon"? My words had been all too rash and careless, and yet, despite being uttered in haste, they were irretrievable. I'd spoken them with such confidence… I couldn't possibly say I couldn't do it now.

I transferred from the Odakyu to the Inogashira Line, then returned from Shibuya to Okachimachi via the Yamanote Line's inner loop, and by the time I got back to my company's Tokyo office, I was prickly with irritation from feeling cornered. There was no way "Rashomon" could fit into or easily link to "In a Grove." But I had no choice. Either way, I had to return home and start writing, and there wasn't a day, not an hour, to spare.

At Okachimachi Station I'd even approached the window for a ticket on the night train, only to give up since all berths would have been booked by then. At the best of times, taking a night train without a bed would be too much on the herniated disc that I so painfully nursed. I would have to leave the next morning—yes, in the morning. If I took an early express train I would arrive in Himeji by nightfall, and everything would work out all right.

My study was my morning and evening train commute—when it came to arranging, grouping, and expanding on crisscrossing thoughts, there was no better place than a carriage in motion. By Nagoya, or at least Osaka, I'd come up with my base rewrite, and by Himeji I'd want to be ready to tackle the real work on the following day.

I got lucky with the express "Hato" [Pigeon] departing from Tokyo the next day.

I waited on the platform to board it, and though I was a third-class passenger, I managed to grab a window seat on the left-hand side, facing the engine. I immediately took my clipboard from my bag, and on a piece of paper I wrote "In a Grove" and "Rashomon." No connecting terms, however, were forthcoming. The departure bell rang as I sat trying to draft, and the express began to leave Tokyo Station. I glanced at the platform sliding by, but I felt weighed down and oddly forlorn.

Scripts were scripts, but weren't the ones I'd shown Mr. Itami essentially different from any that I'd meet with Mr. Kurosawa to discuss? With Mr. Itami, the quality of the content had been everything, and he'd given various opinions, points of caution and directions for revision. But whether or not my rewrite proceeded well—for someone as bad at it as I am, it mostly didn't—that was that.

With Mr. Kurosawa, though, that wouldn't cut it. Quality of content was still fundamental, but there was the very real problem of things like length. A scenario *per se* could be thirty minutes or three hours long. But that wasn't permissible when the premise was to film it and something of an ironclad rule of the industry mandated an hour-and-a-half to two-hour timeframe. Moreover, the screenplay was the detailed project plan, the writ of command for seamless, efficient shooting, according to which each part of filmmaking was arranged and prepared, and dozens of staff and a myriad performers from stars on down put in motion; it was the complete design plan necessary for production.

The scenarios I'd written to show Mr. Itami were done once he'd read and critiqued them. That is to say, they were practice scenarios whose ultimate end was to be read. With Mr. Kurosawa, however, far from done, they were brought on set as a film's clear design plan, accurately ordering and designating practical tasks—a fundamentally different stance.

We neared Shimbashi Station and the dense thicket of Hamarikyu Gardens came into view front and left. The sky above Tokyo Bay was gloomy, the sunlight suffusing a shadowy thin layer of clouds that spread across the heavens.

Mr. Kurosawa didn't necessarily fall in love with Shiyu *at first sight.*

He hadn't looked over the script for *Shiyu* that I'd written in three days and decided then and there to make a movie of it. That was impossible. Yet something about it as movie material must have appealed to him. Ninety-three half-sheets was less than half the length of a regular scenario. There was no way it could be filmed as-is. To make it movie-length… He had mulled it over and arrived at some method. That way, the flavor of the theme, "In a Grove," wouldn't be diluted, but actually brought out. Having arrived at the shape and direction of a rewrite, he'd contacted me through Sojiro Motoki, the producer, to tell me he was going to direct it. For him, a scenario was a film's blueprint. Without a concrete and sure-fire plan to bring it up to the necessary length, there would have been no decision to shoot it.

"This *Shiyu* you've written, it's a bit short, isn't it?" Mr. Kurosawa had said.

If I'd either kept quiet and not answered or asked him if there was a good way to lengthen it, he probably would have offered, "For example, this is one way to think about it… What do you think?" and explained the particulars of the direction and form of his own plans for a modification. Since I simply hadn't given any thought to lengthening it, I would have agreed on the spot, and everything would have been decided according to his thinking. Instead, immediately and with apparent confidence I'd said, "Rashomon," throwing Mr. Kurosawa for a loop; thinking, however, that including "Rashomon" might be interesting in its own right, he'd responded: "Well then, can you add 'Rashomon' to this and rewrite it?"

The steam whistle of the express "Hato" sounded, and we passed over the iron bridge at Tama River.

Across the bridge at Rokugo was Kawasaki City, and the lingering whistle seemed to bid farewell to Tokyo like a sentimental traveler. At this I let out a low mumble mixed with a sigh.

A scenario is a film's design plan...

A strange sight floated high above Kawasaki's urban landscape.

It was the image of the design section of our factory's manufacturing department. At that time, I was the head of the accounting department, but when I began working at the company I had done cost calculations as the factory accountant, so I knew a lot of the engineers there as well.

All of the products made at the factory were the work of the manufacturing department's design section. Destroyer ship bulwarks, midget submarine periscopes—they drew up plans for each part based on original drawings forwarded by the navy in addition to drafting plans for the large variety and quantity of civilian necessities. Without a design plan, nothing could be manufactured on site.

The work directive, and its blueprint the design plan, relied upon by every production unit at the factory, issued from the practiced, swift hands of the design section's engineers, who worked standing. In front of large, slightly tilted draftboards they wielded their compasses, rulers, and drawing pens.

One day, as I watched in fascination the speed with which experience allowed the engineers to work, one of them took a break and lit a cigarette. So I asked him something. The young, handsome engineer wearing black-flamed glasses had only graduated from university the year before.

"The plans you're drawing here are easy, but a Zero fighter's engine must be something else."

"It's the same."

"Huh?"

The handsome young engineer didn't even smile. "It's not a matter of large or small or complex or simple. Whether it's a plane that flies in the sky or the battleship *Yamato* or a tiny piece on the order of a hundredth millimeter that requires a microscope, or whatever, drawing the lines is the same...as long as you have a ruler and a compass."

Recalling, some seven years later, the conversation at the factory's design section, I started and raised my face. I felt done in and could hardly breathe—at the time, I hadn't imagined in my wildest dreams that the scenario was a film's design plan, but now it was inescapably important.

If the scenario is a film's design plan...I need a ruler and a compass?!

I hadn't noticed our arrival in Yokohama, and the express "Hato" had already passed Odawara.

At some point, the light clouds had given way to clear sky over the blue horizon of Sagami Bay, visible out the window beyond hilly slopes where they grew tangerines.

I looked at the clipboard on my lap. "In a Grove," "Rashomon," I'd written before departing Tokyo, and nothing else, which made me sigh. I hadn't taken a single step on the film's theme since leaving the Kurosawa residence the day before. Despite my enthusiasm for getting it done on the Tokyo-Himeji express train, I kept chasing after things that, while related and important, lay far from the problem at hand, purposely avoiding the issue of theme.

The sky might be clear but not so my heart, as they say.

Even if I faced the problem head-on, there was no ready solution in sight. So I was avoiding it. I was running away from the critical point. But that wouldn't do—I couldn't avoid it, I couldn't escape. So, what was I to do? I could only take the dive and begin from square one...no, from zero.

Half in desperation, I took up my clipboard and wrote:

"Meeting Mr. Kurosawa"—unprepared—

In meeting Mr. Kurosawa, I'd been all too improvident. I'd met him casually as if I were giving Mr. Itami a visit to have him read and critique a manuscript. If I'd been less aloof about filming it, that ninety-three pages was too short would have been obvious. When I wrote it, I hadn't even imagined that it would be made into a film, so it was what it was; at the very least, though, after Mr. Kurosawa had selected it to be made into a film, going so far as to meet with me to discuss it, length was bound to become an issue. It was common sense, and the duty of the person who'd written the scenario, to arrive having considered and made plans for how to extend it.

Had I realized this, where would I have begun and how would I have revised or transformed it? It was bothersome and a chore, but slow and steady would win the race, and if I began from there, I might figure out why I had blurted "Rashomon" out of the blue.

"Rely on characters"—potential to extend work—

The main characters were Tajomaru, Takehiro Kanazawa, and his wife, Masago.

Other than these, there was a woodcutter, a traveling monk, a policeman, and Masago's mother, but they were bystanders on whose back I couldn't place the burden of extending the heavy drama.

Tajomaru was a carefree bandit so any drama could be centered on him, but it would be meaningless if that drama didn't play a direct role in causing the events of "In a Grove." Yet, the happenstance encounter was what made "In a Grove" interesting, and a preceding incident was anathema. Really, anything I set up would be an unrelated prologue to the main event, extremely difficult to tie in.

Moreover, because the scenario for *Shiyu* began with the trap set by Tajomaru, his part in the drama already stood out. Since this was a drama about three people owning three different versions of the truth, if possible each of their stories would carry roughly equal weight. In which case, it was difficult—no, impossible—to stretch out Tajomaru's pre-story.

How about Takehiro Kanazawa and Masago?

My heart skipped a beat, and I swallowed. Something like a flash of light raced through my mind. This could work! If I expanded on their pre-story, the whole tale would become surprisingly more interesting.

For instance, I could make Masago the daughter of an impoverished courtier of the fifth order or so. There's talk of adopting her into the Fujiwara clan of regents. Powerful courtiers adopted attractive girls to present as ladies at the imperial court. If she caught the right wise eyes and even grew pregnant, there would be no end to the power and the glory, so Masago's clan goes wild over the opportunity and hustles to make it happen.

Masago, however, has set her sights on someone. This is her distant relative, Takehiro Kanazawa, a samurai serving the Wakasa government who is currently residing in the capital after having been dispatched there to present a tribute of dried fish.

Uninterested in a woman's highest honor and fortune, Masago is determined to be united with Takehiro Kanazawa. He, for his part, is in marriage talks in Wakasa but abrogates them and pledges his love to Masago. Despite the impoverished fifth-order courtier and family's mad hustle to get her adopted, Masago stubbornly refuses to comply, and Kanazawa, too, cleaves to his plan to make her his wife. In the end, worn down by the strength of the pair's intentions, Masago's family has no choice but to consent to the marriage and hold a wedding ceremony.

In this way, the two of them set out for Wakasa as a legally wed couple—but as they're crossing Yamashina, the bandit Tajomaru falls in love at first sight with passerby Masago, setting the stage for the absurdist main drama of "In a Grove."

I had entitled "In a Grove" *Shiyu* because the story was about women and men…relationships. If its opening were extended thus, Masago and Takehiro's parts would gain texture and sharpness to vie with the dramatic Tajomaru, there'd be overall cohesion, the ending's absurdity would take on an accelerating intensity, and in one stroke, *Shiyu*'s scenario would improve by leaps and bounds.

But there was no place for "Rashomon." I could force the gate into an opening scene of Takehiro Kanazawa entering the capital from Wakasa with his tribute of dried fish, and into a shot of the newly-wed couple leaving the capital to return to Wakasa, but it would just be as a backdrop, which wouldn't be including the story at all.

When Mr. Kurosawa had said, "It's a bit short," what if I hadn't mentioned "Rashomon" but instead proposed to extend the beginning with Masago and Takehiro Kanazawa's story? I imagine he would have given me a big nod. Because there was no other way of extending what was inherent in *Shiyu*, I even suspect that Mr. Kurosawa's own thoughts on how to stretch it out had been the same.

No, as creative a person as he might have conceived of something completely different with his innumerable rulers and compasses, but I have no way of knowing.

I berated myself. *Bosh! What "Rashomon"? Extending it with the couple does it.*

The express "Hato" arrived at Shizuoka Station, so I bought a standard boxed lunch and tea.

They talk about people going without sleep or food when they're obsessed, but I've never been one of them. During this time in my life, I went to Tokyo frequently on business, and putting aside when I took the night train, whenever I left Himeji for Tokyo around noon, I'd buy lunch not at Osaka or Kyoto but further along at Maibara. The station lunches at Maibara were cheaper and tastier. When I returned from Tokyo, noon didn't come around until Nagoya, but the ones at Shizuoka, before Nagoya, were cheaper and delicious. This was common knowledge amongst those of us who made third-class roundtrips on the Tokaido Line.

It's a little early, but why don't I eat around Hamamatsu and then take up "Rashomon"?

By the time I finished lunch we had passed Hamamatsu, and out the left-hand window was the ocean, and out the right-hand window was… the ocean again? No, to the right was Lake Hamana, and to the left was the Pacific Ocean around Maisaka, and it was around there that I looked over what I had written on a fresh page on my clipboard.

—Why did I say "Rashomon"?—

It had been instantaneous and reflexive, and I couldn't come up with a reason or basis.

So, what was my "Rashomon" about? No, what was "Rashomon" the short story about?

It was one of Ryunosuke Akutagawa's early works, widely acclaimed, and collections of his stories were often titled after it, making it his representative work.

As for its content—it's the late Heian period. Famine has beset the land, a plague is raging, the capital itself is in shambles, and even the second level of the gate edifice to the city, Rashomon, has become a thieves' den and a disposal site for unclaimed corpses.

One night, a manservant dismissed by his employer and with no place to go climbs up to the gate's second story lured by a faint seeping glow. There, in the meager light, an old woman is pulling hairs, one by one, from a female corpse. The stunned servant chastises the hag, to which she replies:

"This woman used to dry dead snakes and go around selling them as dried fish. But if she hadn't, she wouldn't have been able to eat. So she'll forgive me—for not being able to eat, either, if I didn't pull out her hair one strand at a time to sell to a wig-maker."

The manservant nods and considers this for a moment, then nods again, with greater conviction.

"I understand, old woman. In that case, you'll forgive me for doing what I must in order to eat." So saying, he tears the ragged clothes from her body, descends from the second story, and leaves through the gate. The old woman, whose worldly possessions have been ripped from her, slowly rises as if to follow, looking in his direction with her hand on the rail, but all she sees is darkness—the servant is nowhere to be found. It's that kind of absurdist tale.

I recalled that when I'd been reading Ryunosuke Akutagawa's stories to turn his work into a screenplay, "Rashomon" had topped my list of projects, but what exactly had I planned to do with it?

I was interested in the ensuing life of the manservant who'd disappeared into the darkness.

At first he rips the clothes away from an old woman because he needs to in order to survive, but theft becomes his regular occupation, he moves on to robbery, and before long even murder doesn't bother him. As the leader of a band of scoundrels he violates a young noblewoman and abducts her to the second story of Rashomon to live there together. But in face of the girl's born goodness, evil falls away from him bit by bit until he blossoms into a pure person with no malice in his heart. It's then that he's surrounded by deputies of the commission and shot from below with arrows, and he dies there on the second story looking like a hedgehog.

So, was there anything in the original story or my plan for it that connected, or might connect, to "In a Grove"?

There was nothing. Zero relation, and forcing them together would just create a mismatch. There was, however, one character from "In a Grove" who could establish a connection. Tajomaru—being a bandit, it wouldn't be strange for him to be living in Rashomon. But even if the gate were his home, it didn't follow that "In a Grove" and "Rashomon" were connected. If Tajomaru used to be a manservant whom the gate introduced to evil, then this was a tie to "In a Grove" in that one absurdity led to another. But as I touched upon in relation to the characters, a preceding incident separate from the events of "In a Grove" would be terribly difficult to incorporate.

Might another character serve as a connection?

Impossible. Whether Takehiro Kanazawa and Masago, or the woodcutter, the traveling monk, or Masago's mother, Rashomon could only serve as a backdrop at best. Even pushing it, they'd only use the place to temporarily escape the hot summer sun or an evening shower.

Then why did you say "Rashomon" in the absence of any basis whatsoever?

Humans say things on the spur of the moment, reflexively, without any forethought. But do they ever verbalize something they never once truly felt, never once expected or been conscious of?

"If we included 'Rashomon'…" Even if the speaker wasn't aware of it, there had to be some sort of basis.

I don't really know how it works. Still, a conjecture like the following doesn't seem out of bounds.

Human actions (speech and movement) are predicated on consciousness, but that's not always the case; sometimes, even without conscious thought, without any relation to the right or left sides of the brain, actions are engendered by the oldest, reptilian brain—that is, by the brain stem and instinctive intent.

When Mr. Kurosawa pointed out that *Shiyu* was short, "short" also meant anything from "small" to "weak," and separately from my right or left brain, my instinctive brain stem had perceived the diminutive nature of what I'd dashed off over the course of three days. Perhaps an intent to bolster it for the sake of self-preservation kicked in in a split second and made me say "Rashomon."

Widely known, "Rashomon" is Ryunosuke Akutagawa's representative work. Compared to "In a Grove" and *Shiyu*, it is large, solid, stately, and even deep. By linking up to "Rashomon," my whole work would become larger and stronger—I think perhaps that was my split-second instinctive intent.

Was this to say as long as no missteps stood out, incorporating "Rashomon" had the aspect and advantage of yielding a stronger, larger work than sticking to *Shiyu*? No, there was no such thing as an inconspicuous mistake. I needed to build the narrative edifice up to a level where error turned into necessity.

As far as I was concerned, in order to turn *Shiyu*, the adaptation of Akutagawa's "In a Grove," into a feature film, it was best to roll out Takehiro Kanazawa and Masago's pre-story, and no other revision was in fact possible. But there was my promise with Mr. Kurosawa, for which I had no one but myself to thank.

So are you going to do this with "Rashomon" in it?

You bet I am!

The absurdism of "Rashomon" developing into the great absurdity of "In a Grove"—I would compose the story around this fundamental theme. The manservant of "Rashomon" is Tajomaru's previous life.

An honest servant in a nobleman's household is told he is discharged.

He wanders the capital aimlessly. Famine, plague, decline and degeneration, peddling, spectacle, women seducing men in broad daylight, vulgarity, chaos, clatter, fighting, no food for stray dogs anywhere to be found.

Various images float past as he resolves to find real work.

The blood-red sky of the setting sun, Rashomon looming enormous and dark ahead, an old woman pulling hair one strand at a time from corpses, a woman selling dead snakes as dried fish…

I glanced to my side. The man in the aisle seat who appeared to be a salaryman took his bag down from the overhead rack and put away some documents that he'd been perusing. Just a while ago he'd asked a passing conductor when we'd be arriving at Nagoya. His seat would open up there. My hunch was that no new passenger would board, which meant the seat would remain empty to Kyoto or Osaka. How convenient.

Between Nagoya and Osaka I would fashion the big box of overall structure, finishing off the smaller boxes between Osaka and Himeji; then, tomorrow, I would begin writing the text. The first scene would be the gate at night... No, night would be dark and hard to film. Dusk? Well, a rainy scene was also tasteful and hard to pass up, but dusk it shall be.

> (F · 1)
> ○ Rashomon
> The blood-red sky of the setting sun, Rashomon looming enormous and dark ahead

"The first scene is Rashomon at dusk!"

I completed the screenplay, *The Tale of Rashomon*, in about a month.

But it was an abomination. None of the works I'd shown Mr. Itami as an apprentice had been nearly as misshapen.

The main cause was a rookie error regarding the dramatis personae, the treatment of the protagonist. While Tajomaru appears from the outset and gives a strong impression of being the definitive main character, he disappears after his part in "In a Grove" and the remainder ends up feeling awfully hollow and odd.

To a certain extent, I foresaw the story's rickety progress and a calamitous end result even as I'd started writing. Yet, I wasn't too depressed or pessimistic about it.

Mr. Kurosawa had his own plan—a revision plan he'd put together in his mind before I threw "Rashomon" out there, so if my rewrites failed, we would naturally fall back on that plan. It wasn't like we were groping in the dark.

As for me, I just needed to finish up *The Tale of Rashomon* and tell Mr. Kurosawa it was a failure and, with his permission, implement Plan B and write a scenario that told Masago and Takehiro Kanazawa's pre-story.

But when it rains, it pours.

I still suffered from a herniated disc, and as long as it was my waist that hurt I could live with it. The pain got worse as it migrated downwards, however, and when it reached my knees I couldn't take it anymore. Commuting was out so I took time off and somehow kept working on the scenario at home, but the pain spread even lower to my ankles, and by the time I finished writing, the big toe of my left foot hurt so much that I couldn't walk. In the end I had to attach a note to the scenario explaining my condition and have my wife take it to the post office to send to Tokyo. Lying on my right side, I was unable to move even a step.

Sojiro Motoki, the Film Art Association producer in Tokyo, got in touch with me.

Upon reading the rewritten manuscript, Kurosawa had tilted his head and wondered if he might not have made a mistaken suggestion. But this was a lie...a lie and untrue. The work had come out so poor that Mr. Kurosawa was covering for me. He hadn't made any suggestions during our meeting.

Moreover, Kurosawa wanted to start work on the final draft. He absolutely wanted to polish it together with me, but how was my condition? If there was no way I could come to Tokyo, then with my kind understanding, Kurosawa would be writing the final draft alone.

The pain in my left big toe was abnormal.

As long as I stayed still and on my right side, it didn't hurt, but when someone stepped into the room, the mere vibration across the tatami, not a hard surface, sent searing pain racing through my body. I was resentful. Sad. If not for the pain in my foot, I would go to Tokyo straightaway, meet with Mr. Kurosawa, and extend Masago and Takehiro Kanazawa's story in two weeks...two weeks would be plenty since the content of "In a Grove" would remain untouched. Once Mr. Kurosawa checked it out I could beg him to make it the final draft, and he would surely understand. It was out of the question, though, thanks to my ailing foot.

About twenty days passed during which night bled into day until I couldn't tell them apart.

The pain diminished just a bit, and I was able to visit the bathroom with the help of a six-foot staff cut from fresh bamboo. This was much easier on me than being bedridden, and upon returning I slid onto my futon on all fours and rolled onto my right side, relaxed a little, and let my mind wander.

Was Mr. Kurosawa writing the script in Tokyo now? No, not Tokyo, perhaps at some *onsen* hot springs in Hakone, Atami, or Izu. Secluded at some *onsen* he was penning the final draft—a design plan for the film.

If the scenario is a film's design plan... I need a ruler and a compass?!

Ah, right, yes. That was on my trip back from Tokyo, in a carriage of the express "Hato." I'd remembered the factory's design section from seven years ago, and it had had an unexpectedly strong effect on me, but because "Rashomon" had been on my mind I'd cut my thoughts short. But this thing about a ruler and a compass might help me going forward—no, remain an important insight for the rest of my life—and now was the time to collect and organize my thoughts as best I could.

It wasn't regret for time lost, but a road leading me to the future.

Mr. Itami's feedback on my practice writing offered much of value, a lot of it good enough to serve as lifelong indices. But on the flip side, somewhat emotional outbursts and many scolding words had gone over my head.

Where is the point of view, where?!
The point of view is wandering!
What are the writer's eyes seeing?!
The characterization is warping out of shape!
Too long, the stage directions are too long!

I couldn't digest such language so it had turned into something unpleasant like accumulated permafrost, but now it was all disintegrating and collapsing in an avalanche.

Mr. Itami had seen my works not as "reading material" but as "film design plans," as constructs formed by the many intertwining lines of a design.

It was obvious, if you thought of a scenario as a blueprint in a design plan.

If a design plan had missing lines, vague lines, excess lines and such, then at just one glance, the whole design plan lost all meaning. Over the many years that Mr. Itami had continued to write scenarios and exercise his craft, he must have come by knacks and hunches that amounted to his own ruler and compass.

As such, when he approached others' works, that ruler and compass instantly functioned as a sensor that clearly distinguished between the excellent and the not-so-excellent, and in the case of faulted works, honed in at once on parts that were needed but lacking or that were unclear or ambiguous, as well as on extraneous episodes and descriptions.

Mr. Itami's scenario commentaries in the journal *Nihon Eiga* [Japanese Cinema] would not have become more than merely popular—lauded as unparalleled masterpieces, they won people's confidence and were said to be contributing to improving the quality of Japanese cinema—if they hadn't been backed by this ruler and compass.

At the same time, while one could simply attribute the unmatched economy of masterpieces like *The Rickshaw Man* and *Children Hand in Hand* to talent, these were works that could not have come into being, or seen completion, without something like a criterion for moulding and implementing that talent—and isn't this numerical standard of sorts that is able to make talent breathe, come to life, the ruler and compass that we call knacks and hunches?

I'd love me some too, someday—that ruler and compass.

In any event, it was only possible to obtain them through an uncompromisingly strong and deep awareness of the scenario as a design plan, and through practicing the craft. If I stuck to what I had done until then, obsessing over the surface adornments of the scenario as engaging reading, I would be doomed never to have a ruler and compass.

There are many people who aspire to become scenario writers who drop out, try fiction, and become famous, and many active scenario writers who only achieve great success after turning to fiction. Those who drop out of scenario writing but succeed at fiction follow such a trajectory because they may feel drawn to the scenario as engaging reading but lack an awareness of it as a design plan. Friction and discord with a film studio can be a cause, but we might also say that such writers find their land of repose in the acceptingness of prose, which forgives some unevenness compared to the endurance and perseverance that drawing the lines of a design plan demands—a matter of a steady hand, the relaxed and casual character of prose compared to the scenario's unforgivingness over a mere rhythmic stumble or slackening. There will probably be many more such cases.

Meanwhile, there is not one example of a novelist who became a scenario writer, and this will remain so. This doesn't mean that scenarios are especially difficult to write. Fiction is meant to be read, and the scenario is a design plan. They are distinct species of a completely different nature, and then there's the matter of it being easier to make money writing novels than scenarios.

A large envelope arrived by mail from the Film Art Association in Shimbashi, Tokyo.

It contained a printed copy of Mr. Kurosawa's final draft, along with a letter from Mr. Sojiro Motoki. Even before reading the letter, I hastily took up the printed script, and its cover page gave me a jolt. *Rashomon*.

"Rashomon" was what I tried and failed at, and I assumed the final draft would naturally feature Mr. Kurosawa's original modification plan, but unexpectedly enough the title was my own *The Tale of Rashomon* minus "The Tale of."

With bated breath, I turned the page and began reading *Rashomon*.

A couple of witnesses returning from the commission—the wood-cutter (a feudal "soma-uri" in the final script) who discovered the dead body and the traveling monk who encountered Takehiro Kanazawa and Masago on the road from Yamashina to Sekiyama—are caught in a sudden rain and take shelter under Rashomon. A man who looks like a ruffian (the manservant) comes flying in as the woodcutter says vacantly, "It's a strange tale," and the traveling monk responds, "I don't believe

Rashomon, which also received high praise overseas. Tajomaru (Toshiro Mifune) and Masago (Machiko Kyo) © KADOKAWA

it." Overhearing them, the ruffian leans forward and says, "What kind of story? Tell me!" and the narrative turns to what the woodcutter and the traveling monk experienced and testified to at the commission: the case of "In a Grove."

It was a pretty amazing beginning and I groaned in spite of myself.

Set up in such a way, "Rashomon" would fit in whole.

In short, it was how you used the ruler. Taking great pains to try and fit "Rashomon" into "In a Grove," I'd used a ruler to draw a line out from "In a Grove," toward "Rashomon." Even if it started with "Rashomon," the line came from "In a Grove." Mr. Kurosawa, however, used the ruler in the opposite way, drawing a line *from* "Rashomon" *to* "In a Grove." That way, "In a Grove" fit naturally, as-is, into "Rashomon"—an exceptional, veteran backhand that you couldn't make your own until you had a certain number of works under your belt.

Yet, since "Rashomon" is only so long, taking that route meant expanding on something in "In a Grove" itself to attain the required girth.

Good intro, flawless story progression, everything proceeding apace. But how does it end? I skipped ahead and went straight to the last scene. But I thought the better of it, returned to where I had left off, and continued anew.

The beginning, the development, and the lead-up to the climax were all ideal. I felt keenly the world of difference, the gaps between the conception and skill of Mr. Kurosawa and poor old me. And inserted into that climax was an episode appearing neither in my script nor the original story.

It was the truth of the case, what the woodcutter saw with his own eyes—the facts of the case falsifying Tajomaru's testimony and Masago's confession and the words of the medium possessed by Takehiro's spirit—a singular situation, which only the most muscled arm and mightiest brawn could establish, superbly pulled off, and extending "In a Grove" itself.

Yet, instead of the three characters' falsehoods gaining relief and vividness and the story greater texture as a result, there wasn't much of a change in the characters' words and actions. In particular, Takehiro Kanazawa's death, the central fact of the case, took the form of a duel instigated by Masago ending with the bandit's blade piercing the nobleman's chest after more than twenty passes, which overlapped with Tajomaru's own testimony. The story as a whole seemed somewhat convoluted as a result. While still absurdist, the theme was shifting away from the truth being unattainable to people being creatures of convenience, the film as a whole becoming somewhat abstruse and hard to understand.

It might be said that the above was inevitable and could not be helped in extending the story, but the problem was the ending, and as I'd feared since I began reading—it fell apart.

After the story of "In a Grove" finishes, an infant abandoned at Rashomon begins to cry. When the ruffian notices the abandoned child and reaches out for the kimono in which it's swaddled, the woodcutter and the traveling monk hasten to stop him, but he mercilessly tears it from the baby and runs out in the rain that's just begun to abate.

The monk picks up the baby who's been left with nothing but his underthings, and the woodcutter timidly holds out both hands. Angrily, the monk says, "Are you going to steal even his underclothes?" The woodcutter shakes his head vehemently: "I have six children. It's the same whether I raise six or seven." The monk apologizes for his misunderstanding and hands over the baby. The woodcutter, who was feeling despondent over the irredeemable story of "In a Grove," tightly embraces the child he intends to raise, and as the rain stops he walks away from Rashomon, which is standing out in the sunset.

This scene at the end stuck out like a sore thumb.

Let alone the traveling monk, even the woodcutter who knows the truth of the matter is a bystander, and the drama cannot rest on their backs. Tajomaru, Takehiro Kanazawa, and Masago alone shoulder the responsibility for the drama that is "In a Grove." It ends when the medium possessed by the spirit of Takehiro Kanazawa says, "I…am going into the deep, black depths of darkness…unending…unending…" and then collapses on the white sand. If this doesn't happen in the present tense but is told by bystanders, you can't twist it off and end there, and naturally things need to be wrapped up after they're done with their story.

Even if the woodcutter delivers the truth again, if the story is over then the result is the same in that something needs to come after it. As bystanders, however, there is no drama for them to shoulder, and anything new that one might add could not but stand out as a glaring veneer.

Fine intro, a quite interesting middle, the meat of it keeps you hooked and ready for more. But at that last moment—a sudden unforeseen snag trips it up.

I read the letter from Mr. Sojiro Motoki.

> The final draft has been completed, so I am sending it along. Kurosawa is very interested in hearing your thoughts on it, so once your foot has improved, we would like you to come to Tokyo to meet with Kurosawa and give him your candid opinion directly. Thank you for your consideration.

I thought about it for three days. But I came to no conclusion.

I thought for a week more, then asked my father, "Father, please go into the grove and cut a piece of bamboo. I'm going to make a staff."

"A staff? How long?"

"About six feet… The joints will stand out, so please shave them off."

"Are you going to work?"

I nodded. "Work, too, but first to Tokyo for a bit."

"Tokyo?"

It's not that I came to my conclusion about the final draft with any ease.

I considered a number of endings, for my part, and tried flavoring them with modifications, but nothing seemed suitable. These were basically peripheral characters who couldn't shoulder any drama so there couldn't be any decent backstory, whereas the present form (the bit with the abandoned baby) was at least short, tight, and straightforward. Extending the work in order to modify this last scene amounted to rejecting the very form of a flashback from "Rashomon" to "In a Grove"—the very setup of the final draft.

In terms of a sharp conclusion, the medium possessed by Takehiro's spirit falling to the ground was ideal, but the only way of ending there was to reel out Masago and Kanazawa's pre-story.

A work with that prologue didn't exist so it was hard to say, but there was no mistaking that the story would be coherent and clear-cut at the very least. *Shiyu* [Male and Female] would be too blunt a title in that case, so reverting to the original's "In a Grove" would be advisable.

In short, because a flashback from "Rashomon" inevitably led to a flawed ending and we couldn't say to what extent it might affect the film, I was wondering if I should or shouldn't recommend to Mr. Kurosawa that we try to extend Masago and Takehiro Kanazawa's pre-story. I could tell him, certainly, but the cause of my reluctance, what was holding me back from making the recommendation, was that a new, cohesive "In a Grove" with the pre-story felt one or two sizes smaller, somehow puny in the face of *Rashomon*. As marred as the last scene was, like a man with a scar on his forehead *Rashomon* had far and away greater impact, a daunting tense air of springing out at something unseen.

Not knowing what to do, my days of being torn between the two alternatives continued.

One day, a thought came to me. Mr. Kurosawa's initial plan was a blind spot that I wasn't considering at all. Before meeting me, what kind of revision proposal had he prepared? This being him, it couldn't have had a marred ending; correct, sure, and steady, it must have been free of any forward or backward contradictions and full of originality. But the moment I mouthed the word "Rashomon" unthinkingly, irresponsibly… I gasped and kicked up my futon.

I clambered up on all fours. Grasping the staff I relied on to go to the toilet, I reached the entryway. I put a slipper on my left foot, which was numb with pain, and a *geta* clog on my right foot, and like a boatman planting his rod in the water, walked hanging on my staff. I could walk… I went outside into the brightness. I could walk, like this I could go to Tokyo. Ignoring the passersby watching me with curiosity, I made my way onto the bridge over Ichikawa. I looked at the river's surface, at the white clouds in the sky. A groan came unbidden from the back of my throat.

Now I understand…the man called Akira Kurosawa!

He'd had an absolutely immovable plan. But when I, no, my instinctive brain stem itself uttered "Rashomon"—he had a flash of inspiration. Instantly casting away that almost freakishly robust assertiveness of his, that will of his no lever could bend, he closed his fist on the lightning flash. If it was to grasp that inspiration, nothing else…no scar that might be left as a result even mattered.

By no means had I arrived at a complete understanding of what he was made of. But this most crucial aspect was growing terribly vivid in close up.

The man called Akira Kurosawa—was a man who caught lightning flashes.

The staff my father had made for me from young bamboo felt good in my hand.

He had removed its knots with an axe, filed it down, and even smoothed it out with sandpaper.

However, it was six feet long, so the passengers on the Bantan Line looked curiously at me.

I splurged for a second-class ticket on an express train from Shimonoseki to Tokyo, boarding at Himeji. When a passing conductor stopped in his tracks to glare at my bamboo staff, I preempted him and said, "Bad foot. A cane doesn't help, and this is the only way I can walk."

Arriving in Tokyo, I stayed the night at my company's place in Okachimachi, and the next morning I took the Odakyu Line to Komae Station to call on Mr. Kurosawa. Fortunately, he was home, and he came with his wife to the entryway to greet me. Mr. Kurosawa glanced at the staff I placed next to the shoe cabinet then averted his eyes. Meanwhile, his wife Kiyoko's eyes went wide as though beholding a strange object, and she stared her fill.

I was shown to the large drawing room and, facing Mr. Kurosawa, I began to give him my thoughts on the final draft. Mr. Kurosawa, his eyes slightly lowered, was holding his breath, but when I finished speaking he lifted his face a little and smiled broadly. And the very next moment, his laughter rang out like a shot.

I had a sales meeting back at the office in Okachimachi, and the next day I met with the Ginza headquarters executive of a bank with which we did business. The day after that, before boarding an express at Shimbashi, I visited the Film Art Association since my company chores were done.

"Oh! Hashimoto, thank you for everything! Here, here!"

Producer Sojiro Motoki stood up from his chair like a spring toy and gestured with his hand.

Considered the film industry's leading producer, Sojiro Motoki had a small build, a stout voice, and a friendly demeanor. Barely waiting for me to lower myself onto the sofa across him, he gushed, "You went to see

Kurosawa, I heard!"

He began to imitate Mr. Kurosawa's voice and manner of speaking.

"That guy Hashimoto came by, and he gave me his thoughts on the script. His impression... On a sumo ring... A sumo ring, you hear? Not a wrestler, but a wild dog. A wolf, a wolf... A-And this frightful creature, crouched on all fours, is glaring blue flashes...lightning...poised to pounce on something unfathomable, big, a-ha ha ha ha ha."

Unable to keep up Mr. Kurosawa's laughter, Sojiro Motoki slid into his own.

"Kk, kk, kk, khek!"

It was a year and a half later, in September 1951, that the film *Rashomon* became the first Japanese work to win the Golden Lion (Grand Prix) at the Venice Film Festival, casting something like a ray of light on battered souls whose hopes had been lost in the war.

Mr. Kurosawa was a mysterious man.

Rashomon was released in August 1950, and one autumn day the following year he told me, "Hashimoto, we've decided where you'll be staying."

I had no memory of discussing or requesting accommodations from Mr. Kurosawa. But Mr. Kurosawa and his wife, Kiyoko, had taken it upon themselves to decide for me. I would be staying in Soshigaya in Setagaya Ward…at Mr. Nishimura's house, several minutes from Soshigaya-Okura Station on the Odakyu Line. A man of means, Mr. Nishimura had been an entrepreneur operating a coal mine in Korea, but he'd liquidated his property and returned to Japan over worries about the escalating Sino-Japanese war. He and his wife had a daughter who'd never married, Tomiko, apparently a good friend of Kiyoko's and around the same age.

My residence in Tokyo was still my company's office in Okachimachi, Taito Ward. I had quit the company at the beginning of spring, though, and at some point I was going to have to leave. Since no one said anything to me directly, and three meals and a room were nice to have, it was easy just to keep hanging around. However, since a new place with room and board had been decided for me, I ended that arrangement and moved into the second floor of the Nishimura residence in Soshigaya, Setagaya Ward.

This change in environment had a huge impact on me.

Compared to the ceaseless noise of automobiles and streetcars on Showa Street, the quiet residential neighborhoods of Setagaya were as still as a forest, and there was no place quite so suited to writing. The Nishimura residence sat on a 1,300 sq. meter plot of land with a spacious lawn, and when I was tired I would go downstairs and out into the garden to relax. When my next project was decided, I could write here without having to relocate to an inn.

It was during this year that I wrote a screenplay called *Miki Hirate* for Shin-Toho.

Previously, Saeki-bro had strongly recommended me to the head of studio at Shin-Toho, Mr. Takei, and we had discussed the possibility of my doing some work for him. Due to *Rashomon* with Mr. Kurosawa and my salaryman schedule not being flexible, we'd kept putting it off. But when I quit the company, I found myself with free time and was able to take on the work. Based on a work by Gishu Nakayama, directed by

Kyotaro Namiki, and starring So Yamamura, the film was well-made and well-received; with its release, requests for screenplays from a few other film studios came in, among them enthusiastic offers for multi-film contracts, of which the one from Toho was especially eager. It all contrasted greatly with the release of *Rashomon* a year earlier, when there were no offers from anyone and I was met with deafening silence.

Maybe having your name appear as a screenwriter alongside Mr. Kurosawa's on a Kurosawa film was ignored by both the industry and the press and wasn't very rewarding? Well, no, the screenplays for Kurosawa films were collaborations and someone else's name always appeared with his. Perhaps it was just that, in my case, they were faced with the debut work of a rookie and had no idea who the heck I was, and lacking any priors to consult, especially given that my body of work was nonexistent, they had a hard time appraising my contribution.

The tranquil days I passed at the Nishimura residence in Setagaya left almost nothing to be desired.

I did, however, feel dissatisfied about just one thing. It was that I couldn't go to the cycling race track. I am a fan of gambling and cycling races—no, not a fan, but a maniac. On that front, the Tokyo office in Okachimachi had been a blessing, a forward base. I would go to the station after breakfast and buy a racing paper. If there was a race at Korakuen, I would hone in on that one, and if not, I would buy the papers to examine a few candidates from among Kawasaki, Kagetsu, Keiokaku, Seibu-en, Matsudo, Omiya, etc., take them back to the second floor of the office, and there decide which one to visit.

Zeroing in on the ninth race, I would examine which circuit's best suited my aim, and once I knew where I was going, I'd also pick a seventh and eighth race, then depart. Betting only on three races out of ten, I would merely watch all the others without buying even a single 100-yen ticket.

This was no easy thing. Just watching and not betting at all in the veritable gambling den that the entire racing track turned into—this was the ultimate in self-restraint. You had to hold on to an intensely stoic something and stay calm and collected and refuse to lose yourself. And waiting thus for my races, I would place my bets as planned.

More than half the time my dark horses failed me, but winning one race out of every four or five equaled never running out of principal. And on the train back, I would think in earnest: if there was anything in my life worth affirming, any moment of fulfillment for which I could pat myself on the back—then was it not (though it was a period in my life) my time as a cycling maniac castled in the Okachimachi office?

But Soshigaya in Setagaya Ward wasn't at all advantageous for going to the races.

There wasn't even one racing track along the Odakyu Line, and going anywhere else was extremely inconvenient. Moreover, I balked at telling the Nishimuras, "I'm going out to the races." I could lie and say I was going to the movies, but lying about it turned a serious affair into some secret amusement. Gambling is a match with naked blades, live or die, and if anything, you should be seen off with sparks struck for luck, or you can forget about it.

So as a means of alleviating boredom during my time with the Nishimuras, instead of going to the gambling den I would dress casually, put on clogs, and go for a walk. Destination, studio—it was a reasonable distance to both Shin-Toho's and Toho's, and if I went I could chat awhile with whomever. Perhaps Mr. Kurosawa had chosen the Nishimuras' home as my lodging so that I would be in a good environment for writing and near the studios.

One day, wearing a casual *kurumegasuri*-patterned kimono and *geta* clogs and strolling around Toho's studio, I spotted five or six actresses (a full notch above walk-ons) chattering away by the fountain in front of the main building. Individually they were all ladies, but in a band of that size they were forward and terribly spirited. My *kurumegasuri* attire and paulownia *geta* must have caught their eyes.

"Hey, who's that? He's not an actor."

"Yeah, and he can't be a walk-on."

"Oh, I know… He's a screenwriter."

"A screenwriter?"

"He was in one of the papers. A new writer who has emerged like a comet… Shinobu Hashimoto, who wrote *Miki Hirate* for Shin-Toho."

"What? That's the Shinobu Hashimoto who wrote *Miki Hirate*?"

I casually raised my left hand and passed in front of the women. They cried out "Ah!" all at once and waved their hands at me. It wasn't a bad feeling. It was a good feeling. But inside I was grumbling.

Girls, girls, mention Rashomon *at the very least. I worked ten, no, twenty, no, a hundred times harder on that than on* Miki Hirate.

And one such day, without any advance notice, Mr. Kurosawa dropped by the Nishimura residence.

Coming downstairs at Mrs. Nishimura's call, I found Mr. Kurosawa taking off his shoes in the entryway. Mrs. Nishimura, who appeared to be well-acquainted with him, continued with her greetings, asking after his family, then showed him not to the second floor but to the drawing room on the first floor facing the garden, so I followed after them.

Sitting with his back to the *tokonoma* alcove and facing me across a large rosewood table, Mr. Kurosawa cut to the chase. "Hashimoto, for the next job, I'm thinking of bringing in Hideo Oguni too."

My heart jumped, but I affected a nonchalant look and nodded to say I had no objections.

"You may not have met him before, but I assume you know his name?"

"Yes, I know of him."

Not only had I heard of him, but just the other day his name had come up in an incident of sorts. The location was a café directly next to the security office at Shin-Toho's front gate, and I was talking with the producer Takenaka to determine my remuneration for the *Miki Hirate* screenplay.

"Thanks to you, the cast and crew screening has also been a smash hit, so let's discuss your script fee. How much do we owe you?"

I had no idea. There was a scenarists association, and they had an arrangement with the studios that guaranteed no less than 100,000 yen. This system was applied to new writers, so I had received 100,000 yen for *Rashomon*. All rookies got paid 100,000 yen, but this was my second screenplay so the fee had to be higher. But I had no idea how much higher it should be.

I asked Takenaka just to be sure. "Right now, who makes the most money for a screenplay, and how much does he get?"

"Hmm, the most expensive? Hideo Oguni or thereabouts—in his case, I doubt he'd write for us if we aren't ready to part with at least 500,000 yen."

"Five hundred thou for one script?" I was astonished. If you wrote two, you could buy a house. It was a vertiginous, an astronomical figure. "Ooh, put me on the same pay grade as this Mr. Oguni."

The next moment, a navy-blue bat flapped its wings in front of me. I was flabbergasted. Takenaka, in his dark blue suit, had suddenly shot up and waved his hands alternately up and down. The great bat startled me out of my wits... No, maybe *I* had uttered something incredible beyond the pale of industry common sense for Takenaka to be so startled. I panicked. Flustered and bewildered, I amended my words.

"I... H-Half of what Hideo Oguni makes is fine!"

As for the sum, after some time, we settled on 300,000 yen.

Later, I discovered that for a newcomer's second effort the going rate was still a hundred thousand, but since the script was better put together than expected, the studio's development department had disregarded custom and apparently been ready to pay 150,000, even 200,000 yen. Two hundred thousand yen for a script was a distinguished mid-career writer's price. The studio and producer had braced themselves to that extent.

Yet I came out and asked for the same half a million as Hideo Oguni, so no wonder he was astonished. The navy-blue bat was a perfectly understandable reaction when I was a ghastly terror in Takenaka's eyes.

It was like finding a game piece in a gourd as the saying goes, an unexpected blessing, and a script fee of 300,000 yen truly helped. The fee is a symbol of where one sits within the hierarchy and ranking of screenwriters, and all of a sudden a newcomer had leapfrogged over the medium grade and risen to the top echelon of scenario writers. It was all thanks to Hideo Oguni and his astronomical screenplay fee, but I dared not breathe a word about this incident to Mr. Kurosawa.

"Oguni, you know, is more experienced than both of us, and as a writer he's a horse of a different color," he continued. "In particular, he's your exact opposite in every respect, Hashimoto, and what you lack he has. If we work together, I think it will be a great learning experience for you. Oguni's home isn't too far from here, so I'll bring him to meet you soon."

That seemed wrong to me. I felt like it made more sense for Mr. Oguni and me to meet Mr. Kurosawa at his house, or if Mr. Kurosawa was set on coming here, for me to accompany him to Mr. Oguni's house to pay my respects. But Mr. Kurosawa was already standing. Once he'd spoken his mind, he was done.

Putting his shoes on in the entryway, Mr. Kurosawa reiterated, "I'll come soon with Oguni."

After he left, I went upstairs to my room.

He didn't have to come all the way here from Komae by train just to say that.

Mr. Kurosawa had said to keep my schedule free, so I made sure it was open. Once work started we'd be meeting numerous times, and he could have just told me then about Mr. Oguni. What was more, bringing Hideo Oguni here to meet me… This wasn't some arranged marriage, so why? What meaning did a meeting of faces have? If I were going to acquaint myself with Hideo Oguni, it would only be proper for me to call on him with—though I wouldn't say this aloud—a box of cakes in hand.

So, what kind of person was this Mr. Oguni, my god of fortune? When I first heard his name and fee from Shin-Toho's Takenaka, I imagined a beard. A person who grew a beard...an association I got from Mr. Itami. Yet, unlike Mr. Itami, not just a mustache under the nose but a wide and pointy one...a face somewhat like the great novelist Soseki Natsume's, but as for his height, nearly six feet tall...resolute, with a commanding dignity, at times scanning everything with piercing eyes... in any case, the great master who commanded the highest fee for screenplays in all Japan.

Four or five days later, I had a phone call from Mr. Kurosawa saying that he was about to bring Mr. Oguni by, and I went down to meet them in the entryway.

My eyes grew wide with surprise. Since Hideo Oguni was standing behind Mr. Kurosawa, at first I couldn't see him behind that large figure, but when Mr. Kurosawa made to step up into the house, his companion's face and body finally appeared. He was a small, slightly plump older man with salt-and-pepper hair but no facial hair of any sort—energetic, bustling, a nimble and mercurial type who was the complete opposite of what I'd imagined. I was forced to admit the poverty and untrustworthiness of my imagination like never before.

Mr. Kurosawa and Mr. Oguni sat side by side with their backs to the *tokonoma* alcove in the Nishimuras' drawing room, and I took my junior seat across from them at the big rosewood table. Then Mr. Kurosawa introduced us.

"Hashimoto, this is Hideo Oguni... Oguni, that's Shinobu Hashimoto."

Mr. Oguni and I bobbed our heads, and I added, "By your leave."

Then, as though he'd been impatient for the introductions to be over, Mr. Kurosawa slouched out of his formal *seiza* and spoke to Mr. Oguni. It seemed to be a continuation of a conversation they'd been having on the road.

"And both are red prints, by Tessai?"

"They're more vermillion than red." Mr. Oguni crossed his legs and his eyes narrowed. "No, this hue... Honestly, there are no words."

It seemed that they were talking about pictures by Tessai Tomioka that Mr. Oguni had in his possession.

"But his red prints, Oguni, if these are from when he was in his eighties, they fetch an astronomical price."

"Yes. Next time you visit I'll show you. They're our family treasure.

I've told everyone in the house that if there's a fire, they must get the prints out first."

A slight flush, intense envy, passed over Mr. Kurosawa's face. "It must have been nice in the film industry in the old days. You could buy a Tessai print on a screenwriter or director's pay."

"Well, yes. In the old days, movies were a dilettante's game, even for scriptwriters and directors. But the world's become an unkind place, and lately scriptwriters have changed too. From being a dilettante's game to making a high monthly salary... They're thinking more like salarymen."

"You've still got a lot of guys who call themselves your disciples?"

"Yeah, the initial tier won't quit so they just increase in number, and now I've got more than twenty."

Speechless, I looked at Mr. Oguni. He wasn't the one and only Hideo Oguni for nothing and had more than twenty formal apprentices.

"Still, it would be okay if it were about ten, but when you get past twenty, close to thirty of them, they start splitting off into factions and groups and quarrel and fight, and no good ever comes of it. Only gaining in quantity is its own problem." So saying, Mr. Oguni looked at me and asked, "By the way, Hashimoto, did you teach yourself to write screenplays, or did you study with someone?"

"I studied with a sensei."

"Who was that?"

"Mansaku Itami-sensei."

Mr. Oguni made a strange face. "Mansaku Itami? Mansaku was famous for not taking disciples... But he had them?"

"There were no others, just me."

"Huh. So you're the only disciple that Mansaku left behind in this world."

For just a moment, his expression lost its mercurial bent, and his eyes gave off a glint.

It was three days later when Mr. Kurosawa called me to his home.

I sat at the table in his spacious drawing room, opened a notebook, and faced him.

Mr. Kurosawa was writing in pencil on pieces of *warabanshi*, straw half-sheets, that he'd cut again in half. Whenever he wrote screenplays, Mr. Kurosawa didn't use manuscript paper but these pieces of *warabanshi* cut in half, on which he fit ten rows of twenty characters each, for a total of 200 characters per page. In my case, the lines bent and characters stuck out of their frames even when I wrote on manuscript paper, but

Mr. Kurosawa always wrote ten neat lines of twenty characters each even on blank sheets with no boxes. Perhaps when he was learning to write screenplays he couldn't afford manuscript paper and used *warabanshi*, which became a habit... No, originally, he was an artist accustomed to facing a canvas, so maybe blank paper allowed his thoughts to flow free and unlimited. After all, a screenplay is also a picture written in words.

Mr. Kurosawa finished writing the characters one by one in the middle of a page using a 3B pencil.

A man with only seventy-five days left to live.

He turned the sheet around and pushed it towards me. Just to be sure, I picked it up and read it one more time.

A man with only seventy-five days left to live.

"Got that? That's the theme."
I nodded.
"Make sure not to deviate from that theme."
I nodded, still silent.
"He can be any profession."
"Any profession?"
"Yes, he can be a minister of state, he can be a beggar, a gangster, a thief—anything is fine."
I thought for a moment. "A *yakuza* would be interesting, but no. You already have *Drunken Angel*."
Mr. Kurosawa smiled wryly. "That's true, not a *yakuza*. Anything else will do... In any case, decide his profession. Then a simple story, simple is fine. No longer than two or three of these sheets."
Mr. Kurosawa added a couple more things. The story should be a general framework. Since we didn't know how it would play out in the scenario, detailed writing was pointless. As for the theme, it often comprised the whole story or indicated the bulk of it. I didn't need to separate theme and story and instead might approach them in tandem.
"Which is to say, themes shouldn't be abstruse, you ought to be able to make out their form and see them clearly... Their characteristic is that they can be put into just a few words, and if it takes more, you're not expressing but explaining. So, in my works, I've set themes that can be stated in a single breath, and I intend to keep it that way."
It was as though he were making a proclamation. But what he was

saying firmly retraced Mr. Itami's demonstration of how a theme should be established in *The Rickshaw Man*. Perhaps it was Mr. Kurosawa who most faithfully and pointedly confirmed Mr. Itami's teachings.

I took up my notebook, lifted my face, and looked at Mr. Kurosawa. "The theme is a man who has only seventy-five days left to live... First I decide his profession...and then a simple story, yes?"

I began work on the second floor of the Nishimura residence.

The profession of the man with only seventy-five days left to live was decided rather easily. To start off, I borrowed thick phonebooks from the Nishimuras and picked out and jotted down doable professions, but this was a terribly inefficient way to work akin to searching for a diamond in the sand.

Yet as I kept it up, a dim outline of the man would appear and disappear, and with each cycle, little by little, his silhouette grew more vivid. His death is his greatest drama, so his day-to-day life, his past months and years, and any future he envisions must be as undramatic as possible, with minimal emotional ups and downs and behavioral swerves; everything is cut and dried, and put in the extreme completely robotic, and the more evidently bland his life, the more jarring his impending death. This limited his profession to a fairly narrow range.

Lay that over a concise story that supported the theme...the story of a man who, having done nothing with his life, accomplishes just one mission before he dies—a civil servant, for example—and actually, his profession arises simply and clearly.

The man who has only seventy-five days left to live isn't a minister of state or an entrepreneur, not a scientist or engineer, not an artist or a company man, nor a criminal like a thief or murderer, but a civil servant—he could be nothing but a bureaucrat at a government office.

Other modest ideas occurred to me. The story of an aging itinerant *shamisen* guitar player, part of a troupe of raconteurs and performers of traditional songs. Neither very good nor very bad, come rain or shine he always bellows out the same song, "Murder at Yoshiwara." But one day, he delivers a superlative performance of "Murder at Yoshiwara" that astounds not only the audience but the rest of his troupe. Then he returns backstage and drops dead. One of his colleagues investigates and discovers that a doctor had told the man that he was dying of leukemia and had only a short time to live. The pathos of an itinerant *shamisen* player—just the kind of thing I liked... A tale about an artisan, like a maker of mannequins or an Ise woodblock artist, could be interesting as well. From a death coming in seventy-five days you could draw a line to any profession. But these were just off-stage possibilities so I left it at that and started putting together the story of the government office worker, my best bet. As Mr. Kurosawa had directed, I kept it as simple as possible.

A local government office worker finds out he has stomach cancer and doesn't have long to live. He tries depending on the love of his family, tries living loose with women and sake. But they do nothing for him. One day, back at work after going absent without leave for days out of despair, he sees a document sitting on his desk at the office. It's a residents' petition for work on an underground drainage system, an item he passed on to the civil engineering section half a year ago that has arrived back on his desk after making a round of more than ten sections. Out of habit he's ready to send it over to the civil engineering section—but stops himself and undertakes an examination of the site. Then he immerses himself in the task of removing the swamp created by leaking water and builds a modest little park in its place—before going on to die.

He has worked at the government office for thirty years. For the most part though, his existence is like a mummy's, neither alive nor dead; he only lives in the true sense of the word during those six months, from when construction begins on the culvert to divert water from the swamp until the completion of the park.

(385 characters—under two pages of half-sheet paper)

The sky was leaden, the wind strong.

But Tokyo had no mountains, and I couldn't tell which direction the wind was coming from. The radio had forecast a winter blast the night before, but from the way the trees in the garden were bending, it wasn't a true north wind but more like a northwester that oddly seeped into my body.

In my hometown, this was the season when the gaminess faded from wild boar and their meat turned fatty, but that day I was grateful for beef sukiyaki. I'd be having some with Mr. Kurosawa and Mr. Oguni. This was the meeting before we brought in the producer, and since it was troublesome and annoying to have to go to Shibuya or the center of the city, we decided on the conveniently-located Nishimura residence. The sukiyaki was scheduled for six p.m., but we were getting together at three…the first meeting for the coming film.

"Today we carve out the characters," Mr. Oguni cut to the chase when we saw one another in the Nishimuras' drawing room. He had already been informed of the planned theme and story by Mr. Kurosawa, so today was character design—carving out the characters.

"Oguni... First, read this, would you?"

Mr. Kurosawa took *warabanshi* half-sheets out of an envelope and handed them to Mr. Oguni, who started reading and chuckling. "This is good, this is good... A government office is just like this," he said and passed the manuscript on to me.

Taking it, I saw that Mr. Kurosawa had penned a script-like memo on the bit about the petition making the rounds, which he seemed to like in my story.

> City Hall, the Public Affairs Section window.
>
> Housewives have arrived to petition about the clogged drain.
>
> "Thanks to the water I got this weird rash." "On top of that, it stinks and there are lots of mosquitos." "Isn't there anything you can do about it?"
>
> The person at the window explains the gist of the petition to the section manager.
>
> The protagonist of the story, the section manager, states without feeling: "Civil Engineering Section..."
>
> Civil Engineering Section: "This issue is the responsibility of the local Public Health Center."
>
> Local Public Health Center: "Ah, that goes to the Sanitation Section."
>
> Sanitation Section: "The Disease Control Section... That's number 12."
>
> Disease Control Section: "Please see the Epidemic Subsection."
>
> Epidemic Subsection: "Um, a lot of mosquitos? That's a job for the Pest Control Subsection."
>
> Pest Control Subsection: "All we can do is spray DDT. Anything to do with waste water is the jurisdiction of Sewage Section, City Hall..."
>
> From there, they're passed on to the Sewage Section, the Road Maintenance Section, the City Planning Department, the Town Planning Section, the local fire department, the Education Section, the house of a city councilman, and finally the office of the Deputy Mayor.

Deputy Mayor: "Please, please, come in... We're grateful for your frank complaints and ideas, and that's why we've established a Public Affairs Section to serve as a window... You, show these ladies to the Public Affairs Section right away..."

At the initial Public Affairs Section, the person at the window and the housewives.

"For this kind of problem, please go to the Civil Engineering Section. Window number 8."

One of the housewives starts yelling, "What are you talking about, stop treating us like idiots!"

In simple summer clothes the first time they were here, the housewives are now dressed in thick midwinter attire.

"Enough. We won't be asking you people anymore. Wherever we go, you treat us like fools—and you speak of democracy!"

The subsection chief comes rushing from the back to whisper in the ear of the clerk at the window.

"Oh, uh... I'm afraid the section manager is off today, but if you could submit your petition in the shape of a form..."

The housewives look at the clerk dubiously, crane their necks, and espy an empty desk set apart from the others in the section.

On the desk from which the protagonist is missing is a triangular sign: "Public Affairs Section Manager."

The hero has taken today off for a doctor's exam—and is told he has stomach cancer.

When I finished reading, I began giggling. It was paced well and could be used as-is.

"May I keep this to use in the first draft?"

"Sure. I have it down in my notebook. Well then, shall we begin?"

Character design started with naming. None of the dozen I'd prepared and listed out seemed to serve, but after batting it around for an hour, considering all the pros and cons, we settled on Kanji Watanabe... The hero of our film was Kanji Watanabe.

"Hashimoto, where was this man born?" asked Mr. Oguni.

"In downtown Tokyo. His family owns a metalworks in the vicinity of Edagawa in Koto Ward...a small enterprise that passes down to his older brother. After graduating from the old system's middle school, our man becomes a civil servant, at age nineteen."

"From his parents' point of view," Mr. Kurosawa confirmed, "the older brother is set since he'll continue the family business, but the younger brother needs security…and so they support him through middle school though it's a strain on their budget."

"Yes, that's it."

"Common sense would have him working at the Koto Ward Office," Mr. Oguni pointed out.

"No, to avoid model issues, we won't identify his workplace. If it's a ward office, we're narrowed down to Tokyo, Osaka, and such, but if it's a city hall, it could be Chiba or Urawa if we're talking Kanto, Amagasaki or Nishinomiya if we're talking Kansai… But we wouldn't clarify which city. A city hall in a city of a certain size you'd find somewhere…anywhere in Japan."

The hero, Kanji Watanabe, public affairs section manager at some Japanese city's city hall, is 52 or 53 years old and the recipient of a local governance commendation for three decades of service.

"At work," Mr. Oguni wanted to know, "is he the hungry sort who tries to climb the ladder to get ahead, a wishy-washy layabout, or a typical bureaucrat who handles his responsibilities well enough but doesn't concern himself with anything else?"

"He's the third, a typical bureaucrat."

"He would have married at age 25 or 26, but was it for love? Or was it an arranged marriage?"

"Arranged. His wife is a diminutive, taciturn woman with a scrofulous feel, and I haven't decided yet how many children he has."

Mr. Kurosawa spoke. "The fewer the… One is fine. His wife died early, he has one son…and raised him as a single father. Now his son is grown and married, and they all live together under the same roof, but they're a self-involved young couple and treat him as coldly as they would a stranger…no, worse than a stranger."

"So then, does the son's wife cook the meals and do housework?"

"No, not the wife. But there's no way Kanji Watanabe can cook. A maid or a housekeeper prepares the meals, does the laundry, and so on, and they keep separate households."

The vague contours of Kanji Watanabe's character were coming into view.

I made note of these bits of conversation, then looked over the memos I had made beforehand.

"This is backtracking, but Kanji Watanabe has a medium build and doesn't wear glasses."

"No glasses?"

"No. He only wears reading glasses when he looks over documents."
I added more to this. He wasn't one to go drinking with his subordinates at stalls after work or to frequent a pub. He could drink when the occasion called for it but didn't spend his own money on alcohol. Naturally, he didn't smoke.

"So then, this public affairs section…" followed up Mr. Oguni. "Aside from Kanji Watanabe, the subsection chief, and the clerk at the counter, we need two or three other roles there."

"Yeah, and we want one who stands out."

I repeated after Mr. Kurosawa, "Stands out?"

"For example, a young woman…who says what she wants to say, does as she pleases, and wants to quit this job because she's tired of it. One such person, and various things will be easier to deal with."

The three of us fell into silence as our conversation tapered off. Then Mr. Kurosawa muttered, "The main character has started to solidify…but I'd like one or two more things that would be decisive."

Mr. Oguni clicked his dentures, then mumbled, "When Kanji Watanabe goes to sleep at night…he carefully lays his suit trousers under the futon to press them while he sleeps, as he's been doing every night for thirty years."

Both Mr. Kurosawa and I held our breath.

"And…he always has an *udon* noodle soup for lunch. First taking the time to slurp the noodles, when he's done he takes the bowl like this (he held an imaginary one in both hands and rotated it slowly), lifts it up, and drinks the soup. Then he turns the bowl again and drinks the soup, repeating this two or three times…but doesn't drink it all down and looks closely at the remaining soup and puts down the bowl… That's Kanji Watanabe lunching, how he eats *udon*."

Mr. Kurosawa and I could not but exchange a glance. Kanji Watanabe had become quite three-dimensional. He was also showing signs of squirming around, and the work itself quickened like a baby in the womb. Such was Hideo Oguni, the possessor of a vast, nearly limitless array of drawers (dramatic essences).

Sengokuhara in Hakone was desolate in midwinter.

The stock of frosted and withered silver grass covered the foothills of Mount Kintoki to the north and Nagao Pass to the west, and the chill creeping under my collar intensified, filling every nook of my body with a penetrating cold that made me shiver.

Senkyoro in Sengokuhara was a large *onsen* hot springs inn, but as it was right after New Year's the place had few guests and felt quiet. Mr. Kurosawa and I arrived there at the beginning of January in 1952.

We had decided the theme, story, and characters, so I had begun writing the first draft at the Nishimuras' home in Soshigaya. When I was stuck or had too many ideas, I went to my old office in Okachimachi and continued writing there. My concentration was deep in the deafening silence of the Nishimura residence, but when I felt down the stagnation was like a bottomless bog. In my case, clamorous surroundings tended to quell any nervousness and to speed up my writing, and I completed the first draft shuttling back and forth between the Nishimuras' in Soshigaya and my old company branch office—and in order to turn it into the final draft, I checked into Senkyoro at Hakone's Sengokuhara with Mr. Kurosawa. Due to other commitments, Mr. Oguni would arrive a little later.

The two of us began working, and Mr. Oguni arrived on the evening of the fourth day.

"This place is really cold. I mean, look—it's become a plank." Mr. Oguni had immediately tried the *onsen* upon arriving at the inn, but while he was walking down the long, unheated corridor back to the room, his towel had frozen stiff as a board.

As Mr. Oguni smoked a cigarette, Mr. Kurosawa wordlessly passed him what we had finished. Mr. Oguni stubbed out his cigarette, took a breath, and began reading, but when he was finished he tilted his head slightly.

"Kurosawa… This is a little off."

Mr. Kurosawa raised his face, and I also looked directly over at Mr. Oguni.

"This won't do."

"What won't do?!"

I looked at Mr. Kurosawa in shock. His face was stiff and livid with anger.

"Oguni! What won't do?!" His voice brimmed with a terrible ire bordering on the murderous.

Mr. Oguni began mumbling some words. Wanting very much not to get caught up in trouble, I began to concentrate on the manuscript I was working on. Since there was no room for me to intervene, and perhaps because I had shut my ears instinctively, I couldn't hear Mr. Oguni's voice well. Mr. Kurosawa was silent now, but I could picture his frightening expression.

Suddenly he yelled, "If you're right, Kanji Watanabe will die halfway through!"

"Can't he just die?"

"What?!"

"It's not like we couldn't write the rest if Kanji Watanabe died."

Mr. Kurosawa fell silent, and Mr. Oguni started mumbling some more. He droned on, with Mr. Kurosawa not saying a word.

In the end, Mr. Kurosawa spat out, "Fine, Oguni!"

I looked up reflexively, startled.

Mr. Kurosawa's face was going from livid to angry red. Reaching out to grab the manuscript that Mr. Oguni was returning to him, he tore it up and said, "It's all because you didn't come as promised!"

In my mind, I gasped. It wasn't yet fifty pages. Still, it was a good thirty or forty, pages we'd eked out considering this and that, and now they were clean gone, and we would be beginning from scratch the next day.

I stole another glance at Mr. Kurosawa and Mr. Oguni. Mr. Kurosawa's face was utterly crimson with rage, his expression that of a richly painted red demon. Mr. Oguni, however, didn't flinch, nor did he look appalled. Regally calm, unwilling to yield an inch over his assertions, he lit another cigarette.

My gaze dropped to the manuscript I was writing. I felt gloomy about the work ahead of us. There was no telling, anything could happen.

The next morning, our work as a trio began.

It was just the same as when it had been the two of us. We got up at around half past seven, warmed up in the onsen, and had breakfast, then turned to our work by ten. At noon, we straightened up the pieces of paper, put them off to the side, and had *udon* or *soba* noodles; Mr. Oguni would then smoke a cigarette while Mr. Kurosawa and I went straight back to work. We finished shortly before five and, having wrapped up seven hours of hard work, we'd bathe and have dinner. Mr. Kurosawa and Mr. Oguni, both heavy drinkers, chatted over whiskey cut with water about everything but work. Our bedtime was pretty much fixed at ten… In such a manner we passed the days as if punching a time clock.

We worked around a large table in the center of the tatami room. Mr. Kurosawa didn't sit with his back to the *tokonoma* alcove but rather on the right side of the table, facing south, toward the garden. I sat at the same table to the left of Mr. Kurosawa, facing the alcove. Mr. Oguni, who'd arrived later, dragged out a small low desk from the corner of the room. Facing south from in front of the alcove, with his back to Mr. Kurosawa, he perused a thick English book.

I filled manuscript paper without uttering a word. Mr. Kurosawa, also mute, wrote away on his *warabanshi* half-sheets. Meanwhile, not putting down a single character, Mr. Oguni continued to read his English book. The manuscript circulated counterclockwise, me using my right hand to pass my work to Mr. Kurosawa. He would look it over and simply pass it back, or fix something, or redo it himself…and when a scene or two were done, he pushed it over to Mr. Oguni with his right hand.

Mr. Oguni would pick it up without a word and read. If he said, "Nice," it traveled back clockwise with him pushing it back over the table with his left hand. Mr. Kurosawa would take it silently and clip together the thickening manuscript, the final draft growing without incident. There were some days when we only progressed five or six pages, but also days when twenty or thirty pages flew by, and as long as nothing disrupted our pace of working seven hours a day, we could count on adding to the manuscript by a dozen, perhaps fifteen pages per day. Thus were Kanji Watanabe's fateful days spelled out, his death drawing closer by the minute.

Told by his doctor that he has cancer, Kanji Watanabe loses his bearings and tries to lean on his only son. But the only thing he and his son share now are memories of the past… His married son is like a complete stranger now.

With no one to turn to, Kanji Watanabe withdraws all his money from the bank. Trying to flee fear and loneliness, and with a shady man he meets at a rundown bar as his guide, he grasps at pleasure like straw, in a world of karaoke, beer halls, cafés, cabarets, strip clubs, and blue and red lights… But such joys neither intoxicate nor uplift him, and eventually the pain of vomiting up the contents of his stomach turns his hayride into a transmigration through infinite hell—yet something like salvation visits Kanji Watanabe unexpectedly.

One of the office workers in the Public Affairs Section, Toyo Odagiri, goes to see Kanji Watanabe, who's been absent from work, at his home, in order to get his stamp on her letter of resignation. When creating the characters we had planned for an oddball, and a young woman who says what she wants and does as she wishes brings unusual color and cheer to the darkening screen.

The two of them leave the house and converse at a coffeeshop, a sweet bean soup shop, a park, a movie theater, an eatery… and Kanji Watanabe comes to life. It's not a December romance, it's just fun being with Toyo Odagiri.

One day, Kanji Watanabe visits a small toy factory in town where Toyo Odagiri has gone to work after leaving city hall. But she tells him to stop following her around and refuses to go out with him, making a present of a mechanical toy rabbit she's made herself at the factory.

Holding the toy rabbit in his hand, Kanji Watanabe futilely pleads, "You live your life to the fullest, the way you like. I want to be like you, even if just for one day… Tell me what I should do."

"I just work, eat, and sleep, that's all… You should just up and quit that place too, manager, and go work someplace more worthwhile."

"No, no, it's too late for that."

Embracing the mechanical toy rabbit hard enough to break it, Kanji Watanabe says, "There's only that place, that place for me… No, even there…if, if I had the will…if only I had the will…"

Kanji Watanabe returns to work for the first time in days and sits in the section manager's chair amidst surreptitious, curious gazes. On his desk is a hefty pile of unprocessed documents. On the very top is the petition from the housewives that got shunted around, with a note saying that it should be handled by the civil engineering section. The window clerk, the chief, and the subsection chief have all affixed their seals to it. As is his habit, Kanji Watanabe starts to put his seal on it as well. But he stops. Then, as everyone watches with bated breath, he reads over the petition one more time, removes the note, and tears it up, and tells the subsection chief, "We're going to survey…survey the site regarding this case. Please prepare a car!"

Everyone is frozen in place, with some even gaping.

Five months later—Kanji Watanabe has died, and there's a black-beribboned photograph of him smiling gently at the wake.

The attendees huddle together in small circles, all telling various stories about Kanji Watanabe, who responded to a citizen petition and conducted a city project to reclaim swampland created by water runoff and had a small park built in its place. Kanji Watanabe had coughed up blood and died at the small park they'd just completed.

Kanji Watanabe (Takashi Shimura) in *Ikiru*'s last scene
© 1952 TOHO CO., LTD.

If the story proceeded in the present tense with him still alive, it ran the risk of being a stinky series of inspirational vignettes, but since it's all posthumous, his passion, his extraordinary acts, and the drama of overcoming obstacles and difficulties are all effectively brought to life. Yet, no one knows the true impetus behind Kanji Watanabe's transformation.

Just before the wake ends, a young police officer appears and says he'd like to offer some incense. He is the officer who witnessed Kanji Watanabe just before his death.

Having overcome various obstacles and difficulties, Kanji Watanabe sits gently swaying on a swing, late at night as light snow falls, in the small park you could say he built. He is singing.

Life is short, love away young maid

After burning incense, the officer tells the hushed crowd, "I saw him during last night's patrol. At first I thought he was drunk, and I approached him to take him into custody… But he seemed to be singing so happily, no, all too poignantly, as if the lyrics were seeping into his heart, that I let him be… If only I had just gone ahead and taken him into custody."

Mr. Kurosawa and I had written a scene cutting back from the police officer's lines to the park at night where Kanji Watanabe sat on the swing,
singing.

Life is short, love away young maid…

For this I was merely transcribing what Mr. Kurosawa had muttered, as if
to himself, so I had no idea how the lyrics went after that.
"Hashimoto, how does the rest of the song go?"
"How would I know? It must be a love song from before I was born."
Mr. Kurosawa asked Mr. Oguni, who was reading his English book,
"Hey, Oguni. What comes after 'Life is short, love away young maid'?"
"Um, what was it, uhm… Uhm, it's right on the tip of my tongue."
I immediately called reception on the phone and asked for the oldest
maid working at the inn to be sent up, assuring them that, yes, we wanted
the oldest.
After a few minutes, a voice at the sliding door excused herself, and in
came a maid. She was small and older, but she didn't seem that old.
"I'm the oldest, what can I do for you?"
I cut to the chase. "Do you know the song that goes, 'Life is short'?"
"Oh, the Gondola Song."
"Gondola, that's what it's called? Do you happen to remember the
lyrics?"
"Hmm, I wonder. Maybe the first verse, if I may sing it…"
"Then sing it please."
The inn maid sat on her knees on the tatami by the entrance. Tight-
ening her fists and placing them on her lap, she took a breath. Mr. Kuro-
sawa and Mr. Oguni leaned forward. I swallowed and held my breath. She
began singing, low, not too loud. Her voice was fine and clear, the sentiment somehow heartfelt.

Life is short, love away young maid
Before the red of your lips fades
Before your hot blood cools
As though there's no tomorrow…

We called it in early that day, at three.
Ever since secluding ourselves at the beginning of January, we had

faced the table whether it was Sunday or a holiday, and now it was already the third of February, the end of winter according to the old calendar... The work already had fleshed-out features, we had crossed the mountain and were feeling a little relieved, and so we quit work early. According to the inn maid who had sung "The Gondola Song" (lyrics: Isamu Yoshii, music: Shimpei Nakayama), the staff would be coming by every room before dinner to throw uncooked red beans as was the custom for the old calendar day.

I bathed and returned to our room, but it was still early so I ventured out into the garden.

This was the first time I'd been in the garden since our arrival, and the view from there was expansive. The ridge from Nagao Pass in the west to Mount Kintoki to the north was black against the light, while Myojingatake and Myojogatake in the east connected bumpily in the bright setting sun. Before them the stretch of withered silver grass undulated in the light like white waves, yet the deep cold that permeated my skin had a hint of spring beneath it.

Spring, already... It gave me a kind of relief. When Mr. Oguni had come and clashed with Mr. Kurosawa, I had felt boundless unease about the future of this particular job, but after that nothing happened, the going was smooth, and we'd be finished in a day or two.

But this was thanks to having laid out the basic theme, story, and characterization beforehand in a precise manner. If we'd been vague on those points, the work could have come apart; it was a lesson in how crucial indeed the basics were.

The most important thing in film production is the screenplay, and for the screenplay the most important things in turn are first, theme, second, story, and third, characterization (and composition). While that has been the standard view from the earliest days of cinema, just as neither the film industry nor the one surrounding it has handled and treated the screenplay as being of paramount importance to a film, not many screenplays are written with the three basic tenets so precisely laid out.

If the majority of screenplays satisfied these basic tenets, then both films and TV dramas would be much more interesting and of a higher quality than they are now.

For the screenplay writer, the scenarist, these three basic tenets are a hard slog, almost physiologically so.

When Mr. Itami was reading my screenplays, if I was slapdash about those three elements he would flare up and relentlessly bellow that I tighten the theme, shorten and shape up the story, and carve out the characters to the best of my abilities. I understood how important it was, but when the time came to write I would cut corners again and have a hard time getting the basics in order. This was the first time I had done it all properly, but only because Mr. Kurosawa had forced me to on every point.

Mr. Kurosawa's script-craft involved meticulously, almost mulishly compiling all of the three basics one by one and, just to be certain, wielding a hammer "to tap a stone bridge before crossing it" as the Japanese saying goes—as upright as it gets, some teetotaler clad in the armor of God. If such straight-laced meticulousness is to be called rational, then when it came to making that most important thing for a film called the screenplay, Akira Kurosawa was utterly rational.

Not just that. Something prior to… Yes…yes, that's it!

He was arrogant, selfish, and unilateral, a man who arbitrarily decided where I would live.

But his attitude towards me as a screenplay writer he worked with was completely different. I was a writer he had discovered, and if he had wanted Hideo Oguni to participate, he could just have informed me at our meeting. Instead, he had gone out of his way to visit my lodging and secure my consent in advance.

Likewise, when he introduced Mr. Hideo Oguni and me, he could have summoned us both to his home or made me visit Mr. Oguni's home together with him, but he instead brought Mr. Oguni to me to introduce us.

I was the lead runner and vanguard for this work, and the quality of the first draft would greatly influence the final draft. He treated his main writer with all possible etiquette and allowance… If, prior to my starting on the screenplay, there was anything he should do as the person in charge, then he saw to all the particulars without even the least omission.

Akira Kurosawa's script-craft—as with *Rashomon*, in order to seize a flash of inspiration he could jettison everything and make a dizzying leap for it, but the underlying essence, as with this time around, was straight-laced and meticulous advance preparation, an almost mulishly thoroughgoing rationalism—or rather, something surpassing rationalism that might better be termed perfectionism.

When I stepped up from the garden and entered the room, I found Mr. Kurosawa not in his usual spot but with his back to the alcove, facing the table, writing on manuscript paper. Not on a *warabanshi* half-sheet but on the framed manuscript sheet I'd been using. Since there was an edict in effect against jotting down a single character after bath time, I eyed him wondering what he was up to. Mr. Kurosawa took the clip off the final draft bundle and replaced the title sheet with the manuscript paper he'd just written on.

"Hashimoto... I did this for the title, but what do you think?"

I took it and read:

Ikiru [To Live]

Not a bad feel—but it seemed a bit stylish. It put on airs. This story was a little crude. I had also become quite accustomed, and attached, to the title since the first draft, *The Life of Kanji Watanabe*. I couldn't come to a quick decision.

"Mr. Oguni..."

Having taken his bath, Mr. Oguni had his English book open as always, but when I scooted over he looked up from his book and turned his gaze to me.

"Mr. Kurosawa says he'd like to do this for the title, but what do you think?"

Mr. Hideo Oguni, who had not written a single word for the script but was the work's command tower and navigator, took the final draft and beheld the title sheet. After just a glance he said, "Ah, Hashimoto... This one, this is good, better than *The Life of Kanji Watanabe*. The title of this script is *Ikiru*, okay, *Ikiru*."

The screenplay *Ikiru* was finished two days later on February 5, 1952.

The film *Ikiru* was completed in October 1952, and it took the Special Prize at the Berlin Film Festival (1953), the International Film Education Culture Association gold medal, and the Golden Laurel Award (America, 1961).

When I speak with various overseas film directors and producers at international film festivals and the like, they often show more interest in *Ikiru* than *Rashomon* and *Seven Samurai* and ask me insistently about the motivation and process behind the screenplay. Perhaps this work has an unusual number of fans amongst film professionals.

Seven Samurai I

It was the end of November, several weeks after the release of *Ikiru* on the Toho circuit in early October of 1952, and we were in the drawing room at the Kurosawa residence in Komae.

Akira Kurosawa's face was livid with fierce anger, his eyes bloodshot.

"Why can't we do it?!"

The producer Sojiro Motoki and two members of the Toho arts department were paralyzed with fear.

"How come we can't do it?!"

Sojiro Motoki and the two arts department staff sat as though petrified.

I lifted my face and looked at the raging Akira Kurosawa.

Come to your senses, Akira Kurosawa... If you have complaints, tell me. The producer and the arts department have nothing to do with it and aren't to blame.

This was how it all happened.

During the filming of *Ikiru*, Mr. Kurosawa had a discussion with me and decided the next film would be a period piece and that I would start off on the scenario. What we settled on between us was *A Samurai's Day*.

The story was as follows. One morning, a samurai wakes up. He washes his face, shaves his pate, ties his topknot, bows to his ancestors' spirits. He has breakfast, finishes dressing with the help of his wife, wears his long and short swords, and, accompanied by retainers, heads to the castle.

His work at the castle proceeds without incident, but when it's nearly evening and time to leave, he makes a trivial mistake, and when he returns to his mansion, he commits seppuku in his yard—and in the golden dusk of his garden nearly all the cherry blossoms are in bloom. A certain samurai's day.

Mr. Kurosawa's intention and goal was to create an uncompromisingly realistic period piece of a kind never seen before...to scrupulously render a day in the life of a samurai who commits seppuku. To that end, the screenplay required reading the necessary monographs and taking notes, asking historians about points that weren't clear, and confirming all the details, from A to Z, of a samurai household and castle duty so it was all accurate.

For most works, someone from the arts department was attached to the producer as an assistant, but since there was a lot of research to do for this project, there would be two assistants, and if necessary a third would be ready to mobilize.

Consulting with the producer just in case, I had made the Toho side go that far, but for my own part I was optimistic and the project had my unwavering confidence.

During the days I'd headquartered myself at the Tokyo office of my old company in Okachimachi, Taito Ward, the National Library in Ueno (consolidated today with the National Diet Library and moved to Nagatacho in Chiyoda Ward) had been but a stop away on the streetcar; it had served as a backyard where I went to indulge myself when I had time. So if I went into the reference room at the library, as I had done with *Miki Hirate* for Shin-Toho and *Kaga Sodo* for Toei, I pretty much knew which card catalogues held what information and how the books related to period pieces (for the Tokugawa period) were organized. If I divided the work between the two assistants from the arts department and myself, as long as we didn't begrudge the time we would certainly be able to compile all the necessary reference materials.

In September I began commuting from Daita in Setagaya Ward to the National Library in Ueno.

In August of that year, because my family was joining me in Tokyo, I had moved out of the Nishimura residence in Soshigaya. Up to that point my wife couldn't be spared back home, where a woman was needed, but she'd been released from housework duty thanks to my younger brother getting married. She was coming to Tokyo with our son, who was in the first grade, and our preschool-aged daughters, so we bought and moved into a house close to Shin-Daita Station on the Inogashira Line.

About a week after I'd begun commuting from Shin-Daita to the National Library in Ueno, by way of Shibuya, with one of the Toho arts department people, I was feeling oddly frustrated. After about two weeks, beset by a slow-burning unease, I was feeling irritated. We simply weren't running into the reference materials we required.

What I needed were details about the everyday life of a *bushi* and his duties at a castle, and since many samurai in different domains during the Tokugawa period had made a habit of writing, there was no shortage of diaries and such. Their content, however, centered on the weather, comings and goings, deliveries and receipts, seeing relatives and acquaintances, celebrations, observances, memorials, etc. One source even offered insight into the finances of a modest family living on an allowance from the domain, but as far as I could see there was nothing novel to give me pause, nothing that couldn't be inferred, and particularly in terms of professional duties, there was next to nothing written with any specificity.

According to the records of feudal *han* domains, duties were ordered in much the same way in the various domains, with the daimyo and the elders serving him at the top, and occupations carefully delineated and enumerated from head clerk, infantry commander, and herald on down to temple and shrine manager, counties overseer, investigator, accountant, head of construction and so on. But what I wanted to know was the specific organization and headcount of a branch, the hours they worked (what time they arrived and went home), and their responsibilities (what sort of tasks they actually carried out), and those hadn't been recorded.

If the home life of a samurai could be inferred, perhaps his duties at the castle needed to be inferred as well.

I had set the work in the early part of the Tokugawa period. The reason for this was the manner of seppuku.

Prior to the Tokugawa period, when *bushi* took their lives they would split their stomachs open, either with a lateral cut or crosswise, then pierce their chests or throats to die. The Tokugawa period, however, saw the introduction of a beheading second. The one committing seppuku thrusted a short blade into his stomach. Immediately, the second parted the head from the neck. By middle Tokugawa, however, no blade cut into the stomach; rather, a white fan or small wooden knife lay on the stand. The moment the person placed his hand on it, the second beheaded him. It is said that this was due to an incident where the would-be suicide entered into a frenzy, seizing the blade, running amok, and wounding and killing people. Yet, a fan or wooden knife didn't make for a good picture. Our protagonist's seppuku had to take the form of him thrusting a short blade into his stomach, to be beheaded by his second, so the story was set in early Tokugawa in the times of the fourth shogun, Ietsuna (in the 1660s).

Serving a domain yielding about 100,000 *koku* of rice, the samurai, a herald working directly under an elder, is worth 120 *koku*. Since this is early Tokugawa when social status and rules were strictly enforced, he appears at the castle with two attendants, one carrying a spear, the other rain gear and a box containing lunches for all three of them.

I made a point of mentioning this to Kanehara from the arts department.

"Kanehara, in early Tokugawa castle attendance, did samurai bring a lunch from home or were they provided with lunch at the castle? Put everything else aside and focus on finding out what they did about meals."

At the castle, the samurai is fairly busy in the morning.

He imparts directives approved by the daimyo to the appropriate underlings—temple and shrine manager, accountant, etc.—and hears reports from the head of construction on the progress of waterway improvements in the realm, from the investigator on the latest developments of a village border dispute, and from the counties overseer on the state of a survey into new areas to be cultivated. When it's time for the noon break, breathing a sigh of relief he takes his lunch at his station. An apprentice brings tea from the teahouse.

As the samurai is relaxing and eating his meal, a mounted guard friend with a status of 150 *koku* drops by. He has brought his lunch, and they eat together. The guard comes to the castle every ten days for his gear inspection, and more than anything he looks forward to taking his lunch with the samurai.

The two of them reminisce about their childhoods, when they used to play at the river—a fluffy white cloud that towered like a behemoth, the two of them splashing up water in pursuit of fish hiding under a rock. Their meals finished, they become engrossed in plans to go fishing the next time their days off coincide.

The guard says to the samurai, "Your Katsuyuki has really improved."

The infantry commander and his thirty-odd subordinates have set up a private school at their barracks and take turns instructing the children of each family—for boys, the combat arts, *bushido*, reading, and writing, and for girls, reading, writing, and warrior household etiquette. The samurai has one boy and one girl, while the mounted guard has been blessed with three boys and two girls. The men expect the ties between their two households to cement further as their children grow up and enjoy bonds, perhaps matrimonial, of their own, and beyond, to when the men have ceded headship—days and seasons of unshakeable peace and tranquility. The two friends truly trust each other.

It happens at three in the afternoon when drumbeats signal the end of the day's castle duty.

A subordinate agent of the mountains administrator arrives with a panicked expression, and the samurai, puzzled, turns to greet him. His face stiffens at the agent's words. At the beginning of March, the samurai received a notice from a mountains official that 3,000 *koku* worth of forty-year-old cedar logs were to be quarried; confirming this with the mountains administrator's agent, he reported it to the elder, who in turn reported it to the daimyo and received permission for it to proceed. A deal was made to send 3,000 *koku* of cedar logs to Itachibori Canal in Osaka, for 20,000 *ryo* from the merchants' main exchange, to be tendered in coins by late May in time for the daimyo's departure for Edo service in June.

The 3,000 *koku* in the mountains official's report, however, contained a mistake and should have been 3,000 trees and not *koku*, the agent reports as though coughing up blood. The amount of wood they're sending doesn't meet even half the promised collateral, and it's as if the domain deceived the merchants' main exchange.

The forests of the domain are vast, so logging the missing amount and sawing it into rounds for lumber is possible, but it would take at least a few months to construct a forest road with bridges over two steep ravines on which a wood sledge could pass... It would take until the end of the summer, and even if the felling and drying were managed, the snows would come, and the lumber would not ship out until the following spring. As such, there is nothing left to do but report the situation to the Osaka main exchange and have them wait until the next year for the remaining supply. The mountains official has taken responsibility for the mishap by splitting open his stomach, but could the samurai go give the particulars to the elder?

With a stiff, brooding expression, the samurai reports the details to the elder, who sits awhile in thought as if turned to stone. In the end, the elder lets out a sigh and says, "If the coin isn't transferred from the Osaka main exchange, it will cause problems for our service in Edo, among other things. We have no choice but to notify the main exchange of all the unvarnished details and request that they allow us to deliver the remainder next year." Then, after a couple of false starts, with a burdened air he mutters, "Enclose the top-knot of the mountains official who disemboweled himself with the letter of apology... No, if we don't include a knot from the castle as well, the honor of our domain will be in question."

His jaw clenched hard enough to shatter, his expression frozen, the samurai stares at the elder, but the very next moment he places both hands flat on the ground, bows his head, and crisply offers, "I am prepared to do my duty!"

The samurai makes his way back to his station, but instead of entering he continues down the corridor. He puts on his sandals at the eaves and exits out the main keep's gate. Down the narrow stone-paved pathway he goes, passing through the gate of the inner wall into the middle courtyard. He proceeds along a stone wall and enters the cool armory. The mounted guard has already finished examining and polishing his arms with his colleague and is preparing to leave. Startled by the look on the entering samurai's face, he accosts his good friend in a hurry, and they leave the armory together.

The spring day is long. The shadows of the two men facing each other appear on the keep's stone wall.

Along the moat by the corner tower behind them stands a row of cherry trees, and nightingales sing in their branches, which are almost in full blossom. Having explained everything from beginning to end, the samurai falls silent. The mounted guard, dumbfounded, is unable to bring himself to believe it, and amidst the silence the nightingales sing on.

At last the samurai takes a breath and raises his head. "And so I have no choice but to commit seppuku."

"…"

"And I have a request for you."

With a start, the guard looks at the samurai.

"My second… Please be my second."

The guard stands ramrod straight, his whole body stiff. The samurai looks at him with bloodshot eyes.

"There's no one else I can ask but you. Please, be my second!"

"Ur…" the guard groans. "I-I accept the honor!" Agreeing with a plaintive cry, he covers his eyes with his right elbow and howls out his tears.

The shadows of the two men on the stone wall of the keep—the still samurai and the lamenting guard, his eyes covered with his right arm, are projected there. The nightingales sing.

From this point until the end there isn't one line of dialogue, the final drive relying on sheer action mixed with music.

Stymied though we were by the lack of sources, the story had swelled into something akin to a scenario. It was the end of October, as we were heading into the final stage, that Kanehara from the arts department hesitantly broke to me, "Mr. Hashimoto, about meals… I think I've got a general idea. During early Tokugawa, attending samurai neither brought a lunch nor received any at the castle. At that time, they didn't eat three meals, but still only two."

"What kind of nonsense is that?!" I immediately rejected his suggestion and dispensed a breathless lecture.

Bento… The custom of calling a meal eaten outside the home "bento" dated back much earlier to the Heian period.

According to one theory, the word derives from "mentsu/mento" (a round box used to apportion servings of rice), and in the Heian period, steamed rice and red beans were formed into egg shapes, and this was generalized to soft cooked rice to become today's *onigiri* rice balls. The more casual synonym *omusubi* (from the verb "to wrap") was the lingo of the period's ladies in waiting, and in addition to *onigiri*, for many years people also ate cooked rice that had been dried. Wrappers and containers for them changed over the times too, from primitive bamboo, oak, and magnolia leaf wrappers to jute and straw bags, wicker baskets, circular boxes...made of cedar, cypress, painted maple, etc., just wood grain or expensively lacquered. The bamboo ones in particular tended to be finely crafted, with decorative fixtures and such, and served Tokugawa-period samurai and townspeople as they journeyed along the routes.

Thus, the history of bento is far older than the Tokugawa period, which was when the practice of daimyo attending on the shogun commenced, with lords from all the domains in Japan traveling to Edo to serve him. When you were on call, you had breakfast and went to the castle and ate your lunch there; a bento was delivered by a retainer from the domain's place in the capital, and from the Tokugawa side a tea server offered tea. That this was the custom at Edo Castle throughout the Tokugawa period, early, middle, or late, is backed up by historical sources.

Ergo—daimyo of the era, the lords of the various domains, took three meals from the beginning of the Tokugawa period. If his servants and commoners only took two meals it would have been a visible status marker, and not just official records but folk ditties would have made note of it. Yet there's not a single fact or instance of the sort. In other words, in those times it was already commonplace to have three meals a day.

Moreover, the domains were organized and run following the centralized system of the Tokugawas, right down to conventions and customs. If a daimyo who served at Edo Castle brought his bento, and the shogunate only provided hot tea, then in his own domain the lord would merely provide hot tea for his attendant retainers, who'd have to bring their own lunch—this was common sense for anyone handling the Tokugawa period.

"I understand what you're saying. You're right. I've read a number of accounts like that too. But...Mr. Hashimoto, have you read the records of the Mouri clan? Not the guys in Hagi, but in Nagato."

"The Mouri clan records?"

"About the forty-seven ronin."

"Ah, that one. I read the Hosokawa Diary" (the memoir of Den'emon Horiuchi).

This was about fifty years after the times of the *jidaigeki* or period film that I was working on. Forty-seven masterless samurai of the Akou clan stormed into the residence of Kozunosuke Kira and scored his head to avenge their lord Naganori Asano, then surrendered to the shogunate.

The authorities separated them into the Edo mansions of four daimyo, the Higo domain's Hosokawa, Nagato Chofu's Mouri, and others, whose records of the ronin remain.

"In that Mouri clan record… " Kanehara said, opening up his notebook, "there's a record of the menu for meals."

I took the notebook and saw the following:

1- Morning and late afternoon meals of two soups and five vegetables
2- One noontime snack (steamed, jellied, or dried)
3- *Bancha* and *sencha* tea provided on request
4- Night meal of one soup and three vegetables, or porridge, or Nara tea (tea rice, miso soup, stew, etc.)

I stared at the words "morning and late afternoon meals of two soups and five vegetables," unable to look away.

Though the provision of a noontime snack, a night meal of soup and three vegetables, and tea upon request was especially hospitable, indicating extraordinary treatment for the brave souls who had avenged their lord and reported the deed—as far as regular meals were concerned, there were just two, in the morning and late afternoon.

"Then, a little later during the era of Yoshimune, the man's character and principles were all geared toward restoring the times of the deified first Tokugawa shogun Ieyasu. He encouraged martial training, and as for meals, he chided that while many were now taking three a day, two were enough to nourish the body, and two would do. From this perspective, I feel that three meals as the norm started in the Genroku era and became established after Yoshimune, in the Bunka-Bunsei era during Ieharu and Ienari's reigns. So in pre-Genroku, early Tokugawa, it would seem as though they had two meals."

I sat silent and still. This was a crucial point that I hadn't foreseen—an issue of paramount importance that could make or break the scenario.

Kanehara continued, "'Asa-yuu' [morning and late afternoon] is a time-honored phrase, meaning the morning and late afternoon meals. It's strongly related to the history of lamps. The light afforded by the bygone ones that used an oil plate was weak and unreliable, so meals were eaten while the sun was still out… By contemporary timekeeping standards, I would imagine around four p.m. So two meals, in the morning and the late afternoon, sufficed."

Cold horror ran up my spine.

"However, going into the Tokugawa period, we had the development of paper lanterns, and particularly with technological advances in lighting during the remarkable economic development of the Genroku era, nighttime became bright in a way it hadn't been before. So, the late afternoon meal got pushed back, and the noontime meal appeared. I understand your views very well, Mr. Hashimoto, but as far as meals are concerned, I would say that two is correct for early Tokugawa."

I said nothing. No, there was nothing I could say.

This was an astounding, grave problem. If we lost the noontime lunch from the samurai's day, his interaction with the mounted guard would vanish, and the scenario itself would break apart and disintegrate. Since they were in the same castle, they could meet somewhere, and it wasn't like I couldn't think up a situation or two. But there was none better suited than lunch and the noontime rest.

To maintain the integrity of the scenario, to force extreme tension and have the story proceed with the audience's eyes riveted to the screen to an almost abnormal degree, there was no choice but to stay in the present tense throughout… Put differently, it's the repose of a noontime break and meal that lets the two men enjoy their poignant interaction and to reminisce about the seasons of their childhood as freely as necessary.

If a scene showing that he has such a friend feels even a little lacking in weight and expository, then the film collapsed at that point and came apart completely. Other situations wouldn't work. In sum, if we took the lunch and noontime break away from this samurai on duty, the film's very concept failed to stand up.

I ordered Kanehara, "Enough of the library, I want you two to go around and ask historians, all the Japanese historians, which is correct: Would a samurai on castle duty during the early Tokugawa bring a lunch with him, or would he receive a meal there? Or, at that time, were there only two meals, so that the samurai neither brought nor received a lunch at the castle? If they say they don't know, don't just leave, but ask who you should talk to, and which books you should be consulting, and extend the range of your research as much as possible. If the two of you aren't enough, get another guy on board, Kakuta or someone… Okay?"

I started going to the library in Ueno by myself from the following day, and the three arts department personnel began interviewing historians at once. If the next Kurosawa film fell through at the planning stage, the arts department, in charge of the planning, would bear great responsibility and take a heavy beating not just from the marketing department but also from the studio where the production was to take place. The planning department personnel were desperate too.

There was one more thing about this project that bothered me, besides the samurai's meals.

That was the problem of the castle…specifically, whether or not a fortress could be the seat of a domain government. As far as I knew, the castle keep was prepared to function as a defensive citadel, but I had my doubts about the structure serving as an administrative one from which domain affairs could be conducted. In the age of Nobunaga, the daimyo also used the castle as a residence, but from the times of Hideyoshi things changed substantially, and palaces and manses befitting the size of the domain were constructed on the castle grounds to house the daimyo. I wondered if the center of the government resided not in the main keep, a defensive structure, but rather in those palaces and manses.

All the castles I knew of, however, had either had the main keeps restored to their original states or built anew, and absolutely no palaces or manses for daimyo had survived.

It wouldn't do just to write "Castle X, Herald's Station" under the scene number and expect the art director to do his research and create something suitable. This project was founded on realism, and if I didn't have a clear, three-dimensional sense of the buildings, the characters' actions and emotions would be vague and the story unmoored.

There were many illustrated references, photographs, and introductory publications about the castles dotting the country, but as I mentioned, most focused on the existing or reconstructed keeps, and there were few records of other buildings such as the daimyo's palace or manse that might have been used for domain governance. However, there were areas with gates and doors in many of the towers and enclosures that made up the keep in which administrative personnel might work. In fact, Cosmetic Tower (Kesho-Yagura) in the elegant west wing of Himeji Castle was where the first Tokugawa shogun Ieyasu's granddaughter Princess Sen, married to Tadatoki Honda, conducted her daily life.

A trip to a castle… I'd love to go visit Himeji Castle. The herald situated close to the daimyo, with his station in the palace or a part of the residence. On the castle grounds over which the main keep looms, amid the remaining towers and enclosures, I might catch fleeting glimpses of the stations of the investigator, the temple and shrine manager, the accountant, and the mountains and construction managers where the samurai treads.

Kanehara's calls came at eight in the evening.

The assistant from the arts department contacted me at my home in Daita without fail every one or two days, but he didn't have good news.

The diffuse scope of the interviews gave the impression that their aimless wandering was taking them further and further afield.

It was about the middle of November, ten days after the three of them had begun running around harried. Kanehara's voice over the phone sounded somehow low and gloomy.

"Mr. Hashimoto, what are you doing tomorrow? Will you be going to the library? If you are, could you drop by the main office either on your way there or on the way back? We'd like to meet with you to discuss what to do next..."

The three men from the arts department had already interviewed more than a dozen and a half historians and expanded their search to include an essayist whose forte was the Tokugawa period and nearly ten novelists who wrote period novels, but their answers had been the same: *I don't know, it's unclear.* Kanehara and company must have felt that further research was impossible, and since they had run out of options they had no choice but to call it quits.

"Kanehara, I'm a bit tied-up tomorrow... Can we push this back a few days? I'll let you know the day and time. But it'll be a few days later."

The next day, I picked up my Boston bag and left my house.

I transferred at Shibuya from the Inogashira Line to the Yamanote Line, but I didn't go to Ueno as usual, instead disembarking partway at Tokyo Station and boarding a Tokaido Line express train bound for Shimonoseki. I was headed for Himeji in Hyogo Prefecture. I would be arriving too late in the day for researching or touring. I meant to stay at an inn near the station and to visit Himeji Castle the next morning to make a close examination of the outer and middle courtyards; if I had any time left I'd go up the main keep, then return to Tokyo by train in the afternoon.

I wanted to do everything I could to turn *A Samurai's Day* into a screenplay.

As far as the issue of bringing a bento for lunch was concerned, according to the pros at interviewing over at the arts department who had scrambled about, historians and novelists couldn't say with certainty that you took a bento, nor that bringing your own lunch for castle duty was unthinkable. In other words, the facts were unknown and unclear, so for a dramatic work, perhaps the author was free to say that you of course did bring a bento.

On top of that—three months had already passed since we'd gotten going at the beginning of September. If the project were shelved, not a red cent of the scriptwriting fee would be paid and I would have worked for free, which really hurt. That wasn't all. No, it wasn't the financial aspect, but the humiliation of tripping up at work that I hadn't tasted until then.

Ever since the days of my apprenticeship, when Mr. Itami read my work, every piece that I wanted and tried to bring into being did turn into a script, putting quality aside. I'd never once abandoned one in the middle. Completing a work requires facing various difficulties and obstacles. One such miscarriage and I might become prone to miscarrying, getting into the habit of giving up and quitting whenever the going got tough.

Moreover... No, it was the number one issue: the project had been initiated with Mr. Kurosawa's agreement. We had considered and settled on the theme and story together, and I had made a promise to Mr. Kurosawa to write the screenplay, so what of my responsibility as a writer? When there was a mountain of conditions and necessities compelling the work's completion, why was there something that seemed to hinder and thwart it?

In any event, if I went to Himeji Castle, some sort of... No, perhaps my trip was no more than the aimless drifting of a rudderless boatman amidst the waves.

It was dusk when the express train arrived at Kobe.

Out the window, the darkening ocean stretched out past the line of city lights as far as the eye could see. The dim deep purple where the horizon and sky melded colored the Seto Inland Sea with each passing moment. I gazed at the lanterns of the boats traversing the coastline and at the fire lures on the fishing boats.

When the bell signaling our departure began to ring, I shot up out of my seat, took my Boston bag from the overhead rack, and quickly went out onto the platform. I had no idea why I'd been overtaken by such an impulse.

Standing there on the platform, I once again gazed out at the Seto Inland Sea. The lights of the city and the deep purple of the sea looked more expansive and vivid than through the train window. Behind me the departure bell finished ringing, and the express train began to pull out. But I didn't look back.

In a flash, a poem from the *Ogura Hyakunin Isshu* anthology shot through my entire body.

> *Like a boatman crossing the Strait of Yura,*
> *Whose oar-cord has broken,*
> *I know not where I'm going on the road of love*

Taking up my Boston bag, I quickly walked down the platform, went down the stairs, and then up to another platform where I boarded a train bound for nearby Nishi-Akashi. And when the train stopped at Akashi Station, I walked straight to the ferry pier and crossed the gangplank for the ferry to Iwaya on Awaji Island.

The wind was a bit cold and biting on my neck. As I stood on the upper deck, the ferry turned towards Awaji, let out a short steam whistle, and lumbered out of port onto the murmuring sea in the deep twilight.

The sea at Awaji—for me, it held a vaguely bittersweet memory.

Since I don't keep a journal I can't recall the exact date or route, but it was the year I absconded from the disabled veterans' hospital so it had to be ten years earlier...in 1942, during the war.

I had grown tired of rehabilitation and stolen away without permission and returned to my hometown, but life on the outside was hard on my weak constitution. Eventually, with the war entering a new phase, labor draft notices began arriving. I was exempted from conscription but not from this draft, and if I were recruited for physical labor, a worsening of my symptoms and even death seemed imminent. To avoid that outcome I had no choice but to go work at some munitions factory, from where I couldn't be drafted, but neither did I trust my health at such a place.

I could either gird up and find work at a munitions factory, or swallow my pride, apologize, and readmit myself to the disabled veterans' hospital... One day, in the midst of my endless indecision and frustration, I suddenly embarked on a journey.

Where my feet led me, without rhyme or reason, was Awaji Island.

I don't remember if I traveled a little ways along the coast to the east of Iwaya, the entry point onto Awaji, or through the central city of Sumoto and onto the eastern shore from there, but the name of the inn where I stayed was—I think it was "Yura House."

I clearly remember a long corridor at the inn lit here and there with electric lights.

An inn maid had taken my Boston bag and I had followed after her. Turning right at the corner at the end, we came to a C-shaped area where the sea came in. We had to cross a bridge to get to the guest room in the annex, and with the high tide rising up and swirling black and ominous, it was fairly frightening.

My room in the annex directly faced the sea on the east and north, and the waves roared loudly.

I bathed and ate, then dove into the thick, high-quality futon that had been laid out, but I couldn't sleep for the sound of the waves. The whole room seemed to tremble with the roar of the sea. From Akashi or Suma on the opposite shore the strait looked calm and even, but the currents were surprisingly rapid around Awaji Island.

A long time ago, when I had been at the national railway training center, I had tried to swim from the shore of Tarumi in Kobe to Awaji Island. It had seemed close enough that I might reach out and touch it if I stretched out my hand.

About a thousand feet from shore, however, I found myself unable to swim. Bloodcurdling fear filled me from head to toe. The eerie suction pulling me toward the bottomless deep, slowly dragging me east, was some extraordinary force impervious to man's power no matter how much he resisted... In terrible fear, mad from despair, I somehow managed to return to Tarumi Beach.

I smiled at the memory of my old wild and reckless self. A wry smile, more bitter than sweet.

I tried to swim across. But I couldn't... I wonder if that's why I came by ship?

But the next moment, I was tilting my head.

It came from amidst the sound of the waves... No, it was nothing, I'd misheard. The only thing I could hear was the roar of the waves. But from amidst them... I could not but pull off the top futon and sit up. I attuned my whole body to the sound and concentrated. From within the roar of the waves that seemed as timeless as heaven and earth came a faint—murmur—speaking to me—in bits—

> *...boatman crossing the Strait of Yura,*
> *Whose oar-cord has broken,*
> *I know not where I'm going...*

Lines composed by the Heian poet Sone no Yoshitada a thousand years ago, originally part of the *Shin Konjaku Wakashu* and included in the *Hyakunin Isshu*—a mirage of an event at an inn on Awaji Island ten years prior.

When the ferry from Akashi arrived at Iwaya on the tip of Awaji Island, I prevaricated at the taxi stand.

The question was where I would stay for the night. Should I remain in Iwaya, or go to Yura Harbor off to the east of Sumoto and stay at the inn in

Yura? But I wanted to arrive in Himeji as early as possible in the morning so Iwaya served me better.

Getting into the taxi, I said, "Driver... Please take me to the inn with the best view of the sea around here."

The inn the driver took me to was on high ground, and from a room on the second floor you could see all of Akashi Strait, a wide panorama in the daytime.

After bathing and eating, I opened a window. Suddenly the deep sound of the surging sea grew stronger. I sat down in a rattan chair on the verandah, but the wind was cold and I reflexively pulled close the padded collar of my yukata. The nighttime strait was a stretch of deep black waves.

The lights of Akashi, Maiko, and Tarumi on the opposite shore... Nishi-Akashi to the left, the lights of ships going to and fro, and the scattered lamps of fishing boats far west at Harimanada.

Because I was at a distance from the shoreline and on high ground, the surging sea's roars weren't what I remembered from "Yura House." Yet the force of the current at Awaji Island, which sat by the strait, the sublimity of heaven and earth, and the seemingly eternal sound of the waves were identical.

In a low voice, I recited Sone no Yoshitada's "Yura Strait" to myself. Ten years earlier it had come to me on the waves, but perhaps in my oblivion I had heard my own unconscious murmurings.

"Like a boatman crossing the Strait of Yura, whose oar-cord has broken, I know not where I'm going on the road to love."

Whether the "Strait of Yura" refers to Tangoyura in Kyoto Prefecture, Kiiyura in Wakayama Prefecture, or Awaji's Yura is said to be unknown. Despite singing of love, the poem expresses a certain resignation beyond passion.

Should a boat suffer such a mishap, there is nothing to do but to trust in the winds and the waves. Resignation means objectively recognizing a self that can only give up, not resisting destiny, and leaving everything to what heaven ordains. Ten years earlier, I hadn't gone back to the disabled veterans' hospital; I'd chosen to work at a munitions company as a result, and here I was today. As for the fate of the screenplay I was now writing—I didn't know yet.

I once again turned my eyes to Akashi Strait and its dark roaring surge.

A poem a millennium old following a syllabic scheme, five-seven-five-seven-seven, offers resignation in the face of destiny...the power to heal. What kind of lifespan do our scenarios and films have, I wonder.

110

The next day was cloudless.

I took a ferry from Iwaya to Akashi, then a local train from Akashi to Himeji. When I arrived at Himeji Station, I left the building and walked straight north up the main street.

Himeji Castle was at the end of the street, and its chalk-white, five-story main keep loomed larger with every step I took. After I deposited my Boston bag at the temporary baggage storage window, I had thought to take a taxi, but since the castle didn't open to visitors until nine o'clock there was no point in my arriving early. Plus, it was a road I was used to walking, and as I gazed on the town for the first time in a while, my eyes catching on its changes, I came upon and halted in the middle of the remains of the south training grounds facing the castle.

The south training grounds had been converted into a cluster of barracks at the same time the war ended, but now it was completely a part of the city. Before the war, however, it had been a large parade ground; the army had used the north training grounds to drill soldiers, while the south had been given over to use by civilians free to come and go. The middle of the space had been a good spot to take in the castle.

In front of me stood Mt. Hime, at 150 feet high more a hillock than a mountain. Upon it sat a stone foundation, and among three lesser donjons loomed the chalk-white, five-story main keep (one basement level, six above ground) for which no words—extraordinary, magnificent, beautiful—seemed enough.

Furthermore, to its left was the western wing, its elegant snow-white feathers stretching out far and away from the starting point, Cosmetic Tower, on Mt. Sagi, the same height as Mt. Hime. Surveying the whole including the main keep, it looked as though a white heron were flapping its wings to fly east, and the "White Heron Castle" as it was also known was more than a pretty sight, but rather the apex of Japanese aesthetics, the height of beauty constructed by Japanese hands.

The castle had been erected by the local Akamatsu clan in the Muromachi period, and during the era of the warring states Hashiba Hideyoshi, sent to conquer the western reaches of the main island, added a three-story keep to serve as his headquarters. After the decisive Battle of Sekigahara, the first Tokugawa shogun appointed his son-in-law Sanzaemon Terumasa Ikeda as governor, endowing him with Harima's 570,000 *koku*, Bizen's 280,000, and Awaji's 60,000, for a total of 910,000 *koku*. The foremost castle in western Japan came into being as the so-called million-*koku* domain lord of Harima-Himeji built on it over a period of nine years to guard against the array of formidable daimyo further to the west, whose loyalty to the Edo regime was deemed less than ardent.

Yet, with the south parade ground gone, so was the best spot for surveying the castle. One could simply put this down to the passage of time, but given the passion and toil expended on maintenance and repairs since the Meiji period, the loss just seemed too great... I looked at my wristwatch and began walking.

I entered Himeji Castle at almost the exact time it was opened to visitors.

I entered through the large Gate of the Water Caltrops and, not looking at the outer courtyard, ignoring the middle courtyard, proceeded straight through the "I" "Ro" "Ha" "Ni" or A, B, C, D gates towards the stairs of the main keep.

By this time, I already knew.

The idea was to inspect towers and enclosures in the outer and inner courtyards of the castle with my work in progress in mind, and to turn it into a screenplay by hook or by crook if I could sense that the samurai was real. But if, walking around such spots, I could not feel his presence and existence, I would give up on the work without a second thought... No, that was a deception, a lie, nothing more than a fixed game between the left and right sides of my brain there at the end of my wits, while unbeknownst to me my instinctive brain stem had come down with an irrevocable ruling. To say goodbye to this work...to part ways.

And I was to say my goodbye at Himeji Castle.

If we turned the work into a screenplay and then into a film, the studio would launch a massive campaign touting in no uncertain terms that this was a new and unprecedented *jidaigeki*, and Mr. Kurosawa would also likely imply as much to critics and journalists. But what if someone claimed that the realism of the film was off, that they had only two meals in early Tokugawa, and that there was no way a samurai would bring his own bento to the castle? There was some truth to the arts department's Kanehara's warning.

Interviewed historians of note had agreed that they didn't know the answer, but if we made the film, we had no way of knowing who might level what criticism. The world is a place where one dog barking sets a whole army of them barking, and it would be a fatal blow to our work.

Moreover, *Rashomon* had won the grand prix at the Venice Film Festival in September of the previous year. At first, "film festival" and "grand prix" were just gibberish, but gradually people were becoming aware of their significance and weight. Mr. Kurosawa had taken a great step from being Japan's Kurosawa to the world's Kurosawa. At precisely such a juncture, how could a period piece he'd thrown all his might into bear a gaping wound that was altogether fatal?

This project could not see the light of day unless we had irrefutable proof that the custom of eating three meals a day was in place at the beginning of the Edo period and that a samurai on castle duty would have brought his own bento—but we'd searched for three months and found no such source. Hence we had to give up on the project and let it pass from darkness to darkness.

At the basement of the keep I took off my shoes and placed them in a plastic bag, put on slippers, and walked down the passage, then started up the stairs.

Although *A Samurai's Day* was heading from darkness to darkness, as the person who had begotten it I at least wanted it to have limbs and to bury it whole. This was a story where a herald samurai asks a mounted guard samurai to be his second, the latter accepts, and we see out the conclusion.

But it was complete, in fact, by the day before.

Without one word of dialogue, accompanied only by the musical soundtrack, the faithful movements of the herald samurai preparing to commit seppuku and those of his second the mounted guard; the solemn movements of the herald's wife, son, and daughter, of his colleagues and subordinates, the neighboring homes, the retainers' residence, of his whole house; all of them merciless gears, the entire castle town grinding like giant wooden gears, a lustrous black harder than metal, and ticking towards the conclusion scene by scene to the gut-wrenching finale, a scenario of great integrity—in my mind the "samurai" already lived and breathed. From the morning, fragrant with *sakura* in almost full bloom in the dawn light, into the afternoon and the faint white of dusk, *A Samurai's Day* had taken full shape and was finished, a fateful and unturning one-way street.

The stairs of Himeji Castle's main keep are steep and taxing.

I somehow managed to get to the third floor, but by the fourth I was short of breath, and I halted on the fifth, unable to move, with just one level left to the viewing platform at the top.

I looked around panting, and my eyes were drawn to two great columns. They were the load-bearing east and west pillars that supported the five-storied keep.

Still gasping, I went closer to look at the east pillar. It had been there

113

since the Tokugawa period, as the heart of the castle so to speak: a giant fir tree from the Daizenji temple grounds in Onuki, Kanzaki near where I was born.

Then I approached the west pillar. The provenance of this one was unclear, but if it was also from the surrounding area like the east pillar, then it might have been a cypress or cedar from Mt. Kasagata in Seka Valley, also close to my birthplace and full of huge trees.

My breathing had finally returned to normal, so I climbed the stairs to the top level of the five-story keep, to the viewing platform overlooking the Harima area. Perhaps because of the time, there were still only a few people there, and I looked out the northernmost of the three eastern windows, towards the northeast.

"Ah!" I exclaimed. *I could see... I could see it!*

Backlit in the slanting light was the embankment of the Ichikawa in Nozato, to the northeast of Himeji—the very banks where I had decided to become a scenario writer.

When they started preparing to shoot *Rashomon* at Daiei Studios in Kyoto, I was still a company man, more oriented towards becoming an entrepreneur than a screenwriter. I intended to keep pursuing scenarios as a hobby but keenly felt that continuing on both paths was a tall order. If I didn't choose one, I would come up empty.

One day, as I continued to waver, I informed my immediate subordinate, the accounting section manager, that "I'm going to the Nozato factory." I left headquarters on a bicycle and headed toward the northeast of the city, but the Nozato factory passed by me on my right—and I came out on the Ichikawa's embankment.

As the head of the accounting department, the company's near prospects were clear to me. In a year or two...three if we were lucky, we'd face deadlock and collapse. So I was at a crossroads: I could start my own business or become a scenario writer—but no, it wasn't about resolve, in truth I was dizzy with exhaustion. Having to come up with funds and make do was overwhelming, and I felt cornered and out of breath as I spent my days harried and obsessed.

If I started my own business, things might be fine as long as conditions were favorable, but the economic cycle was ever fickle. The employee roster and families' livelihoods would weigh on my shoulders, and the searing hellish hardship of scrambling for funds might dog me for the rest of my life as it did at the moment.

Meanwhile, if I became a scenario writer, I only had to think about how to feed myself, my wife, and my three children. What a cakewalk.

I parked my bicycle on the embankment's path, walked away, and looked up at the sky.

"I'm going to be a scenario writerrr!"

What was this blue sky, this dazzle, this weightlessness? Greenery sloping down onto the banks in the early summer sunshine, a herd of cattle chewing on grass, and beyond, the sparkling light reflecting off the stones and the flowing Ichikawa. When I turned around, a chalk-white five-storied keep towered, lit directly from above—Himeji Castle in relief. Surveying the Harima plains stood the castle of Himeji, impressive.

That was the moment the seed of *A Samurai's Day* came into existence in my bosom.

Gazing out the east window of the chalk-white five-storied keep, at the Ichikawa's embankment to the northeast, I stood still holding my breath. After a while, I exhaled and walked over to the south windows, to the middle one of five, to take in the view. The streets of Himeji spread out below; before the war, the area south of the Sanyo Line had been pastoral, but now city blocks extended as far south as Shikama, and the horizon on the Seto Inland Sea hovered unexpectedly high.

I turned away from the south-facing window and went down the keep stairs.

Descending down a level to the fifth floor, without hesitation I accosted the east pillar, reached out my arm, and patted Onuki's Daizenji temple's huge fir tree, slightly darkened over the course of a few centuries propping up the keep. It felt cool to the touch. I could discern something like a faint warmth too, though.

Touching the supporting pillar at the heart of the keep again, I murmured, "This castle gave birth to the project, so I render it back to the castle. There."

I returned to Tokyo, and the following morning I went out into the front garden and burned all my notes and materials for *A Samurai's Day*, and in the afternoon, at a coffee shop in front of the Toho headquarters in Yurakucho, I faced the producer, Sojiro Motoki, and Kanehara and the other member of the arts department.

When I announced that I was discontinuing the project, Sojiro Motoki went pale, and even though the arts department guys could foresee this outcome, now that it was a reality their faces completely lost color too.

The next Kurosawa project, with him out of the loop, passing from darkness to darkness… It was no joke for the studio, but also inexcusable vis-à-vis Mr. Kurosawa, a massive debacle beyond salvaging.

"All right, Hashimoto… I'll have to inform Kuro-san, and the sooner the better. You'll come with me, won't you?"

I nodded, and Sojiro Motoki said to the men from the arts department, "You guys too… I'll contact him now."

Having been informed of the situation through Motoki's phone call, when Mr. Kurosawa confronted the four of us at his home in Komae, he was ill-tempered from the moment he showed his face. Rebuking eyes blazing with anger, he shot glares at the arts department men and Motoki. For some reason, he didn't even glance at me.

When, facing him in the guest tatami room, Sojiro Motoki announced anew that there was no choice but to call off the project due to a lack of sources, Mr. Kurosawa exploded in anger.

"Why, why can't we do it?!"

Shaken, the two arts department members began trembling in fear. Akira Kurosawa's anger was terrible. A blue vein popped up on his temple.

"Why?! How come?! I've waited patiently for two months!"

Akira Kurosawa's anger wasn't ordinary; it was extraordinary. Yet he was hardly to blame. For him, who reigned at the top of the world of Japanese cinema with a run of numerous brilliant and fine works since his debut, *Sanshiro Sugata*, having a film he'd decided to make canceled unilaterally at the planning stage, extinguished without his input, must have been a first. The immeasurable humiliation and resentment over treatment such as he'd never before received wasn't something that I didn't understand.

For me too, putting quality aside, I'd turned anything I set out to write, to handle, into a work, and quitting as I was doing now was an unbearable disgrace. In Mr. Kurosawa's case, this had happened without his input, and with his considerable ego and much greater pride than mine, it made sense that his anger would be exponentially stronger and harsher.

Mr. Kurosawa was persistent. He sometimes glared down Sojiro Motoki, but mostly he alternated his bloodshot eyes between the two arts department men, repeating why, how come it couldn't be done. Perhaps the planning personnel had reported to Sojiro Motoki how I was proceeding with the content of the work, and Motoki, ever the talker, had embellished its potential to Mr. Kurosawa—and the swelling of a story into a scenario had gotten him completely on board and he'd given thought to sequences, like the climax to the end after the mounted guard agrees to be the second, and drawn pictures… In any case, he may have been waiting on pins and needles for the first draft. And then it was canceled all

The author (left) and Akira Kurosawa meeting about work, circa 1960.

of a sudden. No wonder his anger was intense, extraordinary.

Even so, Mr. Kurosawa's bloodshot, vein-popping ire passed the point of hysteria. He hounded them without mercy: Shinobu Hashimoto wasn't writing, no, couldn't write the script, because you fellows hadn't gathered any materials to speak of, you are to blame.

That was wrong, the planning personnel had done well. In fact, they had done everything they could, and I wanted to praise them. Moreover, they hadn't called a halt to the project, I had, and there were limits to barking up the wrong tree.

The mood was tense, physically unbearable, distasteful. It wasn't unlike a cat tormenting a mouse, a one-sided bullying of creatures who couldn't fight back. And it just went on and on.

I couldn't hold back any longer.

Come to your senses, Akira Kurosawa, enough is enough. If you have complaints, tell me… I was the one who decided to nix it.

I lifted my face and looked at Akira Kurosawa, who raged on as if obsessed.

"Mr. Kurosawa."

He glanced over. It was the first time his pointed glare had been turned on me.

"Mr. Kurosawa, how many meals do you eat a day?"

"What?!"

"I eat three, and I imagine you eat three as well. But I don't know when Japanese began eating three meals... That's something that no one, anywhere, no matter the historian, knows."

Mr. Kurosawa fixed his pointed glare on me. He looked as though he might spring at me.

"Japanese history is a history of incidents. When and where what manner of incident took place is scrupulously written up every which way. But not one line of accurate history touches on how people lived, how they ate and bathed... Mr. Kurosawa!" I faced him and declared head-on, putting an end to it. "Our nation has a history of incidents. But we lack histories of life!"

Ten years later, I wrote a screenplay with the title *Seppuku [Harakiri]*. It wasn't commissioned by a film studio but completed according to my own whim.

I'd given, at the castle in Himeji, a proper burial to the samurai committing seppuku, or so I thought, but perhaps never having crossed he wandered out of the realm of the dead, and when he sat himself down again to carry out the ritual, his fury was weirdly intense. Directed by Masaki Kobayashi and well-regarded, it won the Special Jury Award at the 1963 Cannes Film Festival and is said to be one of my representative works along with *Castle of Sand*, this reincarnated *Seppuku*.

Subsequent to the cancellation of *A Samurai's Day* and Mr. Kurosawa's extraordinary rage, I'd been hanging around at my Daita home for a few days when I had a phone call from Sojiro Motoki.

"Ah, Hashimoto, Kuro-san…yes, Kuro-san got in touch with me. He seems to have put the samurai seppuku idea behind him. Yes, yes…and he seems to have come up with something new and wants a meeting… The sooner the better, a meeting with you, Hashimoto."

"I'll go now."

"Huh?"

"Well, it's not like I can take on any other work, so I'm just hanging around the house. I'd like to settle things with Team Kurosawa as soon as possible… I'll go now."

"All right. Then please do, and I'll let Kuro-san know."

I left home and took the Inogashira Line, transferring at the next stop at Shimokitazawa to the Odakyu Line. When I arrived at Mr. Kurosawa's house in Komae, Mr. Kurosawa, who had been waiting, greeted me and showed me to the Japanese-style drawing room.

In sharp contrast with the other day he had a calm expression, and without even touching on *A Samurai's Day*, he began talking.

"Hashimoto… Those master swordsmen of yore, Ise-no-kami Kozumi, Bokuden Tsukahara, Musashi Miyamoto… Each of them was amazing in his own way, yes?"

I nodded. It was true.

"The impressive things about these swordsmen, the most interesting episodes, what astounds people, makes them sigh and feel moved… Picking out such anecdotes, lining up seven or eight swordsmen, and the order could simply be chronological, we do an omnibus."

"Hunh…" I leaned forward slightly. "And then you'd have *The Lives of Japanese Swordsmen*."

"I won't be sure about the title until we have the script, but something like *The Lives of Swordsmen*, yes."

"That, I could do in three weeks…no, in two weeks."

"Huh? You could, so easily?" Mr. Kurosawa, in disbelief, looked at me as if to bore a hole in my face.

"Mr. Kurosawa, have you read the swordfighting stories of Sanjugo Naoki?"

"I recall reading two or three of them a long time ago."

"Then, what about Kosuke Gomi?"

"I haven't read those, no."

"There are a mountain's worth of tales of master swordsmen, from Sanjugo Naoki in the past to Kosuke Gomi today. But there's only one source...*Honcho Bugei Shoden*, published during the Tokugawa period."

"*Honcho Bugei Shoden?*"

"If I borrowed it from the library, I could whip up a script in two weeks."

"Well then, Hashimoto, will you try your hand at this omnibus?"

"Yes, I'll do it."

A faint wry smile crossed Mr. Kurosawa's face. "No need to hold yourself to the two weeks business."

"No, work demands a reckoning... It'll be fine."

Without ado, I took on *The Lives of Japanese Swordsmen*, title tentative. Since I was in a hurry I asked to use the Kurosawas' phone and got in touch with the Toho arts department, requesting that they borrow the book from the library in Ueno.

The next evening, *Honcho Bugei Shoden* [A Brief Account of the Combat Arts in Our Land] arrived from Toho headquarters, so I began working at home the day after.

Since the job needed to be turned around quickly, Toho offered a stay at an inn or hotel in Tokyo though resorts like Hakone or Ise might be tough on such short notice. I turned them down, however, and began working in my own four-and-a-half-tatami-mat study.

The front yard of my home was as long and narrow as an eel's bed. On the left was a bamboo fence we shared with the neighbor, and on the right a concrete wall that set us off from a vacant lot on which stood two cherry trees. My house was the cul de sac of a long and narrow alley so to speak—and my study on the second floor facing the yard got a lot of sun and afforded peace and quiet, separated from the nearby eight-mat room by a hallway. I liked it, and rather than search high and low for a place to seclude myself, getting to it at home with due haste promised better progress.

I took notes as I read *Honcho Bugei Shoden*, and when I was done I wrote down names in order in an organizational chart on a dedicated sheet.

Leading off:
Sword saint Ise-no-kami Hidetsuna Kozumi

Followed by:

Bokuden Tsukahara
Shinmen Takezo Masana (Musashi Miyamoto)
Tajima-no-kami Muneyoshi Yagyu
Jiroemon Tadaaki Ono
Samanosuke Matsubayashi
Shusaku Chiba
Kenkichi Sakakibara

That made eight, which seemed like enough.

The leadoff man, Ise-no-kami Kozumi, also known as Musashi-no-kami Nobutsuna, founded the Shinkage school. When a bandit kidnapped a child and hid in a storehouse, he went in disguised as a monk, robbed the bandit of his blade, and killed him with one strike, an all-too-famous episode.

Bokuden Tsukahara et al. are all familiar master swordsmen, foremost experts of a school, and though Samanosuke Matsubayashi isn't all that famous as a theorist, I chose him because his story was terribly curious. Having slain his opponent in one blow at an interschool match and provoked enmity, he was attacked in broad daylight by several men. He swiftly felled five, while the survivors fled. The other school did not let up, but Samanosuke, well-prepared, never left home unguarded by disciples and offered not the slightest opening. The other school hired three ninja, who sneaked into his residence in the middle of the night to stab Samanosuke while he slept, but one was cut down instantly and the other two killed in the next breath. Samanosuke laughed heartily and boasted, "I am never unprepared. There is no assassin in the world who can kill me." One morning, he went to the toilet and squatted down. An assassin hiding in the shit-hole thrust up a half-length spear, skewering him from butt to bosom, and he died then and there.

The last, Kenkichi Sakakibara, was an exceptional swordfighter, but the shogunate collapsed, and in the Meiji period the way of the sword no longer put food on the table. He demonstrated his *iai* quick draw at street corners and made his living by accepting money from people. The way of the sword had become little more than a show.

From the founder of the Shinkage school, Ise-no-kami Kozumi, who brought about a revolutionary golden age for the sword-alone philosophy, to Kenkichi Sakakibara, the forlorn practitioner humbled into street performance after the warrior class perished and the way no longer paid the bills, I would write *The Lives of Japanese Swordsmen* as an omnibus film.

With the characters in order and their stories ready I got down to writing, starting with the opening scene. From the first day, I threw myself into it headlong, extending my workday by an extra hour.

Usually, I was a typical day person who began working at 10 a.m., finished at 5 p.m., and didn't write a word after dinner—this time schedule had become my custom as a writer who'd been de-enlisted for a bout of consumption, whose after-effects were here to stay.

I was terribly lucky that when Team Kurosawa hunkers down it follows the same writing schedule.

When I actually tried it, however, beginning at nine-thirty and ending at five-thirty turned out to be hard on my body. With nothing else for it, I went the salaryman route of Sundays off and set aside a day of rest for every six of work.

On that seventh day of rest, I reread the first half of the draft I'd completed, from the first scene with Ise-no-kami Kozumi through to the fourth entry, Tajima-no-kami Muneyoshi Yagyu. The flow felt terribly curious and contrary to experience. There was an oddity here not present in past scenarios… I thought it might be the special characteristic of an omnibus work, of eight independent stories each with its own protagonist.

I rested for a day and, returning to work the next, made progress according to schedule.

At this rate, I expected to shave one day off my projected fourteen and be done in thirteen, but the truth of screenplays is that you never know what will happen. When I got to Shusaku Chiba of the Hokushin-itto school, I stumbled. Since Samanosuke Matsubayashi's end was rather gruesome, the next scene at Shusaku Chiba's *dojo* training hall was a spectacle with dozens of people wearing gauntlets mixing it up and trading blows, but what to follow it up with didn't come easily and gave me trouble. In fact, by the time I finished the last scene with Kenkichi Sakakibara, I'd exceeded my projection by a day and had only finished on my fifteenth.

Still, if a day later than the two weeks I'd promised Mr. Kurosawa, *The Lives of Japanese Swordsmen* was completed.

For the time being I might call Sojiro Motoki—but hesitated. If I called Motoki, an assistant would come to collect the screenplay and bring it to him. At the moment, however, Motoki was busy running errands as a different team's producer, and I didn't know if he would read it promptly. Either way, if the hands-full Sojiro Motoki were to read it and hand it to an assistant to take to Mr. Kurosawa, it wouldn't be today or tomorrow but would take a few days, perhaps even four. I was a day late, but since

I'd gone to the trouble of finishing in fifteen days, I wanted to show it to Mr. Kurosawa as soon as possible.

Mr. Kurosawa happened to be in when I called his home, so I told him the work was done and, out of momentum, that I was bringing it over.

Mr. Kurosawa read drafts thoroughly.

No, it went beyond thorough or meticulous. He held his breath and stilled his head, his entire body not moving in the slightest, and rather than looking at each character and each line, he seemed to take in each 200-character sheet as a whole, less reading than absorbing everything written there. Even when he turned pages, he shifted neither his face nor his frame, nor his eyes. It was like some unending tense standoff, a seasoned blade hand pointing an unsheathed katana right at an opponent's face and watching for moves with his entire body and soul. As I confronted this, the oppressive tension bore down on me too, and I almost lost my sense of time.

I have no idea how much time elapsed since he'd started reading. He spent a certain amount of time absorbing a sheet, moved on to the next, and then to the next... When Mr. Kurosawa finally finished reading the manuscript of 297 half-sheets, he let out a breath. A long sigh. Long enough to make me wonder just how much air the human body could possibly hold. Then, through the lingering note of his sigh he murmured, "Hashimoto... Scenarios require *kishotenketsu*, it would seem."

Kishotenketsu, a venerable piece of scenario terminology, referred to the introduction (ki), development (sho), climax (ten), and conclusion (ketsu). The term itself, however, was musty, so we said Start, Development, Climax, and Last, using the English words for all but Development (for which we preferred the modern "tenkai"). Since these were divided and placed into four boxes, we called *kishotenketsu* "the four boxes" or even "big box" for short—as in "What happened to the big box?" or "How's the big box?" In any case, it meant that the structure (assemblage) of a scenario had four indispensable elements and stages.

With a self-deprecating, bitterish smile Mr. Kurosawa said, "Trying to string together climaxes from beginning to end to make a movie was woefully wrongheaded in the first place, I guess."

I sank into silence. Halfway through, I'd felt a strange something I'd never experienced before; it was the overstrain and contradiction of completely ignoring the four stages of assembling a story, the "four boxes," and composing a film out of nothing but climaxes. So dumb a folly—

123

my mind went dead silent like a vacuum. Not just *A Samurai's Day*, but now *The Lives of Japanese Swordsmen*, was kaput.

Eventually, I managed to utter, "Right...no way a film can be all climax from beginning to end."

Yet Mr. Kurosawa was the great Akira Kurosawa, and I myself an up-and-coming writer of whom much was expected, and we, of all people, had been foolish enough to become besotted with something that even a total novice understood to be impossible, that could not be turned into a scenario? At times, humans could be remarkably foolish and do stupid... No, it was all due to *A Samurai's Day*. Not only I, but Mr. Kurosawa as well, were shaken by that bungle, and our impatience for the next work, more like our irritation, in some way ended up begetting a fey baby like *The Lives of Japanese Swordsmen*.

Mr. Kurosawa changed the subject somewhat. But it wasn't as if he'd severed all attachment to our goblin *Lives of Japanese Swordsmen*. "By the way, Hashimoto... What were these traveling swordsmen?"

I looked at Mr. Kurosawa, unable to discern his point.

"Tacticians of old were like today's pro baseball players."

"...?"

"You could command a high endowment with just a sword, and some even became daimyo. Just like a pro ball player who goes from team to team fetching a high price on the strength of his bat alone."

I nodded. "Yes, I see."

"As a trend, an astonishingly large number of people must have rushed to the way of the sword...but aside from famous ones that might come up in these lives of master swordsmen, I doubt most of them would have had the money to become traveling swordsmen... I mean the expenses of being on the road. Without some silver on you, how do you ever roam the country on a journey to hone your skills?"

"Hmm, I wonder... That, I think we could find out if we looked it up though. Mr. Kurosawa, I'll look it up."

It was the middle of December, and though a sunny day the wind was biting.

The request I'd made of planning personnel at the Toho arts department had been attended to right away, and I got word that the findings, reported to Sojiro Motoki, would be conveyed to me in person by him. But since this had come from Mr. Kurosawa, I thought it was only right to hear it together with him, and so I asked Sojiro Motoki to meet me at the Kurosawa residence.

There I was holding my hands out over a large brazier, face to face with Mr. Kurosawa, when the diminutive Sojiro Motoki arrived looking all busy. The tip of his nose was red, no doubt due to the cold.

"Ah, I'm late, sorry, sorry…" Sitting between the two of us, and with our heads together, he cut to the chase. "About traveling swordsmen… A phenomenon from the late Muromachi through the Warring States era, tacticians could wander freely all over Japan even if they didn't have money."

Both Mr. Kurosawa and I remained silent.

"That is to say, if you went to a *dojo* and undertook a bout, they'd treat you to dinner and give you a handful of dried rice when you departed the next morning. This dried rice, boiled rice that had been dried out, you could either bite into as-is or soften back with hot water. So as a tactician all you needed to do was arrive at the next *dojo* within the day."

"Mr. Motoki," I asked, "it's all good and well if there's a *dojo* the next day. But what if there isn't?"

"No problem. You just go to a temple."

"A temple?"

"Yeah, because this was in the time before inns. Temples would protect travelers with no place else to go. So, if you went to a temple, they'd feed you and allow you to stay the night, and in the morning when you left they'd hand you that handful of dried rice."

I asked further, "If there's neither a training hall nor a temple, what do you do then?"

Sojiro Motoki, however, was completely unruffled. "We're talking from late Muromachi to Warring States, crime was rampant all across the country, and the wilds were full of bandits and brigands who'd pop up. So if you simply went into some village and spent the night on lookout for burglars, any village would let you eat your fill…and hand you dried rice when you set out."

My heart skipped a beat, and I asked Motoki to make sure. "Farmers hiring samurai?"

"Yup."

I looked at Mr. Kurosawa for a moment. Mr. Kurosawa, visibly struck, was also looking at me. As our eyes met, we unconsciously gave each other a firm nod.

"Done," Mr. Kurosawa said in a low, deep voice.

"Done indeed."

Mr. Motoki watched our exchange in puzzlement, but the next instant he gulped with expectation.

I confirmed with Mr. Kurosawa, "The number of samurai… How many samurai should the farmers hire?"

"Three or four is too few. Five or six, maybe seven or eight… No, eight is too many, I'd say seven."

"Then it'll be seven samurai."

Mr. Kurosawa lifted his face and looked out into space as if to issue a challenge. "Yes, seven samurai!"

Sojiro Motoki, who had been holding his breath, began to smile. Two scenario writers had buried their sharp fangs into some huge prey. The theme and story could be gleaned from our snippets of conversation. Farmers would hire seven samurai, fight incoming bandits, and win… Material where the story and theme were this concise and complete, and this perfectly overlapping, was rare; it was a one-in-a-hundred project.

The work was pregnant with something that could make it incredibly fun.

"Hashimoto!" Mr. Kurosawa flung out at me. It was like the rebuke of an animal trainer dispensing reminders to a too-eager horse or groom at the starting gate. "Don't try to write cleverly or skillfully. The first draft just needs to line up the necessary elements."

I nodded and he continued, "And there's a lot of action in this scenario. If there's too much action in the stage directions, it'll lag and be hard to read. For scenes where stage directions stretch on, don't stick to the present tense of scenarios, just go ahead and use the novelistic past tense here and there, got it?!"

Minakuchien in Atami is a high-class inn known for its many stand-alone cottages scattered across expansive, foliage-rich grounds.

It was mid-January of 1953 when Mr. Kurosawa and I set up in a cottage room at Minakuchien to finalize, with Mr. Oguni, the first draft of *Seven Samurai* I'd written at my home in Daita oblivious to end-of-year and New Year observances.

This was the same time of year that we'd secluded ourselves a year earlier at Senkyoro in Sengokuhara for *Ikiru*, but since it had been too cold in Sengokuhara, this time Mr. Kurosawa had apparently consulted with Sojiro Motoki and chosen warm Atami. Mr. Oguni's schedule was packed, however, so he couldn't make it on the appointed day, and as with *Ikiru*, only Mr. Kurosawa and I checked in to Minakuchien.

After spending the night there, we began our first day of work.

Everything was the same as it had been back when we were at Senkyoro in Hakone, a large table set out in front of the alcove with me seated facing it in the junior position. Mr. Kurosawa didn't have his back to the alcove but sat to my right…the table wasn't square but rectangular so there wasn't much room on his side, but there he sat to my right facing the south garden. The *shoji* screen was closed though, and you couldn't see the garden.

As I arranged manuscript paper and pencils on the table and prepared for work, Mr. Kurosawa also took his tools of the trade out of a red Boston bag. This time, however, it wasn't his usual *warabanshi* half-sheets but a thick college notebook.

Wondering why, I peeked over and saw a circle, drawn in pencil and labeled "Kambei" underneath, containing a portrait of the central figure among the seven samurai called Kambei.

Starting with his height, about five foot five, and medium build, the notes went into great detail. The way he wore his straw sandals, his gait, how he answered others, how he turned around when called to from behind, his demeanor and behavior vis-à-vis all sorts of situations, with ample illustrations throughout, sprawled on and on in the college notebook.

I felt like I'd been smacked in the head with a club out of the blue.

It had felt like me alone for *A Samurai's Day*, me alone for *The Lives of Japanese Swordsmen*, me alone for *Seven Samurai*—always me alone suffering exhaustion and hardship while Mr. Kurosawa went fishing by the Tama River or attended art exhibits, ball games at Korakuen, and Noh plays, enjoying himself without a care in the world. I'd resented being the one to pull the lonely, short end of the stick, but mutely Mr. Kurosawa, too, had been working on the foundations of a giant structure as the muscle propping up the whole edifice out of sight, continuously fraying his nerves.

But what was with this breadth and depth of characterization?

It was in no way customary or ordinary and surpassed the limits of thoroughness, approaching the bizarre.

In writing a scenario, everyone first slaps together a theme and story of sorts, but characterization, carving out the characters, is tiresome and also where you can cut corners. Once you've organized the story to a certain degree and built the big box (the four boxes of composition) and decided on how it will begin, you're prone to shirk on carving out the characters, their settings, and just start writing. Everyone knows how important it is, but it's tiresome and annoying and even seems redundant given that personalities and such naturally begin to be established once you do start writing and the characters get going.

Seven Samurai, in which farmers hire samurai. From left, Shimura Takashi, Kamatari Fujiwara, Yoshio Kosugi, Kuninori Kodo © 1954 TOHO CO., LTD.

But that's wrong. Even though people have a frightening number of commonalities, each of us has special characteristics and is different. That's how we get drama. If you don't flesh out the characters, if you write them in a hackneyed way, then the actors will express them in a hackneyed way. It's only when you sculpt the characters and imbue them with characteristics that ingenuity and effort come into the players' performances.

A work's tension and richness of nuance are determined by the clarity of the scenarist's image of his characters going into the writing. If you don't attend to it thoroughly before you begin on the text, no matter how seasoned you are, your experience and technical proficiency won't cover for you.

It's not an overstatement to say that the quality of a script hinges on the tiresome, annoying, and oft-shirked sculpting of the characters.

Mr. Kurosawa silently turned the pages of the college notebook in which he had carved out the characters.

Kambei, being central, took up nearly half of it, but Heihachi, Kyuzo, Katsushiro, Gorobei…images of the seven samurai probably filled up the thick notebook.

Predicting that this time the work's outcome hinged on the coloration of the personalities of each of the seven samurai and adamantly refusing to cut corners that bore no cutting, expending the maximum amount of effort afforded by one's talent—it could be left at that, but what was this gluttony and determination for fleshing out the characters?

Akira Kurosawa—the greatest characteristic of the man's screenplay writing was not cutting corners that shouldn't be cut and, to an unthinkable degree for ordinary people, sparing no accumulation of effort.

Didn't his godly bolt of inspiration in the case of *Rashomon*, and his perfectionism that exceeded rationalism in the case of *Ikiru*, both owe to this power of execution, to this refusal to cut corners, to sparing absolutely no accumulation of effort?

I sat unmoving in front of my manuscript paper, my eyes fixed on a point in space. I couldn't put down a single word. The first shockwave had passed, but now the second was beginning. It was more vivid than the first and exposed something that had been lurking in the back of my consciousness.

Someday, not so far from now, as a writer I will surpass Akira Kurosawa. It's only a matter of time.

I'd never thought it very deeply or consciously. A notion, wriggling within the recesses of my heart, that while I had Akira Kurosawa in my sights and worked under him for now, I'd surpass him and eventually take the lead as a scenario writer, accepted as fact, never doubted, was yanked off like a mask...exposed by a real college notebook that smashed my self-serving self-regard to smithereens.

At this rate, forget about surpassing him.

In order to overtake him, I would have to be even more scrupulous than he was in fleshing out characters. But even if I could make up for it with energy and stamina, the problem was—the pictures. He could draw pictures, but I couldn't. What could make up for this handicap? Unless I made up for it, I couldn't possibly surpass him.

And for that... In any case, once this job was done, sidelining everything else, I had to get to this...

"Hashimoto..."

Startled, I raised my face. Mr. Kurosawa had finished reading his notebook, lain it on the table, and turned toward me as I'd just sat there in front of my manuscript paper.

His arms were crossed; there was a frown on his face and something seemed to be on his mind. "About this script... Hashimoto, do you know Dvořák's New World?"

"Yes, it's a favorite of mine. I have a record too and listen to it sometimes."

"I want that New World music to be the original work... Do you know what I mean?"

"I get it," I answered without missing a beat.

Mr. Kurosawa seemed to be holding his breath as he gazed at my face.

"The feel of the script we're going to write...the rhythm or sense of sound, the inflection, that reading the script imparts to you."

"That's it, yes, yes..."

"For the beginning, we could just go with the first movement, and the Negro spiritual in the second movement can be used to good effect for the farmers' plight too."

Mr. Kurosawa nodded. He seemed somehow relieved.

"And then the nimble, awfully crisp third movement, that's for some jolly part in the first half. Especially the end, the grand end...the final battle, right? The fourth movement's massive swell, the phrase la-si-do-si-la-la repeating like churning waves, on and on... There's nothing else for the final battle but that."

Mr. Kurosawa gave a few big nods. Relief welling from the bottom of his heart seemed to spread over his face as a smile.

"Good... Well then, Hashimoto, let's do *Seven Samurai* with 'The New World' as the original."

Mr. Oguni arrived in the evening a week after we began working.

"What a luxurious inn. They do have a main building, but it's almost all cottages. I had no idea there was an inn like this in Atami."

"Mr. Oguni, will you take a bath?"

"Yeah."

"Since the bath is attached to the cottage, it's small and takes only one."

"It'll do if it takes one, no?"

The maid who had shown Mr. Oguni to the room bowed low on the floor and said, "Then I'll start filling the tub. In twenty to twenty-five minutes, please turn off the water."

When Mr. Oguni hung his overcoat on a hanger in the anteroom, entered without changing his clothes, and sat, Mr. Kurosawa silently passed him the manuscript, fastened with a clip. Mr. Oguni took it without a word and began to read.

I was sharpening my pencils with a folding knife for the next day's work. Twelve B3 pencils was the amount per day. If I sharpened them in the morning before we started work, my hands would turn completely black and I would have to wash them, so I always attended to the task after wrapping up for the day and before taking my bath. But today I felt distracted as I sharpened them. I was concerned about Mr. Oguni's reaction. I remembered the clash between him and Mr. Kurosawa over *Ikiru* like it was yesterday. Putting it nicely, Mr. Oguni was without artifice; put not so nicely, he was impulsive and lacked reserve and consideration whoever it was that he was addressing, and you had no idea what he might come out with.

In the tense atmosphere I continued to sharpen my pencils, occasionally glancing over at Mr. Oguni. When I was sharpening my eleventh with just one more to go, Mr. Oguni finished reading the manuscript, placed it on top of the table, and looked at Mr. Kurosawa and me.

"Neat, entertaining!" he said, and with more feeling, "We've got something here... This is going to be good!"

As per Mr. Oguni's words, *Seven Samurai* proceeded smoothly.

First, the theme and story were concise and clear.

A tale of farmers who hire seven samurai and fight incoming bandits, and win... A rare and almost unheard-of plan with a simple, pellucid theme that could be put in one line and which was simultaneously the story.

The second factor in the scenario's smooth progress was the character settings that Akira Kurosawa had carved out. Through his extraordinary efforts, so contrary to the norm, each character's distinctive flair shone through, but beyond that, there was another aspect unrelated to his efforts—no, which trenchantly underlay and supported his efforts—that made the tale entertaining to a surprising degree and gave it a vibrancy that brimmed with realism.

The central figure among the seven samurai whose entrance makes the tale vastly more entertaining, Kambei, is Ise-no-kami Kozumi. His lieutenant and advisor Gorobei is Bokuden Tsukahara. The ferociously skilled swordsman who lives by his blade, Kyuzo, is Shinmen Takezo Masana (Musashi Miyamoto)... These weren't personages that a scribbler's imagination or whimsy could ever create; they were legendary swordsmen whose anecdotes the classics retained, and each had scooted over from *The Lives of Japanese Swordsmen*.

That reckless wild child of an omnibus, *The Lives of Japanese Swordsmen*, was what begat *Seven Samurai*'s protagonist and other crucial figures. And *The Lives of Japanese Swordsmen* was the splash made when the upstanding, stoic *Samurai's Day* fell flat—an intense rebound, an unexpected blessing if there ever was one.

In other words, *Seven Samurai* swallowed whole *A Samurai's Day* and

The Lives of Japanese Swordsmen as great live bait, and with them in its belly, how could it not be entertaining?

With Mr. Oguni's arrival, the nightly drinking really got going.

I don't drink, so when it was just me Mr. Kurosawa idly poured for himself, but now paired with Mr. Oguni, the two of them drank whiskey with water like it was some competition, waxing eloquent and finishing off a bottle in no time. This was all thanks to our work humming along at a good clip, our almost too eventless days unmarred by brooding, belaboring, or soul-searching.

The sign of dark clouds looming ahead *Seven Samurai* visited me around the time the white plum tree in the garden began losing its blossoms petal by petal. We'd gotten quite a bit written by that point; the seven finally had been brought together and were ready to leave town for the village, a major punctuation mark.

There were 163 sheets... Assembling the samurai was supposed to take up about a third of the screenplay, so the whole thing would be three times that length, or 480 pages? We had to be kidding, a scenario close to 500 pages was, boy, no, what on earth was it turning into? As its length was really troubling me, I conducted a broad review of the plot from the beginning to see if there were any repetitive situations or scenes that seemed to stagnate.

> A mounted troop of brigands who have attacked a village at midnight look down on another village from a pass at dawn.
>
> "Should we do this one, too?"
>
> "Not so fast. We just took their rice last autumn."
>
> Even if they attack the village, there will be no spoils.
>
> "Then we'll be back when that barley's ripe!"
>
> The gang of brigands rides off in a whirlwind of dust.
>
> One of the villagers shows his face through a thicket of striped bamboo and runs down the pass for dear life, and hearing his report the villagers meet in the square to discuss countermeasures.
>
> "We should have the magistrate do something!"
>
> "You think we can count on the magistrate? Let's make bamboo spears and stab them to death!"
>
> "As if we could do that... All we can do is meekly hand over the barley and beg them to leave us enough to eat!"

Opportunism, warmongering, pacifism, a riot of every kind of opinion refuses to die down, so a representative and a gaggle of villagers visit the water mill in the outskirts where the elder dwells.

The old man listens to their various opinions, but hearing out the case of the faction that wishes to fight, he says, "Let us!"

When people gasp, he explains, "We'll hire samurai." On the way here after their last village was burned, the only settlements left untouched were those that had hired samurai.

The group falls quiet, but after conferring with the person next to him in hushed murmurs, one of them asks, "But are there any samurai who will fight for us just to be fed?"

With his eyes closed, the elder replies, "Look for hungry samurai. When it's hungry, even a bear will come down from the mountains..."

Thus four village representatives, Manzo, Mosuke, Rikichi, and Yohei, leave in search of samurai. As the opening this level of sell (amount of text) was inevitable.

Finding samurai, however, is no easy task. They call to an itinerant tactician only to be beaten terribly for even suggesting such a thing when they're mere peasants, and at their cheap lodging in town, they treat a ronin to sake and food only for him to turn tail and make himself scarce.

A coolie who shares their lodging regales them with derisive laughter. "So, any luck finding your cheap, strong, fanciful samurai? No one's so fanciful in this day and age. Go home, go home."

The four men redouble their efforts to find samurai but can't handle the sound ones who look like fighters. Feeble specimens and freeloaders who bum a meal and a night's rest are the only ones who show any interest. At wits' end the four men discuss the situation and decide to stop searching and return to their village. They set out from their lodging.

On the road home, they come across a strange sight in another village.

There was a crowd outside the home of a wealthy farmer.

They peeked through the crowd to see a traveling monk shaving the head of a ronin on the bank of a river. According to the crowd, a bandit had forced his way into the home at daybreak but had been spotted by someone from the household, upon which he'd grabbed the three year old of the family and hid in the barn. They tried to capture him but with him bawling that he'd kill the kid their hands were tied.

Clinging to a passing ronin, the child's mother explained their situation and begged for help. The ronin sought out an itinerant monk in the crowd and proceeded to have his head shaved bald with a razor.

The four men watched breathlessly—the ronin, his head shaved, handed his long and short swords to the itinerant monk and borrowed his robes to assume a monk's figure. Then, taking the two rice balls that the mother had made in a hurry, he briskly walked away from the riverbank and passed through the gates of the house.

The gathered crowd timidly followed him through the gates. Without hesitation, the ronin disguised as a monk approached the barn and opened the door slightly. There was a terrible cry from inside.

"Don't come in! If you do, I'll kill the kid!"

The disguised ronin said, "I'm a monk, I'm not here to capture you. I thought the child must be hungry and brought a rice ball. I have one for you, too."

"Don't come in! Throw them in from where you are!"

"Here…" the disguised samurai said, tossing one through the slight opening in the door. He waited a moment and tossed in the other, but the next moment his foot kicked the ground and he leapt into the barn. A sharp, booming war cry came from inside, followed by a short, breathless groan.

The door to the barn fell and out came the bandit. The crowd drew back instinctively, but the bandit wobbled and staggered to a halt, his stomach bleeding profusely, and crumbled to the ground.

From within the barn emerged the disguised ronin with the child in his arms.

The mother made a beeline for them and took the child. The disguised ronin flung away the bloodied sword he'd taken from the bandit.

The stunned crowd could hardly speak.

—The bald ronin has taken to the road, and Manzo and the other farmers follow a little ways behind.

Rikichi says, "We have to ask him, no matter what. That samurai more than cuts it."

But when Rikichi rushes to approach him, someone brushes past to stand in front of the ronin and then to kneel and bow low to the ground.

It's a young man still wearing his forelock who watched in awe from the front row of the crowd.

"I'm Katsushiro Okamoto. Please, take me as one of your disciples!"

"I'm Kambei Shimada, a ronin who lives hand to mouth. I neither have nor need a disciple."

"No, please, take me as your disciple... I'll follow you even without your leave."

"Well, stand up. If you want to talk, I'll listen as we walk."

Relieved, the forelocked Katsushiro stands, but without a moment's respite Rikichi bounds between them and grovels on the earth like a flat spider.

"A plea! A plea for your ears!"

Yohei is boiling rice in an earthen pot behind the cheap lodging in town.

Inside the dim lodging—Kambei's arms are crossed, Katsushiro sits at his side, and across them are Rikichi, Manzo, and Mosuke, all three with stooped shoulders, crestfallen.

With a cornered look, Rikichi says, "So is there no way..."

"Can't be done," Kambei answers.

Katsushiro says, "Master, I would arm the farmers with bamboo spears and—"

"Quiet. This isn't like playing at war. And I'm not your master. (To the three:) They may be mere brigands, but you can't defend against forty horsemen with just two or three samurai. There are fields out front, but until these are flooded they can attack on horseback. Guarding just the four sides would require four, and with two in reserve... Including me, you'd need at least seven..."

As if clinging to his words Rikichi says, "Seven, then? If we had seven..."

Laughing, Kambei says, "No, no, I'm just speculating, it's not like I've accepted the job. For one thing, it's not going to be easy to gather seven trustworthy samurai. Plus, feeding them won't be enough. And I'm tired of battle. Old age, you see."

Silence falls. Laborers sit by the hearth warming unfiltered sake over a fire, and mixed in with the popping kindling comes the sound of Rikichi's sorrowful weeping.

Nonplussed, a laborer sips his sake and thanks heaven he wasn't born a farmer. Another says it would be better to be a dog, that they should die, just die, hurry up and hang themselves, and find some peace.

Reprimands Katsushiro: "You scum, watch your mouth!"

The laborer becomes angry. "Have some sense, I'm only telling the truth."

Katsuhiro flies into a rage. "What do you mean, the truth? Don't you feel these farmers' chagrin?"

"Don't make me laugh, you are the ones who aren't feeling it."

"What?!"

Kambei's taut gaze is also sharply focused on the laborer.

"Listen, if you get it, why don't you help them?" one of the laborers says.

Snatching away the bowl of rice that Yohei, having come in from the back, is offering to Kambei, he holds it up to the old samurai's face. "Look at this—this is for you guys. But you know what these simpletons eat? Millet, they eat millet. They're eating millet and giving you the white rice!"

Kambei calmly gazes at the bowl of rice—then speaks softly. "I get it, so pipe down." He receives the bowl and raises it a little to give thanks. "I won't be having this white rice lightly."

Hence Kambei accepts the farmers' request, and by now we were over 100 sheets, at 104... The subsequent selection of the six samurai—to the tune of Dvořák's New World's nimble third movement—had a pleasing rhythm and a brisk pace.

But Kambei was The Lives of Japanese Swordsmen's Ise-no-kami Kozumi, his lieutenant and advisor Gorobei was Bokuden Tsukahara, the one who lived by his sword alone, Kyuzo, was Miyamoto Musashi... Each had his own distinctive episode, and moreover, Heihachi Hayashida, chopping wood behind the lodging to pay for his stay, Shichiroji, a former subordinate whom Kambei happens upon in town, and especially the curious Kikuchiyo, born a farmer, a samurai who isn't a samurai, needed more than cursory treatments. Combined with Manzo returning to the village to report that they've decided to hire seven samurai, and the village's reactions, the assembling of samurai took up another sixty pages. When they come together and finally set out for the village—it's all tied in, taut with tension, with no room for cuts or deletions, so it had to take 163 pages up to this point.

But since the plan was for this to be a third of the whole, combined with the rest of the manuscript, was it coming out to more than 480 sheets? For a film scenario, 280 was appropriate, with 320 or so the upper and 250 the lower limit, a leeway of about thirty to forty sheets. A scenario exceeding the average by more than 200 sheets, going beyond 480 pages, was unprecedented, and I figured the length of the film would be over four hours, but there was no way a single picture could take up over four hours.

But Mr. Kurosawa didn't say one word about the length.

As with *Ikiru*, Mr. Oguni, not writing a word and reading a thick English book, inspected the manuscript coming from Mr. Kurosawa and vetoed some things as the command tower—but said nothing about the number of pages, the length.

Mr. Kurosawa had a philosophy about scenarios.

"You cannot rest even for a day."

According to him, the work of writing a script was like running a full marathon. You had to keep your chin down and your gaze lowered, fixed on a point just ahead, as you silently ran. If you didn't look up and continued to do nothing but run, you eventually reached your goal.

The average daily output of Team Kurosawa was fifteen sheets. We might be seated for the same seven hours from ten in the morning until five in the afternoon, but sometimes we did just five or seven pages, while on other days we'd hit a groove and get out more than twenty or thirty pages, for an average of about fifteen. So if we shut ourselves away for three weeks, or twenty days of actual work, we could finish a screenplay of three hundred pages or so.

Mr. Kurosawa liked Noh theater, and when the day's work was done he would often talk about Noh over dinner, and he always spoke of Zeami. A historical figure of the Muromachi era who enjoyed the backing and patronage of the Ashikaga shogun, Zeami produced numerous masterpieces and established Noh as an artform continuing to the present. One day, as this Zeami crossed a river on a boat, at about the midway point another boat came from the opposite bank, and the ferrymen called out to each other: *Oh, the weather's good. Mm, I'm glad for the good weather, but I'm tired out today. Huh, why? Well, because I took a day off from work yesterday.*

Zeami could not but slap his knee. That was it! That was the trick, if you rested your body you just ended up feeling tired. When it came to practice, you could not rest even for a day.

Just as Mr. Kurosawa said, scenarios were like running a marathon, and looking ahead because it was too much led to discouragement, the end... I understood in my heart that, even when things were painful, keeping your head down and persevering was the only way.

But that was for writing a scenario coming out to the usual three hundred pages, and I wondered if the mindset and law worked when the page count rose to four or five hundred. If you tell marathon runners at the 20 km point of a 42.195 km race that the goal has been pushed further to a whopping 62.195 km, the runners' mood and performance might— can only risk extraordinary, irrevocable chaos.

Mr. Kurosawa collapsed at about page 320.

It was a severely cold morning with icicles in the garden.

He woke as usual and took his bath, then summoned a maid and asked her to lay out his futon. Skipping breakfast to sip on the gruel he'd ordered, he got into his futon and lay there still as death. Because of Mr. Oguni's untimely return to Tokyo on business, it was just me and Mr. Kurosawa.

"Do you want a doctor to take a look at you?"

"No, it's all right. I'll be fine after a rest."

With nothing for it, I shoved the table to the alcove and, with my back to the sleeping Mr. Kurosawa, continued to write.

But when noon arrived, Mr. Kurosawa didn't eat anything, and he had only gruel for dinner as well. The next day too, he ate only gruel in the morning and slept for a long time in his futon.

And with nothing for it, shoving the table to the alcove like the previous day, I continued writing the script with my back to the sleeping Mr. Kurosawa.

The work was about to head into its climax at long last.

Entering the village, the seven samurai settle into the home of Rikichi, who lives alone, the housewives of the village taking turns to provide the meals. Rikichi had been married, but three years ago, negotiating with a brigand struck by his wife's good looks, he'd offered her as a sacrifice to buy peace for the village. But that was the only year the brigands didn't come, and the next year they blithely rescinded the agreement and attacked. Rikichi had become such a warmongering extremist thanks to his intense hatred, surpassing a grudge, for the brigands.

There is friction and animosity between the samurai and villagers, but through Kambei's calm responses, the elder's ministrations and mediation, and in particular the eccentric and ferocious ex-farmer Kikuchiyo's priceless role as a catalyst, the issues are resolved one by one. Amidst days of setting up anti-cavalry fences against the mounted brigands, and the villagers dividing into squads, women and children excepted, to train in the use of bamboo spears, a fleeting love blossoms between Shino (clad in male attire and hair shorn by father Manzo on account of the samurai) and Katsushiro, counted as one of the seven—all this is the Negro spiritual of Dvořák's New World's second movement.

The barley ripens more every day, is cut and harvested, and the hour of battle, the brigands' assault, draws nigh. The southern fields are ridden of their footpaths and flooded in preparation for the mounted assailants. Yet the brigands don't appear, and an odd tension builds. One day, three scouts on horseback are seen lurking in the water god's forest behind the settlement. When the villagers promptly report this, Kyuzo and Kikuchiyo rush to the spot and, in a flash, kill two and capture one. Interrogating the prisoner, they learn that the brigands' stronghold is no sturdy fort but a simple thatched mountain hideout.

Hence a surprise night attack might be launched. They could set the place on fire, cut down a few, several, even ten or so who scramble out in a panic, then retreat swiftly before the counterattack. In preparation for the final battle, they need to reduce the number of assaulting brigands by as many heads as possible. A night attack on their own initiative would serve. By horse it is a half-day's journey, so on the brigands' three mounts and Yohei's, Kyuzo, Kikuchiyo, and Heihachi leave the village with Rikichi as their guide.

From the point at which the party leaves the village at sunset for the surprise attack, I wrote alone.

I felt rather abandoned. Unsure. Terribly alone.

Having gotten into scenarios for the pleasure of it, I'd never once felt anxiety or pain, difficulty or suffering as regards to writing. But after one person in a collaborative work collapsed, I came to the bitter realization that writing a screenplay is akin to a battle with some invisible thing. If that makes you run out of breath or puts you over your head, all that's left is the discouragement of defeat…

The oppressive burden on my shoulders, the solitude of fighting alone after one of us, our team leader and brother-in-arms, had fallen wounded battling something unseen, really got to me.

I'd thought that for this job we'd hum and skip along throughout but now there was no telling. No, in marathon terms, we were already past the 42.195 km mark, and this was unfamiliar territory, a *terra incognita* that we were running through, gasping for breath. At this rate, I might also crash.

It was the third morning after his collapse. Mr. Kurosawa woke and took his bath, and when the maid cleaned the room and started to lay out his futon, he said, "No need today." Though he had gruel for breakfast, once he finished sipping it down, he took his seat at the table, now in its usual location. I silently handed him the manuscript I'd worked on over the two days, and he read it and began revising it little by little—but his cheeks were hollow and his face pale and dreary.

Thus our work regimen returned to normal. But the rate of fifteen pages a day did not. I was exhausted too, and my unsteady pace was that of a wounded beast crawling sluggishly on the ground.

The surprise attack by Kyuzo, Kikuchiyo, and Heihachi is successful, Rikichi setting the mountain hideout on fire, ten brigands getting cut down one after the other as they come flying out in a panic. Heihachi, however, is felled by a matchlock gun blasted off by a brigand. Rikichi encounters his wife as she comes out fleeing with one of the brigands, and they lock eyes, frozen in place, but the next second his wife turns and leaps into the flames behind her.

Placing Heihachi's corpse on the back of a horse, Kyuzo and the others return to the village. They take out his sword and plunge it into the new burial mound in the village's east.

Kambei says to Gorobei, "You said he'd be a treasure in hard times, but the hard times are just beginning."

Rikichi breaks down in tears, and wailing rises up from the gathered farmers.

But right away, everyone turns as one to look up the western hill at the sound of thundering hooves. Clouds of dust rise up into the air, revealing a band of brigands surveying the village—thirty-odd riders. Livid over the surprise attack of the previous night, they've come to kill everyone in one fell swoop.

"Wa ha ha ha!" Kikuchiyo laughs brazenly. "Guys! They've come! Here they are!"

At last, it's the final battle.

From somewhere sounds The New World's fourth movement.

I knew it, and Mr. Kurosawa knew it as well. It would be between at least 160 and 180 pages from here to the end. The first part, from the beginning to the gathering of the seven samurai, and the middle part, from their getting to the village through preparations for battle and the brigands arriving, were each 160 to 170 pages, but it was unimaginable for the last part to be shorter than the previous two. This work had three longish stages, a trio pattern, one-two-three.

Ideally, it sat better if the final battle had the same or somewhat larger page count compared to the other sections. Insofar as the gist of the film was seven samurai teaming up with villagers to do battle against brigands, the money sequence couldn't be shorter than the first and the middle, or the film wouldn't feel consistent. But 160 to 180 pages more from this point… It was a vertiginous amount enough to freeze my spine and send shudders through my body.

Mr. Oguni returned from Tokyo.

Honestly, I wanted Mr. Oguni to help. To write just one word. But, as always, he read his thick English book without putting down a character, only examining the few pages of final draft that Mr. Kurosawa would pass to him.

Mr. Kurosawa and I were on our last legs, but still we continued to write.

As for the nightly parties, since Mr. Kurosawa wasn't imbibing after his episode, Mr. Oguni, too, drank only a little, and one cheerless day followed another.

My entire body felt wrung out, my mind was fuzzy, and I had no idea what I was writing. I bathed upon waking, ate, then turned to the table, wrote something and handed it to Mr. Kurosawa, wrote more and handed it over, and in the evening I sharpened my pencils, bathed, ate, and slept. How many days passed like this? Five, a week, ten, twenty… Plum trees bloom for a long time, but at some point the petals all fell, and the buds of cherry trees began to grow fat. Had we spent nearly two months secluded at the inn?

A newspaper reporter once asked me bluntly, "How does a scenario writer work?"

"By going from studio to studio like a vagabond."

"Vagabond?"

"Yes. If I like the work offered to me, I hide away in an inn and complete it in exchange for room and board, then pick up my traveling hat, and head to the next studio… It's a carefree career. Above all you don't incur expenses."

"Oh, no expenses?"

"You can wear the same pair of shoes for ten years because you don't

141

get out much. You only wear a white shirt and necktie to weddings or funerals, so just a few times a year... A padded kimono at the inn covers your clothing needs."

Dumbfounded, the reporter didn't say a word.

"No matter how fancy the inn, no matter how long I stay, the studio picks up the charges. The only thing I spend money on is my supply of manuscript paper, but even that half-sheet is studio paper, so there's nothing I need to pay for but pencils, and when they get short I can attach them to a holder, so if I buy a dozen they last a year... No line of craftsmanship is more efficient."

It was more than half exaggeration and sarcasm, but there was certainly such a side to it. The explanation, however, glossed over a crucial bit.

When I was secluded alone, once I passed the two-week point, with the permission of the manager as passed along by a maid, I would take meals not in my room but in the kitchen. I would have the same food that the clerks, maids, and cooks ate every day. The lavish dishes that the head chef prepared with flair were delicious for, at most, two days, and then you started to get tired of them. Plus, the food's flavoring is key. High-end cuisine tastes delicious because it's seasoned sweetly. It's not as though we eat such sweet fare ordinarily; at home, we have salty, spicy foods more than we think. Thus sticking with lavish dishes means building up stuff that doesn't suit your body, and you start feeling tired from the core and awfully sluggish.

With Team Kurosawa, there was no way I could go alone to the kitchen, so for thirty days, or even if it went to fifty days, it was all lavish dishes. I understood that the chef took care with the menu and made various adjustments since we were staying for so long, but basically the flavor stayed on the sweet side, so my body utterly wilted and lost all vitality.

Film studios refer to sequestering us at an inn as "canning" (*kanzume*).

Left at home to write, writers tend to take their time, so they send us to inns to, yes, "can" us... There is no more appropriate word. For scenario writers, working in seclusion at an inn amounts to being packed into a can. For humans though, the inside of a can is not a positive environment or a favorable condition.

You yearn to slip out of the environment just a day or even half a day sooner, but until the manuscript is completed, there is no escaping. So you lash yourself, quicken your pitch, and wrap it up speedily, even if it means blindly. For film studios, this isn't a practice meant to pamper scenario writers nor a means of ensuring good work. "Canning" just happens to be efficient for the mass production system that is filmmaking, so they look the other way and bear the expenses.

I wondered just how many days, how long, we'd been holed up at Minakuchien.

Minakuchien was a gilded cage. Our room faced south toward a garden, but Mr. Kurosawa, eschewing the distraction of employees delivering meals and showing guests, kept the sliding door tightly shut. Unvarnished wood faced us on all four sides.

The three of us canned in our gilded cage had long since traversed, in terms of a marathon, our 42.195 kilometers—or were we past sixty?—and were running, tottering on in total exhaustion like somnambulists. Yet now and then somewhere far away and faint to our ears played The New World's fourth movement.

There's just one thing I clearly recall from that period.

One day, as we were working, I glimpsed out the corner of my eye the sliding door of the anteroom opening and a maid trying to enter with tea for us. They came to serve you tea every day at three. But the maid stopped dead in her tracks, took one, two steps back as though repulsed, and stood stock-still. Then she calmed her breathing and, after a moment, entered the room.

That night, as she was setting our meal on the table, I asked her, "This afternoon, you were about to come in but didn't. Why was that?"

She answered hesitantly, "At our inn, we sometimes host *go* and *shogi* title matches. Not so much on the first day…but on the second when the contest is decided, the air is so frightfully tense from the masters' tremendous fighting spirit, it's difficult to enter to serve tea."

Mr. Kurosawa and Mr. Oguni were silent. I also remained quiet.

"But today… Pardon me, but lately it's always like that… *Go* and *shogi* don't compare. Something more seething and chilling…coming from Kurosawa-sensei and Hashimoto-sensei, writing your manuscript, tenses up and clogs the whole room, and it's scary…so frightening that I couldn't enter. I apologize."

I'd thought Mr. Kurosawa and I were both utterly exhausted, winded, and writing on nothing more than inertia. Surprisingly, that wasn't the case, and the two of us, mustering the last of our stamina, were writing on sheer spirit and will.

Then—somehow through spirit and tenacity of will alone, and across 174 half-sheets, we finished writing every meticulous and detailed scene of the showdown between the seven samurai and the brigands…the implementation of diverse tactics against the incoming marauders, an intense battle to the death where the seven samurai, wringing every last drop of their wits and stamina, the villagers assisting them, wipe out the brigands to the last man.

Neither the samurai nor the villagers, however, are spared casualties.

Lined up in the east of the village are four burial mounds, each with a katana thrust in.

Kambei stands before them, with Shichiroji and Katsushiro on either side.

Gorobei, at the height of the battle, and Kyuzo and Kikuchiyo, just before its conclusion, fell to the ranged weaponry of the brigands, their guns.

The wind sweeps over the burial mounds with the standing katanas.

Kambei says, "Again we've survived."

Shichiroji nods without a word.

Kambei adds, "But again on the losing side."

Shichiroji and Katsuhiro look at Kambei with curious expressions.

"No...the ones who won aren't us, but those farmers."

Kambei and the others turn to look at the south of the village.

The village is out in force, men and women all planting rice.

Rikichi beats a taiko drum in time with the singing of bright voices.

Kambei's words travel on the breeze swaying the seedlings.

"Samurai sweep across the earth like this wind, passing through. But the soil ever remains...and together with that soil, farmers survive."

Over paddies of seedlings resonant with singing voices and the beat of a drum, the June wind blows again—passing through.

F · O (Fin)

By the time we finished writing, *Seven Samurai* exceeded five hundred half-sheet pages, at 504.

Sagami Bay, dark all across, painted Hatsushima Island into obscurity ahead.

Yet the wind that brushed my cheeks didn't feel that chilly. It was March something. A Boston bag containing a just-finished 504-page manuscript at my feet, I stood on the platform of Atami Station. It was past eight-thirty in the evening.

Set against the jet-black of the wide sea, the lights of Atami City below glittered prettily. Atami City, where I hadn't once set foot over the last two months.

Mr. Oguni had left the inn slightly before me to hurry to Kyoto, and I wondered if the express he'd boarded was running west near Shizuoka or Hamamatsu.

The Tokaido Line train bound for Tokyo arrived, so I took up the Boston bag with the fresh manuscript inside and boarded. Mr. Kurosawa's wife, Kiyoko, was coming to Atami, and he was staying at Minakuchien to relax for a day or two before returning to Tokyo.

The second-class car wasn't crowded, and I placed the Boston bag on the overhead rack and took a seat.

At the outer edge of exhaustion when I left Minakuchien and got into a cab, I assumed that I'd collapse in my seat once I boarded and slump over like the dead and arrive in Tokyo that way. When I got out of the cab at Atami Station, bought my ticket, and began to head to the platform, however, my feet remembered the sensation of walking with every step I took, and the messy muck filling my head seemed to peel off layer by layer, my whole body reviving with something like vigor.

In the same way that, no matter how horrible your seasickness, your sense of equilibrium is restored the moment you set foot on solid ground, once I boarded the train, the seat in which I had expected to slump over like the dead served as an extremely comfortable and stabilizing cushion. I plunked myself down, and when I was settled in, the train began to move—at which instant a jolt shot through my limbs and all my veins rippled, and beyond mere wakefulness, that something like vigor gained force and spread through me, completely contrary to expectation.

It was a fresh sense of power, self-confidence, and ambition that I was fairly certain I'd never forget for the rest of my life.

After this, I'm capable of writing anything.

The 504-page *Seven Samurai* had given me something precious.

Nothing comes from work that admits any slack. There is a kind of writerly assurance and confidence which you come by, which only becomes your flesh and blood, after you've depleted your wits and stamina and exhausted your energy and willpower, after you continue writing despite feeling like you might start coughing up blood, and manage to finish the job.

That wasn't all. There was also an exhilarating sense of freedom, as if a window had popped open in my congested bosom. I was intoxicated by the grand feeling of having been liberated. It wasn't liberation from "the can" and seclusion. I was liberated from Team Kurosawa—from Akira Kurosawa.

Mr. Eijiro Hisaita had done *No Regrets for Our Youth* and *The Idiot*; Mr. Keinosuke Uegusa, *One Wonderful Sunday* and *Drunken Angel*; Mr. Ryuzo Kikushima, *Stray Dog* and *Scandal*... You graduated from Team Kurosawa after two pictures. I, however, had done three: *Rashomon*, *Ikiru*, and *Seven Samurai*.

But it wasn't simply a matter of the number of works. I had given my all for *Seven Samurai*, and Mr. Kurosawa had gone all the way too. We two coming together again, when the pair of us were like used tea leaves, couldn't possibly yield any meaningful piece of writing let alone another *Seven Samurai*.

Either way, Mr. Kurosawa probably wasn't going to tap me for work again, and even if he did, I was done with Team Kurosawa. The great, invisible chains that dominated my schedule—unbound by Team Kurosawa, from now on I'd fly about the film world as freely as I pleased.

"Hashimoto... Good for you."

When I lifted my face and stared out the window, we had already passed Yugawara, and across the dim scenery off Manazuru, beyond the darkness of Sagami Bay, I saw Mr. Itami's face floating like a phantom. It looked like a portrait of Mr. Itami in black and white film.

"So you've finally found your own compass and ruler."

"Yes... I feel like I can write anything, everything, now. But, sensei, there's just one thing troubling me."

Saying nothing, Mr. Itami just kept looking at me.

"If I put my mind to it, I can write anything. But I'm not sure that anything I write will ever surpass *Seven Samurai*... I just have that feeling. Since I still have a kid in elementary school and two in kindergarten and need to make a living from scenario writing for years, decades, it makes me sad and dejected to think that I can never top *Seven Samurai*, and I wonder if a scenario writer worthy of the name should accept that."

"Hashimoto, if you ever face difficult times or worries, think of Akira Kurosawa."

"...?"

"He'll buckle down for real to film this *Seven Samurai*, and it may well become his representative work. For him, too, it will be impossible to do any better, and for the rest of his life he won't surpass it. But he's still only forty-three…and has a lot of directing left to do, and the anguish, the pressure, the hollowness, and the vexation that he will experience every time he makes a work, the extraordinarily intense agony, which he won't be able to share, of being unable to surpass *Seven Samurai*… That is what the gods bestow on those who make something excellent and win renown…that is their punishment."

I stared fixedly at Mr. Itami.

"Hashimoto, when you face difficulties or worries in that regard, think of Akira Kurosawa. Compared to your own, his suffering will be ten, twenty, no, a hundred times worse."

Back in Tokyo, at the writers' hangout Hirata in Soshigaya, Setagaya Ward, Mr. Kurosawa and I considered things, locked in conversation, and cut forty-odd pages from the first part.

That made the finalized draft of *Seven Samurai* 460 pages long, and the running time of the filmed and done work came out to three hours and 27 minutes.

If any of us—Akira Kurosawa, Hideo Oguni, Shinobu Hashimoto—had, at some point, voiced concerns or misgivings about the length of the film, the work could have run aground or even fallen apart. Even if it didn't meet such an end, the second half of the film would have been quite abbreviated, and compared to the finished product it would have been considerably less entertaining, a tongue-tied and malformed thing.

The work took its actual form because the three of us took the single-line theme and story as a talisman and never let go of the tripartite structure as the way to express it, and because, firm in our conviction that the film would be entertaining if the scenario was entertaining, no matter how long, none of us ever exchanged a word about its length or brought it up.

In the 1960s—while I was in Moscow for a joint film symposium with the Soviet Union, the University of Moscow's cinema program asked me, through their film academy, to deliver a lecture on *Seven Samurai*. As I'm bad at public speaking I declined on the spot, but when I asked, "Did *Seven Samurai* show here in the Soviet Union, too?" the woman director of the academy gave a big laugh.

"Mr. Hashimoto, you really know nothing, do you? Decent film schools everywhere in the world have one text in common. That would be *Seven Samurai*."

CHAPTER THREE:
THE LIGHTS AND SHADOWS OF
COLLABORATIVE SCREENPLAYS

The "Writer Leading Off" Approach

> *Bad films can be made from good screenplays.*
> *Under no circumstances, however, can good films be made from*
> *bad screenplays.*

This was the first article of Mansaku Itami's Film Constitution.

In the Japanese film world, it was Akira Kurosawa who most conscientiously and methodically demonstrated this in his work—but, taken by surprise by the particular method, Mansaku Itami might have cried out in admiration were he alive.

Once I asked Mr. Kurosawa point-blank, "Though you could write alone, you always write the book with someone else, and the films you direct are always co-scripted... Why is it that you work with others?"

"Well, Hashimoto, I'm a director. There are difficult, tiring aspects to writing the book. I'd skimp on it at times because I know I'm going to be out there and I can do this here and that there when we shoot. But when I'm with another writer I can't cut corners, and so naturally we're able to produce scripts with few holes and a high degree of perfection. That's why I write with another writer."

The response, delivered fluently without pauses, had a persuasive tone rare for Mr. Kurosawa.

But it was a lie, a complete lie. No, Mr. Kurosawa wasn't someone who lied to people. When newspaper reporters and critics asked him in interviews why his screenplays were co-scripted, he'd respond with something along that line each time, and through endless repetition the delivery took on flavor and persuasiveness until it flowed easily. It not only sounded plausible to third parties, but at a certain point he himself also wound up believing that that was why he co-wrote his screenplays.

Those weren't the facts, though. Everyone who'd worked with Mr. Kurosawa knew. He wasn't someone who could write half-baked scripts with bits like "[insert swordfight here]." Whether alone or with someone else, he conscientiously saw through every scene, connecting each via a certain feel (tempo and rhythm), and was the type who couldn't abbreviate anything at all. It was a bald-faced lie to say that working with a writer yielded scripts with no holes and a high degree of perfection, and this will be obvious to anyone who checks out the screenplays he wrote alone for other directors.

So why did he collaborate with other writers on screenplays for films he would direct?

The answer is clear and simple: the quality seemed at least a little... no, manifestly better than when he wrote alone. Commissioning another writer was a serious matter involving time and a budget. The initial meetings and the writer's first draft took up more than a month, and subsequent meetings for a revised second draft, and his participation on the final draft on top of that, meant three or four months to half a year for the script to be finished. If the work's content was comparable, it was a stupid loss of time and a pointless waste of planning funds (script fees).

Which is to say, Mr. Kurosawa had to be getting something in exchange for all the headaches and toil, as well as the time and money, that collaboration required.

Then what of the writers who co-scripted with him?

As soon as you accepted a job, you had to be prepared to spend three times the usual time and effort. Following a meeting, everything through the first draft was the same as with other projects, but as soon as it was done everything changed completely. Typically, making a few revisions yielded the final version, so the first draft was actually the full product.

With Team Kurosawa, however, the first draft wasn't the full product but simply a kind of springboard (design) for the purpose of judging and examining whether the work was staying true to its aim, whether the aim itself didn't suffer from oversights or errors or a too optimistic outlook, and what changes in form might afford a deeper and more interesting work. Put differently, far from full products, the first and second drafts were just a further step in planning, a test of faith, a stepping stone, live bait for reconstructing the theme and story. As such, the finalized draft that built on these assessments and prospects retained little of the outline or main elements, whether of the first or second draft, other than traces now and then.

But no matter how much time and effort it took, these were factors that strengthened the screenplay's foundation, and Mr. Mansaku Itami wouldn't have been especially surprised or impressed. The question was the next stage—the way the final draft was written.

"About co-scripting a Kurosawa work... How do you approach that final draft? Do you divvy it up so each person has his own part to write?"

"Nope, no divvying. Everyone writes the same scene."

"Everyone writes the same scene?"

"Yup, whether it's three people or five, it's ready, get set, go and we all start working on the same scene."

"So it's a competition: whose will be best? The best and most interesting entry becomes part of the main final draft."

"Well, that's about it."

"But that must be tough." The questioning young scenarist sighed, appalled. "That's like having your flesh and blood scraped away for the writers, every single day a fight for survival."

As the appalled questioner said, writing the same scene in competition isn't easy. At first, it's perpetual vexation and discouragement, an uncomfortable feeling that your thought process needs a repairman... Your mental makeup is shorting and burning out amidst a shower of sparks, and you even fear that at any moment now it's all going totally bonkers.

Once you slowly become used to competing over the same scene though, it's not such a big deal. In scenario writing, three or four scenes linked together make differences in skill, whether you're good or not, extremely clear, but if it's just one independent scene, what comes to the fore are different voices, and skill is harder to discern. You end up with two if there are two people, three if there are three, and four patterns if there are four, and it's harder to say which ones are good or bad, superior or inferior.

Mr. Kurosawa, who didn't like laws and theories of filmmaking, seldem mouthed any.

There is a piece he contributed to the journal *Eiga Hyoron* [Film Criticism] nevertheless. Regarding what other artforms films resembled, he considered music to be the most similar. Music communicates a sensibility to the audience but is unable to explain things.

It's the same with cinema. Explaining something that requires an explanation doesn't get through to a film audience, explication is simply impossible, and on that essential point cinema and music share quite a similarity.

I am in great agreement with this, and if someone were to ask me what a screenplay most resembled, I would answer without hesitation that it's like a musical score in its written form.

The sheets of a score are a writ of command to the performers to stage music, and the screenplay is a writ of command to the film crew from the director on down to come up with the image and sound, but in addition to both being writs of command, they have an important thing in common in terms of content.

In the screenplays that we write, the most important thing is the modulation birthed by the series and arrangement of words...the tempo and rhythm, and likewise the musical score is all about tempo and rhythm. For me, writing a screenplay is a different world from penning novels, plays (stage scripts), and the like—I can't help but feel that I'm composing a symphony.

With Team Kurosawa, you started writing the same scene at the word go. Each person had a different voice, but we all knew more or less if the scene was a vivacious duple meter (4:2), an ordinary-paced quadruple time (4:4), or a lamenting, perhaps admiring, triple time (4:3). Just as, in the case of music, replacing a phrase (substituting a phrase in a measure) is a simple thing, for scenarios too, exchanging and swapping out among the finished scenes, on a phrase and measure basis, is surprisingly easy.

For example, let's say Mr. Kurosawa has in front of him his own manuscript, and to his left and right what Mr. Kikushima (Ryuzo Kikushima) and I have written. For this scene Mr. Kurosawa might want to go with his own voice. Yet, both Mr. Kikushima's and my writing include terms, idioms, particular word orders, and feelings evoked by them that he wants to keep.

Incorporating them is surprisingly easy. He removes the portion in question from his own manuscript and replaces it with what someone else has written. Because it's an exchange of phrases, fixing a little of what comes before and after suffices. In this way, what Mr. Kikushima and I have written are inserted into Mr. Kurosawa's writing. It has no traces of editing, and the screenplay appears to have been born fully formed. At the same time, our voices mingle with Mr. Kurosawa's in the script, resulting in an unprecedented mixed-choral screenplay.

There was another way of going about it too. Mr. Kurosawa would read the three versions of the scene, and if he thought Mr. Kikushima's was interesting overall, he'd take up Mr. Kikushima's manuscript without hesitation and modify it into his own voice, then insert anew any bits he wanted from his own manuscript and mine to come up with a rich final version.

Writing the same scene all together in this fashion made it possible to edit them in any way, and from there you created a rich, fresh, and lively screenplay.

Team Kurosawa's co-scripting was about multiple people writing the same scene through various perspectives (compound eyes), editing them, and creating a screenplay with the feel of a mixed chorus—that was the chief characteristic of a Kurosawa work.

There are many examples of collaborative screenplays in the film world. Ninety-nine percent of them, however, end up being collaborative when the scenarist refuses to respond to the producer or director's ideas for a revision and a different writer is brought in. Very rarely, writers who get along well do accept a commission as a group and apportion the work amongst themselves. But Team Kurosawa was unique in all of Japanese cinema in that one writer took the lead to work on drafts that were springboards, and especially in how the final version lined up different versions of the same scene and sifted through them to create a rich, fat, but also fresh mixed-choral screenplay without gaps or weaknesses. Even my mentor Mansaku Itami might have opened his eyes wide at this method of screenwriting and extolled its virtues.

No, I'm afraid this way of screenplay writing has no parallel not only in Japan but in the world, and was unique to Team Kurosawa as led by Akira Kurosawa.

In a nutshell, it was Mr. Kurosawa who made it possible with his singular and transcendent eye for people.

Among his collaborators, Eijiro Hisaita was celebrated as a playwright rather than a scenarist, Keinosuke Uegusa was an old classmate from middle and high school and a bit player in Toho films, Senkichi Taniguchi was a directing contemporary who'd never written a scenario for anyone else, Ryuzo Kikushima was a disciple of Toshio Yasumi but a rookie and total cipher, and I, despite my tutelage under Mansaku Itami, was a rank amateur… None of us he chose to work with were top-of-the-line pros.

Akira Kurosawa's eye for candidates whom he thought might not only be on par with a pro, but capable of turning out stuff beyond a top-line pro's given the right work process, was more than just sharp. It's vaguely frightening.

Akira Kurosawa said that film essentially resembles music.

A singer who has taken the world by storm has many hits at the peak of his popularity. But his repertoire, in the true sense of the word, is limited to his first song, which the world greeted with great applause, and all the songs that follow are mere variations on it. Perhaps Akira Kurosawa instinctively understood that everyone has his own unique repertoire but that it's just one song.

He made his debut with *Sanshiro Sugata* in 1943 and followed up with *The Most Beautiful*, *Sanshiro Sugata Part II*, and *The Men Who Tread on the Tiger's Tail*, but after writing and shooting three works that each had a different feel, namely *Sanshiro Sugata*, *The Most Beautiful*, and *The Men Who Tread on the Tiger's Tail* (since *Sanshiro Sugata* and its sequel were cut from the same cloth), hadn't something like uncertainty crossed his mind…that no matter what he wrote next, it would resemble one of those three films?

Perhaps that was why he cast the playwright Eijiro Hisaita in the leadoff role for *No Regrets for Our Youth*. And perhaps in the process of creating the final draft of that collaborative screenplay, he experienced firsthand the unexpectedly efficient method of utilizing the same scene, his and Mr. Hisaita's voices coming together in a mixed chorus to give rise to a screenplay with a completely new feel.

A not only efficient but effective method of creating a script, once tried and mastered, naturally rules out any desire to go solo; however, even with a mixed chorus, the first work and the next may feel fresh, but to the extent that each person has only one repertoire, any more sounds like nothing but lazy echoes. Thus, to go on working, you have to swap out your collaborative partner one after another.

Eijiro Hisaita	*No Regrets for Our Youth, The Idiot*
Keinosuke Uegusa	*One Wonderful Sunday, Drunken Angel*
Senkichi Taniguchi	*The Quiet Duel*
Ryuzo Kikushima	*Scandal, Stray Dog*
Shinobu Hashimoto	*Rashomon, Ikiru, Seven Samurai*

With me, the fifth one, he finally exceeded two films and collaborated on three.

These works (co-scripts where a writer led off) all basked in the limelight of their times, amply satisfying audiences and winning full-throated accolades and repeated praise from critics. They made people look forward to the next film, and always breaking new ground, the next work responded with a freshness and appeal surpassing the previous offerings. His renown a multistage rocket, he rose from up-and-coming director to grandmaster of Japanese cinema in no time flat, and thrust beyond the realm of Japanese films after *Rashomon* fetched the Golden Lion at the Venice International Film Festival, he became a world-class grandmaster of cinema—Akira Kurosawa.

The Straight-to-Final Draft

After we finished writing *Seven Samurai*, I did a few works for Toho, Nikkatsu, and Toei. While I was preparing for my next Nikkatsu film, I had a phone call from Sojiro Motoki, the producer.

"Ah, Hashimoto, it's Motoki. Been a while... Well, *Seven Samurai* is a huge hit, the biggest hit since the dawn of Japanese cinema. The company's feeling bold, and in the low-end theater free market it's been, 'If you want *Seven Samurai* then buy ten other Toho films,' ten films, ten, all right? And what with this and that, Kuro-san's been dragged around and it was nuts, but finally he can take a breather. He says he'd like to get together with you, what's your schedule look like?"

"Hey, Mr. Motoki, if this is about a job, forget it," I declared, throwing consideration to the wind. "The others have mostly done two films... but I did three, okay? I'm graduating from Team Kurosawa."

"No, I have no idea if it's about work... Filming dragged on, and it was a rigmarole after the premiere so he hasn't seen you and absolutely wants to, he says. Isn't there some way you could make the time?"

If Mr. Kurosawa had indeed said so, I couldn't refuse outright, and I reluctantly promised to go to Komae. Since we didn't hang out in private, any meeting would have to be about work, and if it did turn out to be about work I planned to turn him down on the spot.

I transferred from the Inogashira Line to the Odakyu Line at Shimokitazawa, arrived at Komae, and went to the Kurosawa residence. He was waiting for me in the large Japanese-style drawing room.

He started in, "Hashimoto, about our next job... I'm thinking of doing it differently."

He'd gotten right to the point. I looked at Mr. Kurosawa in silence.

"Up until now one writer led off, but quitting that, we all get together, have a brainstorm, and create the final draft from the get-go... I want to take the leap and try doing it that way."

Jolted, I just kept looking at Mr. Kurosawa. The immense shift in the method of collaborative screenplay writing was nothing other than a blessing for the writer, a welcome, revolutionary, and grand reform that changed everything.

While competing on the same scene for the final draft was tough, it wasn't a big deal once you got used to it. Just the final draft meant the customary schedule would be shortened to a third, which was easier on the writer, mentally too. You had to gird your loins when you took up a

Kurosawa project, but the new system made it only a bit more of a hassle than a regular program picture and fairly easy to sign on to. But—this new system came as an unexpected shock to me. Now I couldn't turn down the next Kurosawa project.

Directors are sensitive to a film studio's climate.

A writer like me might have a contract with Toho, but since it was for a certain number of films and non-exclusive, I could go freely to and between Shochiku, Daiei, Toei, Nikkatsu, etc. Even if I clashed with one studio and things went sour, I could easily remain indifferent to that studio's direction and climate. Directors, however, are different. To switch companies is to switch your workplace, your studio, and it's a serious career event. As a result, directors are sensitive to a company's climate and pay constant heed, and Mr. Kurosawa had this side too.

Masumi Fujimoto, who was close to Toho's chief of production (and who later became vice president), said to me, "As far as the company is concerned, Hashimoto, we don't want you to do jobs for Team Kurosawa. Even without you, whoever it is, Team Kurosawa scripts get done… The company wants you to work on other stuff… For the time it takes to do one Team Kurosawa, we can turn out at least three mid-list films. That serves the company better, sales-wise too."

When I responded with silence, Fujimoto chuckled and dealt the coup de grâce. "I assume it would be better for you, too. You get paid for only one script with Team Kurosawa, but three times that for three other types of films. Don't you think it would be more convenient for both of us?"

Mr. Kurosawa may have gotten wind of the company's climate and how it was administering writers. No, even if he had, he wasn't the kind to worry or fret over it. More than that, the issue at hand was that there were no replacements in sight for the role of leadoff writer.

Plus, after the war, he'd transitioned from solo scripts to collaboration with a writer leading off and already made ten films that way. Perhaps he thought a change in direction may well have been due. What's more, the change in style wouldn't affect the quality of the work.

From past experience, the final version only retained traces of the first and second drafts by the leadoff writer, when it did any at all. Every single film went through great leaps and bounds, so lacking a first and second draft wouldn't influence or affect the final draft. Thus, if everyone got together from the beginning, brainstormed, and started in on the final draft…the "straight-to-final draft," then not only would the work quality be the same, but it would also be a more efficient use of time. He seemed to have judged so, and—either way, it was impossible for me to turn down this next job.

I felt rather forlorn and empty.

Mr. Kurosawa... Could we two pairing up at this stage yield anything surpassing Rashomon, *or* Ikiru *and* Seven Samurai?

That's what I wanted to say. But it was verboten. To the extent that I was a writer, there was nothing I could do but always bet on possibility. Even if your past successes are never to be surmounted, if you settle into such a stance you can't get down to new work.

I hurled a bone of contention at Mr. Kurosawa, a far smaller matter, a trivial peeve not even worth mentioning compared to the melancholy in my heart. "Mr. Kurosawa, this time around let's have Master write as well—Master Oguni too!"

Mr. Kikushima and I and others called Mr. Oguni "Master Oguni," or just "Master," as a sign of our affection and respect for our great forerunner.

Mr. Kurosawa looked confused for a moment, but a wry smile crossed his face. "Yeah, we can't let Oguni not write a little something."

The eastern coast of Izu has many cliffs and reefs.

But if you go past Inatori as far as Imaihama near Shimoda, a sandy white beach spreads out before you. Cherry trees in full bloom peek between gaps in the pine groves close by, and the shoreline of green pines against white sand is itself picture-pretty. The sea bulges in along a deep curve—the cape of Inatori to the left and Izu Oshima Island straight and far ahead, scenic is the spring peace and calm that is the Imaihama shore.

The inn "Maikoen" sat on high ground overlooking the bay.

Originally a private second house, it was small in scale, with two eight-mat guest rooms in the main edifice and a new wing on a lower level against a cliff slope. All the staff were family, the mother serving as the madam and the oldest son as the head clerk, and even the receptionists were a pair of sisters in the prime of youth, a cosy inn.

Mr. Kurosawa, Master Oguni, and I began work on the "straight-to-final draft" within the excellent environment of the main building of Maikoen.

I Live in Fear.

It was the story of a man overwhelmed by fear of the atomic bomb.

Mr. Kurosawa, who had collapsed during the writing of *Seven Samurai* at Atami, had gone for a physical at a hospital in Tokyo after we'd finished the script. Apparently he'd nursed a large tapeworm that they extracted. Because of this, and in consideration of one another's health, at Imaihama we cut our work regimen short by an hour and headed down to the shore for a walk every day to relax and to relish the spring sea and the *sakura* in full blossom.

One day though, past fifty or sixty half-sheets, a worry began to niggle at the back of my mind. The development section, which felt a little sluggish, continued in that vein.

Was what I said downright dumb?

"Let's have Master Oguni write as well," I'd proposed at Mr. Kurosawa's Komae residence. The excruciating stint on *Seven Samurai* stayed with me, and perhaps because Mr. Kurosawa's memory of writing *Seven Samurai* was also drenched in pain, he'd easily agreed, "Yeah, that's good, let's do that." Mr. Kurosawa wasn't just a writer, however, but also our team leader, so shouldn't he have given it some more thought? "No, Hashimoto… You and I write, with Oguni as the command tower."

From the start of this project, Master Oguni had braced himself and competed with Mr. Kurosawa and me over the same scenes. What I wanted from Master was help when we were stuck in a maze with no way out—to assume the position of navigator, and at other times the command tower. I imagine Mr. Kurosawa felt much the same way.

But when Master Oguni actually began writing and entering the multi-scenarist fray over the same scene, no cakewalk, it taxed his nerves and exhausted him, and his hands full, he could hardly serve as the command tower.

With Master also writing, the work had started rolling without a command tower or navigator.

As the command tower, Master Oguni would no doubt issue a warning about this development section and arrange a fix; however, Mr. Kurosawa, too, continued to look only at what was in front of him, and we just skidded on. Given his extreme distaste for peering too far ahead, if I expressed concern it was as clear as day that Mr. Kurosawa would treat me to an emotional outburst and go on raging. Only Master could serve as his brakes or accelerator—but Master Oguni was too wrapped up in his own writing process, and if nothing was done the force of the moment would rule, and it would be like careening down a slope without breaks. My neck and shoulders grew abnormally stiff, and a cold something ran up my spine. If we continued like this, the work might flounder and even stumble.

The "straight-to-final draft" was missing more than a command tower or navigator—prior to that, a major and even fatal flaw had been built in.

The screenplay for *I Live in Fear* was completed near the end of April 1955. The picture went into production preparations at the studio from May, and after rehearsals, it began production in August, wrapped on October 18th, and opened in movie theaters on the Toho circuit on November 22nd.

It was late autumn at Imaihama, and the surface of Sagami Bay was aubergine under the bright rays of the sun just before dusk.

I was working on a job for Toei in the eight-mat tatami room in the main building at Maikoen. The sisters came flying in with enough momentum to crash through the sliding screen had I not left it open toward the garden.

"Sir! Kurosawa-sensei has arrived!"

He had come with no prior contact or notice, completely out of the blue.

Mr. Kurosawa didn't step up into the entryway but instead walked through the garden. He approached the eight-mat room from outside, muttered "Hey" in my direction, then turned around and stood looking down at the ocean. He had an awfully haggard look on his face.

The sisters hurriedly laid out a cushion on the porch, and Mr. Kurosawa sat down without a word and again stared out at the ocean. I stood, and then went to sit cross-legged beside him on the cushion the sisters had placed next to his. Yet, Mr. Kurosawa continued to look out at the sea in silence. I also said nothing and looked out at the sea. It was almost sunset, the sky a rosy pink, and the sea's aubergine was slowly becoming tinged with black.

Still saying nothing, sunken in silence in the slowly strengthening wind, Mr. Kurosawa continued to gaze at the sea. His distressed, anguished countenance was that of a man who'd fallen into the lower depths.

I more than understood how Mr. Kurosawa felt then... No, the problem was mine too, and as the two of us watched dusk come over the sea, a wan feeling, of hollowness, of desolation, filled my bosom.

I Live in Fear, released on the Toho circuit on November 22nd, had been an unspeakably terrible box-office flop with record-setting low attendance.

That aside, how did Mr. Kurosawa know I was here? If he'd called my home to find out my whereabouts I would have had word, and even if he'd requested Sojiro Motoki to find out... Well, if Motoki had contacted

Toho headquarters, the arts department would have known my schedule and that I was currently on a job for Toei. He'd have had to ask the producer in charge at Toei, however, and if he'd gone that far, he'd contact me by phone of course—but there had been no such call.

So how did Mr. Kurosawa find out that I was working at Maikoen in Izu's Imaihama?

Mr. Kurosawa's face was still sunk in bitter doom.

The horrid box-office failure of *I Live in Fear* defied the imagination; none of my past works had flopped so badly, either, and I couldn't believe that it had happened. *Seven Samurai* had been the most successful film since the advent of Japanese cinema, and *I Live in Fear* the next Kurosawa work. The film's promotion had been thorough, with novel and unique poster art by the director himself. Nonetheless, from the day of its premiere, no one came to see it. If theatergoers had flocked to it to some extent but thinned out after finding the work unentertaining or too difficult, that was that. But from the outset no guests graced the utterly empty houses. It was a woebegone flop descending straight into a bottomless pit. At the same time, shocked by our customers' acumen, their sharp instincts, I trembled.

A film about the travails and sorrows of atomic bomb victims may have had a chance depending on how it was made. But the life of a man consumed by fear of the bomb—how to cope with, think about, and put to rest the most absurd thing in humanity's possession—had occasioned a thoroughly adverse reaction. Downright sure that those of us who made movies lacked any such philosophy, theatergoers had called out the film's true nature at one glance and rolled their eyes.

It had come to this due to the plan's own misconception and the screenplay's resulting inadequacies, but the error's root cause was the "straight-to-final draft," which dispensed with a writer's preliminary work.

If some scenarist had led off and produced a first draft, I believe Mr. Kurosawa would have intuited with one reading how meaningless and futile it would be to make the film.

Fear of the bomb—depicting it without the calamity of suffering the bomb, without the visuals to convey the crucial horror, amounted to explaining the fear through speech and behavior. The whole drama could only unfold as exposition.

Mr. Kurosawa's cinematic credo, however, was that things that needed explaining couldn't be explained in a film, and since we'd only be forcing something that couldn't be comprehended on the audience, Mr. Kurosawa would have aborted *I Live in Fear* without hesitation at the screenplay stage.

It was an everyday occurrence in the film world for a writer to produce a lousy first draft, but when Mr. Kurosawa led the charge and brought in two writers, a master and an up-and-comer, removed to an inn at great expense, all the while keeping staff at the studio on standby, they had to start shooting with the resulting screenplay, regardless of whether it was good, bad, or terrible, as the final draft.

In truth, however, this was no final draft but a mere first draft written by three people. Until that point, a Team Kurosawa first draft was live bait (a test of faith, a stepping stool) in preparation for the final draft and existed for the sake of reevaluating a project and, further, discerning what needed to change to make the work deeper and more interesting. With the "straight-to-final draft," that precious live bait didn't exist at all—so a suspect first draft with numerous flaws and lacunae had to be treated as the final draft.

With a writer leading off, more importantly, the scenarist tasked with the job attended to the preliminary work of crafting the theme, story, characters, and also structure in advance of writing the first draft, putting its eventual quality aside.

With the "straight-to-final" style, on the other hand, it was unclear who had which part. Thinking we might need material, I did ask our producer Sojiro Motoki to arrange a meeting with the physicist and nuclear researcher Mitsuo Taketani. He spoke to me in detail about things like why nuclear fission occurs, how the atomic bomb is structured and built, and the scale of its havoc and effects. Regarding the fundamentals, the theme and story and such, however, I'd done nothing, and I doubt Mr. Kurosawa or Mr. Oguni had, either.

(I have a fragmentary recollection of an interview or roundtable discussion in a film journal or some comparable venue according to which I led off on the screenplay for *I Live in Fear*. I performed the role in meeting with Mr. Mitsuo Taketani for research—not on the scenario itself.)

In any case, since we were going to brainstorm about the theme, story, and such, I'd assumed we'd put our heads together upon secluding ourselves at the inn and then start, but when we settled in at Maikoen (Mr. Kurosawa was a few days late), the reality was different. All we discussed was the first scene, how to open, and we ended up diving into the main writing.

In sumo terms, seclusion at an inn is like the wrestler being called and ascending to the ring. The rest is a fight to the finish, and your fight plan should be something you decided on prior to entering the ring.

Put in plainer terms, there is no scenario without the dope and works in place, but in the case of *I Live in Fear* we started with absolutely none of that advance preparation.

All in all, a misbegotten plan plus faulty screenplay equaled box-office rout for *I Live in Fear*, and its misfortune owed to the new "straight-to-final draft" system of screenplay writing that came equipped with a fatal defect. And this fact, Mr. Kurosawa understood better than anyone, had felt more than anyone.

Izu Oshima seemed boundless in the evening haze, the sea a darker purple than aubergine.

As before, Mr. Kurosawa sat on the porch at Maikoen and looked out at the ocean.

Seated next to him in silence I also gazed at the sea, but the late autumn sun dropped like a sinker, and the rose-pink sky, shining orange for a moment, soon took on the hue of watered-down ink, and the sea grew yet blacker.

Eyes turned towards the darkening sea, his expression bitter, sunk to the lower depths—Mr. Kurosawa still didn't speak.

Everyone spouts that if you work in film you're bound to have hits and misses. Facing the reality of it head-on is nowhere as easy as that.

It's true that a hit brings profits to the studio but doesn't mean a cut for the director or writers, and naturally a miss inflicts losses on the company while the director and writers don't have to take concern or responsibility. One might say that, but it's not exactly how it works in reality. You're terribly worried about attendance and wonder if those box-office receipts aren't inextricably linked, related on an essential level, to the work you put in.

No, on this point, I have a frightfully vivid, if rather sad, impression borrowed from the real world that might count as incontrovertible proof.

It was autumn of the year *Rashomon* was released, and I was walking through Asakusa. I'd shacked up at the Tokyo branch of my company in Okachimachi, so if I wanted to go to the movies, at the time Asakusa was closest, and as I like bustling places, I often puttered around there. Sunk in thought I walked aimlessly through the hustle and bustle of the old-school Rokku district.

What, in essence, is a scenario writer, which I'm about to become instead of a salaryman?

I stopped in my tracks with a start. In front of the Tokiwaza, a Shochiku theater, two barkers were calling out in their husky voices, "Ey, welcome,

welcome!"

Unable to move, I stood watching those men as if nailed to the spot. What if...no, this, no mistake...this. The essence of the work I was about to begin wore jackets there outside the theater, wiped their dripping noses with their fists in the cold weather, and called out, "Ey, welcome, welcome!"

A curious hallucinatory fantasy turned me into the barker.

Next to me was another barker—Akira Kurosawa.

Outside an unpopular, empty theater, we two were hollering at the top of our lungs like pathetic clowns, barking on and on.

"Ey, welcome!"

"Ey, welcome!"

—Akira Kurosawa was sad.

It had been an intense shock. His first humiliation in fifteen films and thirteen years as a film director, the decisive damage of box-office failure.

Yet he was composed. He put on a façade. Inside, though, he was extremely regretful and terribly sad. Wailing from the lower depths. Yet he endured, somehow endured. After the premiere, he just stoically persevered.

One day, however, he couldn't take it anymore. He was unable to stay standing or to sit still. This suffering and sorrow wasn't something that anybody...that even his parents, siblings, wife, or children could comprehend.

But there were two people in the world who could, who alone bore joint responsibility...Hideo Oguni and Shinobu Hashimoto. On impulse he phoned Hideo Oguni, but he was away from Tokyo, working in Kyoto.

"Then where's Hashimoto?" Working somewhere... No peep from the guy since April at Izu's Imaihama. Maybe Hashimoto was working in Imaihama, in Izu... He boarded the Odakyu Line like a man possessed.

Getting off at Odawara and on the Tokaido Line, transferring to the Izu Express at Atami, it was a straight shot—no, the same route he'd taken before, getting off at Ito and taking a cab, passing through Kawana, Yawatano, Atagawa, and Inatori, to the eastern shores where neither cliffs nor reefs but a curving beach of white sand spread.

There at Imaihama, off the national road onto a narrow

side path, winding once, twice, toward the familiar sight of Maikoen on a rise, and in the inn's main building... There! Hashimoto was there! Just as he thought, Shinobu Hashimoto was working at Imaihama. But exchanging nary a greeting, except a groaned "hey," they sat side by side on the porch and watched as dusk fell over the sea.

He'd wanted to see someone who could share his sorrow. If he did, his sorrow and suffering might ease just a little... Well, it was the opposite. When the person by his side was a direct conduit for the sorrow and suffering, the anguish and grief simply spread without end, intensifying.

As twilight descended, Mr. Kurosawa and I just sat gazing out at the sea at Sagami.

Oshima in the foreground already lost in the evening gloom, lights flickered on over Inatori Cape, the left tip of the concave coastline, and the ocean grew darker, blacker, and wider.

Perhaps the wind had picked up a bit. The sound of the waves faintly strengthened.

The Maikoen sisters prepared his lodging in the new building down the cliff and set our dinner in the adjacent room, and it was only when we sat facing each other at the table that Mr. Kurosawa began to talk to me in bits and pieces.

"Actually, Hashimoto..." he started out, taking a sip of his watered whiskey.

An American producer had contacted him about making an omnibus film with two famous European filmmakers and one from the United States, Akira Kurosawa from Japan making a fourth. The aim was to make a single film with four renowned top-class directors who led world cinema...but with the material restricted to tense thriller-likes.

"The material could be a thriller or a ghost story, but can you think of anything that might work?"

"A thriller or ghost story?"

"Yes..."

"Then how about this? *The Cursed Nail*, it's called."

"*The Cursed Nail?*"

For just a period when I was still a salaryman, I was put in charge of the lumber department. One day I was making the rounds at the factory when a sharp metal clang rang out. As I watched dumbfounded, the sawing platform came to a halt. The foreman jumped down to turn off the switch to the electric band saw and climbed onto the platform to examine the cross section of the giant piece of lumber. Suddenly he whirled around and yelled angrily at an older factory worker responsible for bringing lumber in from the yard.

"Hei-san, look here! If it's thirty or fifty years old and buried in deep then I'd be willing to understand, but this ten-inch nail is just a few years old at most. You've got eyes and hands, so how could you not tell? I warned you to be careful about trees from shrines!"

Twenty minutes later, Hei-san and his assistant had unloaded the huge cedar log from the platform and levered and rolled it back to the lumberyard where they performed a careful inspection under the bright sun. Hei-san kept grumbling foul-mouthed complaints to his assistant, however, perhaps still resenting how the younger foreman had yelled at him.

"I thought I told you to be careful, since this is a tree from a shrine? Where do you all keep your eyeballs? If it were fifty or a hundred years old, it would have rusted, but a brand-new five-inch nail like this could ruin the band saw!"

"Hei-san," I said.

He was holding up in the sun the five-incher, now split in half, that he'd dislodged with a crowbar and nail remover. Seeing it sent cold shivers down my back. Nails of that length had once been used to pin straw figures in order to lay curses.

"It wouldn't have been strange a long time ago," I ventured, "but do we still have this today?"

Hei-san glanced up at me. "It is now as it was then."

His gaze contained equal parts respect and contempt for the young factory manager from headquarters who couldn't even tell the difference between cedar and cypress.

"Factory manager, even you must have someone in this world you'd like to bludgeon to death. A bastard, or two."

I was pretty much done...and Mr. Kurosawa's body was leaning forward.

"That could work, Hashimoto, that could work... But it ought to be set in the Heian era."

"The Heian era?"

"Yeah, it happens in a Noh piece as well, and it's really something else. The next time they perform it, we should both go see it at Nohgakudo Hall in Suidobashi. At any rate, in the event that the omnibus film happens, let's say we're going with *The Cursed Nail*."

I nodded, and Mr. Kurosawa emphasized, "I have a feeling your aim is a modern piece, but this is Heian, absolutely Heian. A Heian-era woman in a white kimono, a black comb in her mouth, going clang, clang..."

Mr. Kurosawa seemed to have gotten back some of his verve, and he poured himself another glass.

The conversation paused. The wind, strengthening since dusk, seemed to have picked up in intensity, and the waves sounded faintly as far as the foothills.

Perhaps not having thought of his next project yet, Mr. Kurosawa didn't say a word about it. Nor did he say one word about the "straight-to-final draft," the biggest factor in the failure this time around, and whether or not he meant to persist with it.

After that—four more film screenplays were completed at Maikoen in Imaihama.

The Lower Depths, *Throne of Blood*, *The Hidden Fortress*, and *The Bad Sleep Well*.

(The order in which the screenplays were written didn't always align with the films' release dates, sometimes ahead or behind for production reasons. In addition, because more writers were brought in for *The Bad*, we moved to an inn in Kawazuhama partway through.)

These films, no slouches, nevertheless lacked the tension, luster, freshness, bravado, and dynamically developing climaxes that had been characteristic of Kurosawa works to that point. They neither wore their accomplishments on their sleeves nor increased his acclaim.

The mixed chorus that made the collaborative screenplays distinct now had a fixed roster and simply betrayed mannerist inertia...particularly because Master Oguni was no longer acting as the command tower.

When Master Oguni was the command tower, he called the shots on breaking and steering, while as writers Mr. Kurosawa and I revved up the engine and stepped on the gas. Without a command tower, however, each person had to be his own brakes and steering wheel; we held ourselves back to avoid failure, eschewing bold risks and picturing sure finishes, and what came out of it only went through the motions, dull and colorless.

Restoring Master Oguni would have done it, but this was no longer possible because being a writer was easier. Never putting down a word, just waiting for the manuscript and passing judgment in the midst of a tension exceeding *go* and *shogi* title matches—how incredibly tough that really was. It was so much easier to turn to writing. If we dared ask, "Be our command tower again," it was evident that Master Oguni would leave his seat irate, veins bulging at his temples, and drop out of Team Kurosawa.

Even so, Mr. Kurosawa's unswerving obstinacy was no ordinary thing. Whether you called it hating to lose or being headstrong, it had an aspect that surpassed my likes' understanding. Having suffered as much as he did over *I Live in Fear*, he still didn't halt the "straight-to-final draft" system and kept to it.

Yet, compared to the writer-leading-off approach with its thorough design plan and the presence of first and second drafts, the do-or-die straight-to-final draft which did away with all that prep ended up with far too many flaws in the finish, and there was no escaping a deterioration in script quality.

Though they were all co-scripted, whenever a writer led off, from the post-war *No Regrets for Our Youth* to *Seven Samurai*, the works dazzled with their living hues; after the 1955 *I Live in Fear* when the "straight-to-final draft" came on like a revolving stage, things took a turn for the worse and slipped into the shadows…plunging headlong into a vague world of darkness with no end in sight.

● *The Lower Depths*

This set Russian literary giant Gorky's play *The Lower Depths* in the Tokugawa period.

I'd gone skiing in Niigata, crashed and fallen on a ski slope in Iwahara, and hurt my neck. I didn't participate in the work, and Mr. Kurosawa and Master Oguni completed it on their own. Thus, I don't know where or for how long they were secluded, but given what came before and after, it had to be Maikoen.

In fact, since the material has something of a dark, gloomy feel, I'm a bit relieved that I didn't take part in this collaborative screenplay.

Thanks to all that, I have neither read the completed script nor seen the finished film.

● *Throne of Blood*

One day, out of the blue, I had a phone call from Master Oguni.

"I'm coming over now. You're home today, right?"

Shortly thereafter, Master Oguni arrived at my house.

"Hashimoto, the next time Kurosawa calls on you, make sure you show up. When you're not there, Kurosawa does nothing but speak ill of you all day. I'm sick and tired of hearing him badmouth you."

"I'll go, Mr. Oguni. My neck was in bad shape for *The Lower Depths*, but next time I'll definitely be there... So, what's it going to be?"

"*Macbeth*... Shakespeare's *Macbeth*."

"Hunh, *Macbeth*? That's difficult material."

I don't really like Shakespeare much. If I were fluent in English and could see famous actors performing it at the best theaters in England, I might appreciate him and learn a thing or two, but as far as reading him in translation goes, it's a drag. The stage directions are extremely brief and the dialogue copious, which turns me off. Many laud his lines as being full of wit and charm, and for plumbing the depths of human nature, but to me it all sounds like overpraising.

Hence I was reluctant to read the work in translation again, and since I mostly remembered the story, I went without rereading it.

When I arrived at Imaihama, I unexpectedly ran into Mr. Kikushima (Ryuzo Kikushima).

"Hey!" "Oh!"

Mr. Kikushima was four years older than me, and his style and inclinations were a little different from mine, but he was my forerunner at Team Kurosawa, and during the time Mr. Toshio Yasumi led the Japan Writers Guild, the two of us formed a solid tag team as managing directors and played a lot of evil hardball. We were dubbed the guild's *hishakaku* (the rooks, in chess) during its golden age—when both the industry and other writers' organizations spoke in awe and fear of "the ruthless JWG." He and I were close enough to ignore etiquette with each other and to blurt out whatever we pleased.

Mr. Kikushima grinned at me. "Hashimoto, we'll be working together on this one."

"Yes, be kind to me..."

With Mr. Kikushima on board, there would be four names lined up this time, where there had only been, at most, three on other collaborations.

I believe that Mr. Kurosawa, who had felt understaffed working with just Master Oguni, worried that I might show my headstrong side and turn him down. He'd called on Mr. Kikushima in advance just in case.

It had been a long time for Mr. Kikushima, who was returning to Team Kurosawa for the first time in seven years since the 1950 film

Scandal.

Throne of Blood, a work that transposed *Macbeth* to the Warring States era, didn't entail any difficulties or hardships worth mentioning.

● *The Hidden Fortress*

Mr. Kikushima, who'd returned to Team Kurosawa after a seven-year absence for the preceding *Throne of Blood*, showed a lot of vim and vigor with this one.

Ever since *I Live in Fear*, Kurosawa projects were like being dragged to church for me, while Mr. Kikushima, particularly concerned with the downward trend of recent Kurosawa offerings, was all in. Collaborating with the team might expand his repertoire and also help to get such projects filmed, and apparently, he had shown as much passion and mettle by pitching this plan himself, visiting Mr. Kurosawa's home in Komae a number of times for meetings.

The aim was an action piece about breaking through enemy lines, reminiscent of Mr. Kurosawa's old adaptation of the Minetaro Nakayama novel *Three Hundred Miles Through Enemy Lines* (a treatment of the Russo-Japanese War's Tatekawa Force Recon Unit).

The time is the Warring States era—succumbing in battle to a neighboring rival, a domain loses the better half of its territory. It owns, however, a hidden fortress where 200 taels of gold are stored inside withered branches designed to look like kindling. With the gold packed on a horse or on a hand cart, the domain's princess and two retainers overcome all kinds of peril, cross enemy territory, and return to their realm to rise another day in this action spectacle.

Meeting face to face at Imaihama, I was taken aback when Mr. Kurosawa and Mr. Kikushima, who had already come up with several situations wherein the trio were trapped, unloaded on Master Oguni and me as "homework" the task of figuring out how they might break through.

Our days at Imaihama felt like an all-star gathering of scenarists, of four lords in their own right, which was fun.

During our customary shoreside walks before evening, I played catch with Mr. Kikushima on the beach. His legs were slightly infirm due to arthritis, but we weren't teammates on the Toho Headquarters Arts Department baseball team for nothing, as sketchy an outfit as that was, and we'd work up a good sweat. Mr. Kurosawa and Master Oguni did dashes or jumped rope nearby, and together we would return to the inn, wash away our sweat in the *onsen*, and move on to dinner and drinks. Mr. Kurosawa and Master Oguni were champions for whom no amount of booze was too much, while Mr. Kikushima and I preferred only a little, but we all passed the time in spirited and free-ranging conversation.

One day, the conversation happened to turn to food.

The eel at such-and-such a place, tempura, sushi, steak, Chinese cuisine…all delicious at the very best restaurants. But also eye-poppingly expensive. No, because you were paying a corresponding amount, deliciousness had to be taken for granted.

Wasn't the truly tasty stuff what we madly gobbled down when we were kids and still growing? Those foods we came to know best, weren't they the most delicious? How about it? Each of us should try and make those.

Mr. Kikushima stepped up to the plate as our leadoff man. "I was born in Kofu, Yamanashi Prefecture, but as a kid I found soy-simmered shellfish the tastiest."

"Kiku-san," Master Oguni said with a puzzled look, "Kofu in Yamanashi Prefecture is mountain country with no sea. Why did you have soy-simmered shellfish there?"

"Master, there's a reason for it."

It went all the way back to Shingen Takeda in the Warring States era. His Kai fiefdom was mountain country, but fearing the pressure of the powerful warlord, domains in the vicinity sent him all sorts of tribute. Over a great distance and across mountainous paths, for instance, Odawara's Hojo clan transported their marine products, shellfish preserved in barrels of sake and soy sauce. Rocked over the long road, the steeped shellfish became indescribably tasty by the time they arrived—and in time, the specialty of Kofu in Kai country.

Mr. Kikushima's eyes narrowed. "Putting the soy-simmered shellfish on warm white rice… There's nothing in this world as delicious."

First thing the next day, Mr. Kikushima made a call to Kofu, and two days later the simmered dish arrived. That night, we were treated to the Kofu specialty.

"This is great," cried out Master Oguni. "Right, tomorrow we'll have the delicacy of my own childhood memories…the specialty of Hachinohe in Aomori Prefecture!"

What Master Oguni had the sisters at Maikoen prepare was a curious thing.

It involved filling a large pot with grated *daikon* raddish; using a hefty kitchen knife to chop up the heads of three large salted salmon, which the eldest son, the head clerk, was dispatched to Inatori to buy; and stewing the mix. When Master Oguni, swallowing, lifted the lid saying "Should be ready," steam rose up out of the pot and the sound of grated *daikon* simmering grew louder.

I put my chopsticks in, apprehensive, and picked up some of the meat from the head and put it in my mouth. Perhaps having soaked up grated *daikon*, the salmon tasted unlike any I'd ever had, utterly delicious.

"Oguni, hey! This grated *daikon* is good…really good," Mr. Kurosawa said. "Usually grated *daikon* is what it is because it's raw, so why?"

Simmering in the salt and fat of salted salmon, the grated *daikon* transformed into a flavorful stewed dish. Just putting some on rice dispensed with the need for sides, and you could wolf down one bowl after another. Master Oguni puffed up a bit at the sight of the three of us diving into the pot with our chopsticks.

"This was the best feast when I was a kid at home…Hachinohe, Aomori's grated *daikon* and salted salmon head hot pot," he proclaimed. Turning his eyes to me he continued, "By the way, Hashimoto, tomorrow it's your turn, but where were you born?"

"Hyogo Prefecture."

"Hyogo Prefecture? So Kansai."

"Yes, to the north of Himeji City in Hyogo…in the middle of the mountains in Nishi-Harima."

Master Oguni gave a deep nod. "Kofu in Yamanashi, Hachinohe in Aomori, and now Nishi-Harima in Hyogo."

Two days later, after we'd finished a light lunch, I announced to the other three, "I'll be taking this afternoon off…to gather ingredients for dinner."

They looked a little put off but said nothing.

Without changing out of the inn's padded kimono, I put on my sneakers and went out the back of Maikoen and up a narrow path into the hills. Spanish mackerel, the lead actor of the dish I was going to make, was a seasonal fish of the Seto Inland Sea and possibly unobtainable in the Sagami Bay area; I'd told the head clerk that red snapper would do in that case.

After a dozen minutes up the sloping path, I came to a good vantage point. It was of a valley stretching towards the southeastern slope of the range, cut off from the sea. Looking out over the vegetation, however, I could see that my quarry, *sansho* or Japanese pepper, only grew at the foot of the mountains.

As a child I ran around hill and country and knew all there was to know about their flora; in particular, I was made to pick Japanese pepper until I was sick of it. I can tell where the *sansho* grows just from the foothills' shape, the shrub thickets, the fern clusters.

"Over there."

When I descended to my spot of choice and looked around, I found shiny green leaves of wild Japanese pepper in the narrow sliver of space between the mountain path and the shrubby growth beyond which rose the foothills' trees. The mountains of both Harima and Izu were tracts of laurel forests.

Taking out my *furoshiki* wrapping cloth and tying the four corners together to make a pouch, I began picking the Japanese pepper leaves. I moved about, and after nearly two hours, gathered enough *sansho* to fill both palms twice.

"Enough, this should be plenty."

I returned to the inn. As I'd requested the previous day, the Maikoen sisters had the other ingredients on hand, bamboo shoots, shiitake mushrooms, lotus root, dried gourd, and freeze-dried tofu, plus rice cooked and deposited in a large wooden tray.

"Sensei, you'll be adding not just vinegar but sake and mirin, right?"

"Yeah, the trick is to make it a little sweet."

You add *mirin* or sweet rice wine to vinegar and sake, turn the white rice in the tray into sushi rice using the sweetened vinegar, and then mix in the other ingredients. Then comes the crux: the freshly-picked, well-rinsed Japanese pepper goes on top of the rice, one leaf at a time, right up against each other and with no spaces between them. Neatly add another layer, and yet another. When you've run out of *sansho*, cover with bamboo mats and white cloth and place a lid on top as a light weight. After three hours or so, remove the weight, white cloth, bamboo mats, and the third and second layers of *sansho* leaves, peel away the first layer so as to leave a speckled pattern, and check the taste. Finally, roughly arrange red snapper sashimi soaked in vinegar on top and finish by scattering thinly-sliced fried egg over the surface.

"It looks delicious," the sisters sighed.

"More than half of it will be left over, so you can have it with your mother and your brother."

It's just ordinary Kansai-style *bara-zushi*—yet a mere morsel suffices to make everyone, anyone cry out "Mm!" The fragrance of Japanese pepper spreads in your mouth and reaches all the way down your throat. After that, seized with a compulsive appetite, you dig in and eat. Eat and eat. You pause to take a breath now and then and get another helping, then go back to eating in silence. Mr. Kurosawa and Master Oguni, who drank, typically ate just a three-quarter bowl of rice, but that day, once they had a bite of the *bara-zushi* they kept on eating without a word, downing only a glass or two of whiskey and water.

I was concerned for the sisters who were serving us. I had told them there would be enough left over for the four family members to eat, but at this rate I couldn't even be sure about the two, no, even one of the girls.

Master Oguni's bifocals glinted, and he asked the younger of the sisters, "Ai-chan, is there more?"

She answered sorrowfully, "There's only half a rice bowl's worth left... not even enough for one."

"What? We've eaten a whole tray's worth. Well, I should give my stomach a break, I'm done."

"Ah, so full, so full..." Mr. Kikushima said patting his stomach. Then to me, "Hashimoto... *Sansho* isn't rare, but it's how you use it, I guess."

"The wisdom of the poor, Mr. Kikushima."

He looked puzzled.

"I was born in a poor village of just tenant farmers."

Mr. Kurosawa, Mr. Oguni, and even Ai-chan stared at me.

"This is a story from when my grandfather was a child, so I think it was towards the end of the shogunate or the early Meiji period."

When the autumn harvest wasn't good, meals consisted of just a handful or two of rice mixed in with barley. At the beginning of spring people picked fresh buds to shore up (increase the volume of) their chow, but there was an age-old warning concerning this.

"Everything else is fine, but stay away from *sansho*. With *sansho* it turns so yummy you overeat and end up a glutton."

Finally it was Mr. Kurosawa's turn.

Yet, two days passed and he'd made nothing. In fact, he didn't even betray signs that he meant to.

On the evening of the third day, Master Oguni demanded at dinner-time, "Hey, Kurosawa... You're from Akita so we're neighbors, right?"

"That's right, I'm from Akita Prefecture."

"So when are you making us something tasty from Akita?"

"Well, the thing is... I moved to Tokyo when I was little, so I don't remember anything tasty from there." Mr. Kurosawa put his whiskey glass down on the table and seemed to gaze into the distance. "What's still with me from Akita...is just that song."

"Song?"

"Yeah, at celebrations and such, a couple dozen relatives would get together, drink sake, and sing."

"Do you remember it?"

"Yeah, only vaguely, though."

"Then sing it. In place of the yummy."

Mr. Kurosawa nodded, took a sip of whiskey, fidgeted, and uncrossed his legs to sit in the formal *seiza* style. Then, after calming his breath, he began singing with a faroff gaze.

I was startled. Master Oguni and Mr. Kikushima immediately exchanged glances. The lyrics were heavily inflected local dialect and we didn't understand a word, but his voice had a luster and bounce, and his sense of melody was exquisite. He lilted line ends with a bopping rhythm, his talent far surpassing the average folk singer's.

The crisp modulation was like Kumamoto Prefecture's "Otemoyan," but unlike "Otemoyan," the melancholy of deep snow country seemed to fill the air in spite of the rollicking tempo.

Hoi kita, sassa, sassa, sassa!

Sometimes including the accompaniment, Mr. Kurosawa was now clapping along as he warbled, simply and innocently, of longing for home. He seemed to have grown lighter, as if his body and mind had been unburdened. But didn't this mean that, whether by his own or others' doing, the everyday Akira Kurosawa was bearing something incredibly heavy (akin to glory, or vainglory)? Nothing of him was free of it.

I had never seen this Akira Kurosawa, and I think that was true for Master Oguni and Mr. Kikushima as well.

Working in seclusion, what we're writing seems only slightly less important and precious than our very lives. Once the job is done, the film is made, and days roll past, that fades and disappears from memory, but some things, never going away, remain as lifelong remembrances, overcoming time with a vivid nostalgic poetry.

Namely the simmered shellfish of the mountain country of Kai, the salmon heads and grated *daikon* of Aomori's Hachinohe, the *bara-zushi* of Nishi-Harima in Hyogo—and above all, leaving the strongest impression, Akira Kurosawa, unencumbered, innocent, warbling an "Akita folksong" from his native country, simply longing for home.

My terms for participation were selfish, disrespectful, and unilateral. I would allot only two weeks but forgo remuneration in exchange, an egotist with only the lightest responsibilities, and no script fee.

It was only when Team Kurosawa moved from Maikoen to an inn at Kawazuhama, dubbing it a second-round camp, that I left Tokyo and joined them, but there with Master Oguni and Mr. Kikushima was Mr. Eijiro Hisaita. Though I was acquainted with Mr. Hisaita this was the first time we were working together, and we were five in all.

If it were four, each of us would take one side of a table, but five meant two guys crowding one of the sides. Moreover, my established place was to Mr. Kurosawa's left, but since Mr. Hisaita was sitting there, I sat next to Mr. Kikushima on Mr. Kurosawa's right. It didn't quite jibe with my way and habit of doing it.

Since I joined the work partway through, I had trouble grasping the story's flow, and I spent the promised two weeks just trying to get my bearings, after which I returned to Tokyo.

Eventually I was sent the completed screenplay, but I didn't feel like reading it, and I haven't seen the finished film either. This is irresponsible, and thoughtless in the extreme, of a writer listed in the credits, but nothing about the work compels picking up the screenplay or attending a test screening or visiting a theater.

Backed by social trends, the contemporary story treats corruption at a public corporation, but it just doesn't shine, and after *I Live in Fear* it was still one somehow lackluster work after another.

Some film industry insiders were beginning to shake their heads about recent Kurosawa works.

Even masters and grandmasters sometimes put out uninteresting fare and subpar stuff that miss the mark. But wait some and they come out with works that meet and even exceed expectations.

Meanwhile, in the case of Kurosawa offerings, while the expectation that in time he would deliver persisted, the actual works kept falling a step short. Although none of them were flops or bombs, none of them seemed to overflow with the charm and fun specific to cinema or to prove as much in the form of satisfyingly voluminous audience mobilization.

At this rate, Kurosawa works would fall from grace and be a matter of past glories—no, his past works shone in reflection only insofar as his present films cast some light. If the current films grew feeble, his older ones would lose all of their energy source and, their glory extinguished,

The five at Kawazuhama: Eijiro Hisaita, Akira Kurosawa, Hideo Oguni
(front row from left), the author, and Ryuzo Kikushima (back row from left).

simply turn into relics of the past.

In any case, even though the situation was grave, the cause of the extended slump had to do with whether one writer "led off" or we went "straight-to-final," craftsmanly arrangements behind the curtains that were altogether opaque to producers and studio executives.

Excepting Akira Kurosawa himself, only three people, Master Oguni, Mr. Kikushima, and I, understood the cause behind the extended slump of Kurosawa works.

The three of us often ran into one another outside Team Kurosawa. But, as if we'd ruled against it, we never so much as brought up Team projects or work. Had one of us said anything, we would have been of one mind that of course an intervention was necessary and that clearly the only way forward was to return from the current "straight-to-final draft" to the "writer leading off" approach.

The question, however, was who would lead off. I absolutely did not want to lead off for Team Kurosawa anymore, and I think Master Oguni and Mr. Kikushima felt the same way. If I wasn't going to myself, then, in arguing that someone ought to, I'd have to recommend another writer; fine if the job went well, but if it didn't work out, I would need to stand in between that writer and Mr. Kurosawa, not an enviable position to be in. None of us wanted to draw the short end of the stick.

In that case, unless Mr. Kurosawa himself did something, there was no changing anything. Yet, Mr. Kurosawa hated to admit defeat and was stubborn, and it was hard to imagine him reverting from the "straight-to-final draft," which he'd introduced, back to the original "writer leading off" approach. Given that fact, perhaps there was nothing to do but to be swept along by momentum and to end up where we may.

No, I—perhaps I don't have the right to say either way at this point. After *The Bad Sleep Well*, my relationship with Team Kurosawa grew terribly thin, and regarding *Yojimbo*, which followed, let alone participating on the screenplay I know absolutely nothing about its proposal plan or production particulars.

● *Yojimbo*

I clapped when the screening finished. Ecstatic, I clapped so hard my hands hurt. The theater was packed, with not even any standing room left, and those who had been standing scrambled to get to the seats of guests who were leaving, in a massively chaotic shift change.

I stayed sitting in my seat, however, and continued to clap.

I was applauding Mr. Kikushima and Mr. Kurosawa, the screenplay writers, and, for maintaining the work's tightly focused visuals and over-flowing force to the end, Mr. Kurosawa the director. What a surprise— the "straight-to-final draft," which I had deemed impossible and given up on, scored a major success, blooming an elegant flower with outsized petals as if to mock me.

When I stood up after a while, wound my way through the audience, and left the theater, I saw people standing in line to buy tickets. It was probably the biggest hit for a Kurosawa film since *Seven Samurai*.

Dogenzaka, the road in front of the theater we commonly referred to as "Shibuto" (Toho-Takarazuka Theater in Shibuya), dazzled in the bright May sunshine.

I felt strangely buoyant and ready for a drink. I was alone though, and it was midday, so my feet took me down Dogenzaka, towards a coffee shop that I frequented. When I entered the place located by the station and under the Yamanote Line tracks, I luckily found an open seat by the window facing the street.

Once the coffee I had ordered arrived, I lifted the cup, once more offered congratulations to Mr. Kurosawa and Mr. Kikushima, and took a sip.

It was entirely Mr. Kurosawa and Mr. Kikushima's achievement—while for me, it brought back a vivid recollection of a certain day at Imaihama during *The Hidden Fortress*.

Around a table plunked down at the center of the eight-mat room at Maikoen, I sat opposite the alcove with Mr. Kurosawa on my right, Mr. Kikushima in front of me with his back to the alcove column, and Master Oguni to my left. The manuscript always traveled counterclockwise: what I wrote went to Mr. Kurosawa, then Mr. Kikushima, then Master Oguni, before returning to me; what the others wrote came to me from the left by way of Master Oguni; thus we confirmed the content of our competitions over the same scenes.

One day, when what I wrote passed via Mr. Kurosawa to Mr. Kikushima, instead of passing it on to Master Oguni, Mr. Kikushima tilted his head, looked up at me, and said, "Hashimoto, when you charge in like this, it gets stuck. Do this beforehand and it handles."

So saying, he began to fix my manuscript himself rather than turn it over to Master Oguni, and when he was done he handed it back to me directly, across the table. I took it and looked, and I couldn't believe my eyes, I was so awed. Such incredible handling. Mr. Kikushima had an established reputation for the way he handled drama, but this was indeed superb.

As I sat entranced with the manuscript, Mr. Kurosawa held out his hand and demanded to see it. Almost as soon as he took and read the revised version, his face twitched and his breathing stopped.

Mr. Kurosawa and I were front-running start-dashers, while Mr. Kikushima and Master Oguni fit the come-from-behind mould; my strengths and weaknesses were also those of Mr. Kurosawa. A manuscript that I considered fine—no, that I didn't always think worked but that I didn't know how to fix, that I lacked the intuition to revise and the technique to handle, Mr. Kikushima could treat effortlessly. Mr. Kurosawa, too, was speechless over Mr. Kikushima's knack for forward handling.

Mr. Kurosawa was aware of Mr. Kikushima's skill thanks to precedents including *Stray Dog*. But after he left Team Kurosawa... The Ryuzo Kikushima who went on to taste plenty of hardship in our rough-and-tumble world was no longer the Ryuzo Kikushima of the past.

What does being good at forward handling mean? Putting it in the following manner might help explain, without resorting to lingo, what goodness at what we're talking about.

In a Toei Studio yakuza film, Ken Takakura, whose sworn brothers have been killed, enters enemy territory to launch a suicidal final raid. On the way, however, Junko Fuji comes rushing out of the townscape. "Wait!" she says, clinging to him. "Please don't go!"

Both Mr. Kurosawa and I would come to a standstill at this point. Ken Takakura is stuck. He can't just keep on standing here, but he can't very well shove off the heroine and run off, so the drama comes to a grinding halt.

Yet writers who work on Toei films would hardly break a sweat. Junko Fuji continues to cling to Ken Takakura, crying without letting go, but after a while she says, "Even if I try to stop you, you're going to go." Then, she wipes her tears and moves away, saying, "So, go... Go!"

"Sorry!" Ken Takakura says, raising a hand in apology, and immediately runs off.

Handled like a charm.

Handling has to do with such drama, and in sumo terms, Mr. Kurosawa and I were like grapplers who took opponents to the edge of the ring by brute force but got stuck there in the face of last-ditch resistance. When pushing didn't clinch it, however, Mr. Kikushima, faking a push, instead pulled and compromised his opponent's stance, drawing him into his own finishing move and bringing him down.

Forward handling involves many of these pulling moves that are invariably effective, but overusing them easily comes across as being too wily and phony. Moreover, since pulling techniques necessitate footwork, relying too much on them leads, in sumo terms, to fancy wrestling...or in theatrical terms, to smoke and mirrors and bluffing performances banking on vulgar appeal.

In the case of a story that seeks to be authentic or to grasp at human truths, this kind of method brings it all tumbling down. If, however, you alert your audience from the start that it's make-believe, complete fiction, then perhaps such wiles could work to a surprising degree.

Because Kurosawa films, whether original, adapted, or translated, sought the truth at heart and overwhelmed with a sense of reality even if it was all make-believe, these measures had been off limits.

But if the material absolutely doesn't need to feel real, if the audience is fully made to understood from the outset that it's fiction, in other words, if it is entertainment fare through and through, the method can come into free play.

Even if you don't hold scrupulous meetings, don't think through the story and theme, and don't sweat over characterization and narrative structure—even if you jump right into it, a "straight-to-final draft" would work for such a screenplay.

Given Mr. Kikushima's bravura forward handling and quick footwork, made in the right way, a new kind of wily entertainment screenplay could issue forth. The rest would be putting his powers of direction to the test on untried, fun entertainment fare.

No, it wasn't as simple a decision as that for Mr. Kurosawa.

Ever since *I Live in Fear*, though he never let it slip to anyone, he must have spent lonely days rife with impatience and anguish. The failed *I Live in Fear* had been an original work, its story an unknown and uncertain quantity, so he turned to adaptations with a clear shape next, to Gorky's *Lower Depths* and Shakespeare's *Macbeth*; yet, while not misshapen, the films lacked the fermenting fertile interest unique to cinema.

With no other choice he changed track and did a historical adventure resembling *Three Hundred Miles Through Enemy Lines*, an action piece he'd written in the past. Yet, even though the meat of adventure is action and the swift flow of images, *The Hidden Fortress* made transporting gold, a heavy burden, its subject; thanks to its speed deficit it was a far cry from the exhilaration of an adventure film.

At last, he went all out and mobilized five writers for *The Bad Sleep Well*, but unable to ride the current of the times, it, too, ended up tepid.

He was out of moves. There was no room left. Failing to catch any upward swell, each film traced a downward curve, and he could lose all fame and glory if the next work fell flat.

Now that he stood at cliff's edge, it was do or die. Eschewing neither pulling moves nor footwork, he had to take a chance, didn't he, on untried entertainment fare… All right, it's a go then, let's do it! And it worked out, worked big time.

The collaborative screenplay has its lights and shadows.

From its inception in 1946 right after the war until *Seven Samurai* in 1954, with a writer leading off, it shone brilliantly, but with *I Live in Fear* and the straight-to-final shift, it plunged into a dark stretch of shadows with no end in sight on to 1960's *The Bad Sleep Well*. With *Yojimbo* the following year, however, the "straight-to-final draft" came to life all of a sudden and, like a galloping horse, dashed out into a shimmer of light.

This world of light would continue for a while. Changing the subject was all it took to turn out two or three more entertainment ("straight-to-final draft") projects. And the central co-writer would be Ryuzo Kikushima, with me no longer tied to Team Kurosawa.

Good… Phew, good.

182

I'd clapped so ecstatically at Shibuto not just to congratulate Mr. Kurosawa and Mr. Kikushima, but spontaneously, instinctively, to applaud myself. I was liberated from Team Kurosawa, tried and cleared of guilt.

Compared to the other writers I was a special case because I made my debut with a script I brought in, *Rashomon*. It was thanks to Mr. Kurosawa's recognition that I got my start as a writer, and if he ever called on me, I was in no position to refuse no matter what difficulties I faced. So when *Seven Samurai* was done I breathed a sigh of relief at graduating from Team Kurosawa—prematurely and based on a self-serving understanding as invisible chains bound me after all.

But this time, without a doubt, the chains would be severed, completely... *Hurray! Three cheers*, as they said, my whole body seemed to tingle, and I felt as free as a horse galloping across the sky...no, a dragon swimming in the air to its heart's content and ready to soar to the heavens.

From now on, I could try to do fewer works and become a writer who didn't get paid by the script but on a film's returns; I also had dreams in the way of film production down along the line. I could really romp around the movie world unrestricted.

In any case, I thought keenly, no, in a heartfelt way, *what strong luck Mr. Kurosawa has.* Thanks to *Yojimbo* and the next two or three films, for the next ten years...no, twenty years, his position as a grandmaster of world cinema would rest secure. His luck was indeed formidable.

But it's such a major transformation, no one could have foreseen it... As though Chikamatsu ducked behind the curtains to come out the next moment as Namboku.

The works of Monzaemon Chikamatsu, who authored *Love Suicides at Sonezaki* and *The Courier for Hell,* and Namboku Tsuruya, who authored *Tokaido Yotsuya Ghost Story* and *Indian Tokubei, a Story of a Foreign Country,* offer a great many hints and lessons for scenario writing, and despite their utterly contrasting hues I have always revered both of the great Edo playwrights.

Yojimbo, the elegant large-petaled flower birthed by the "straight-to-final draft" against my bet, in a way seems like a ferocious avenger to me... a mad out-of-season blossom that is not so much elegant but bewitching— an astoundingly huge, purple blossom.

CHAPTER FOUR:
HASHIMOTO PRO AND MR. KUROSAWA

Two Assistant Directors

After *Yojimbo*, Mr. Kurosawa's path was many-colored, bumpy, dramatic.

He followed up *Yojimbo* with two big entertainment offerings, *Sanjuro* and *High and Low*, both of which met with great box-office success, and two years after *High and Low* came the less flashy but ambitious *Red Beard*, a historical drama set at the Tokugawa shogunate's Koishikawa clinic. With his next film, however, he ran into an unexpected bump and scandal.

In 1964, during the filming of American studio 20th Century Fox's *Tora! Tora! Tora!* at Toei's Kyoto studio, he had to step down as director (was terminated) for running behind schedule, an extraordinary event.

Rumors that Mr. Kurosawa had been suffering a nervous breakdown when he stepped down from *Tora! Tora! Tora!* spread through the film world and mass media, so he needed to make a picture to demonstrate that he was fine. The directors' group *Shiki no Kai* or The Four Horsemen Club (Akira Kurosawa, Keisuke Kinoshita, Masaki Kobayashi, Kon Ichikawa) devised a project, *Dodes'ka-den*, based on a story by Shugoro Yamamoto. I was marshaled in a hurry, along with Master Oguni, and had to write a script with Mr. Kurosawa for the first time since *The Bad Sleep Well* ten years earlier.

My ties to Team Kurosawa had been severed and another job had been a tall order, but given the extraordinary circumstances I had no choice.

Only, I was concerned that Mr. Kikushima wasn't participating. When I asked about it, Master Oguni explained that the trauma of *Tora! Tora! Tora!* had precipitated a vindictive tit-for-tat between Mr. Kurosawa and Mr. Kikushima and that the two had parted ways permanently.

Since there was no choice, Mr. Kurosawa, Mr. Oguni, and I moved forward on the work, but as material, *Dodes'ka-den* was too small for Mr. Kurosawa, who specialized in painting big pictures on a big canvas. The project, more like drawing a single flower on a small frame, took only two weeks or so to write.

The episode that followed, Mr. Kurosawa's suicide attempt, came as a great shock to me.

His deeply embarrassing dismissal from *Tora! Tora! Tora!* and the box-office failure of *Dodes'ka-den*, now compounded with this scandal of a suicide attempt... Not just Japanese but American film funding would no longer touch Mr. Kurosawa, and any sort of comeback as a filmmaker seemed like a pipe dream.

But Mr. Kurosawa was a man of strong luck, an unsinkable battleship.

His unparalleled, peerless cinematic talent, denied a place in capitalist nations with their utilitarianism, could only blossom in a communist country that appreciated art. Seeing the matter thus, the Soviet Union invited him as a *de facto* guest of state and ruled in favor of producing a project close to his heart, *Dersu Uzala*, based on Vladimir Arsenyev's work. Mr. Kurosawa left for the Soviet Union with a small group of staff and undertook shooting in an arduous Siberian location. The film was finished and released in 1975.

It was a miraculous comeback, like a phoenix rising from the ashes. However, attendance was surprisingly low and the receipts unexpectedly meager for *Dersu Uzala*, which was released in Japan and the Soviet Union.

For three years, for *Yojimbo*, *Sanjuro*, and *High and Low*, the "straight-to-final draft" was a large flower blooming under a bright sun, but after a two-year blank and from around *Red Beard* the rays dimmed, leading to *Dersu Uzala*'s poor performance, and once again, like some revolving stage, it all plunged into a dark and hazy fog with no end in sight.

Hashimoto Pro (founded in 1974) and Mr. Kurosawa aren't really related in any way.

At the same time, Hashimoto Pro's first feature, *Castle of Sand*, was directed by Yoshitaro Nomura, and its second, *Mt. Hakkoda*, by Shiro Moritani, both former assistant directors to Mr. Kurosawa. Neither, however, was just one of many assistant directors.

Moritani had been master filmmaker Mikio Naruse's assistant director before sliding over to Team Kurosawa to serve in the same capacity. For a long time the Team's weakpoint had been its dearth of good people in that role, but Shiro Moritani as the chief assistant director, Masanobu Deme as the second, and Kenjiro Omori as the third accounted for a golden age of satisfying ADs. At the Toho Studio in Kinuta, all eyes were on the gifted Moritani as a future filmmaker who could fill the post-Akira Kurosawa hole. He and I were quite tight, and together we did *Neck, Yet Our Days... [Saredo Wareraga Hibi...]*, *Tidal Wave*, and *Mt. Hakkoda*.

Meanwhile, there's no word but fate to describe my encounter with Yoshitaro Nomura.

One day, I visited the Kurosawa residence to discuss *The Captain of "The Coffin"* (a collaborative screenplay with Mr. Kurosawa that, in the end, was not made into a film).

Shiro Moritani (1931-84)

Mr. Kurosawa, however, was too irate that day for the discussion to go anywhere.

While he had finished filming *The Idiot* at Shochiku's Ofuna studio, it had a long running time, and right around then he was in the middle of a spectacular head-on dispute with Shiro Kido, the vice president, about whether or not it should be cut.

"Hashimoto…" Mr. Kurosawa lamented with a gloomy expression, "I went to Shochiku's Ofuna and made two films, *Scandal* and *The Idiot*, but nothing good came of it. Still, Shochiku's Ofuna has Yoshitaro Nomura, the best assistant director in Japan."

"The best assistant director?"

"Right, neither Toho nor Daiei has anything on them. He's Japan's best."

Be that as it may, since we weren't talking about the work at hand, I was ready to leave after having chatted for about half an hour. That was when Takashi Koide, *The Idiot*'s Shochiku producer, arrived to relay Mr. Kido's intentions, with Mr. Nomura in tow…the same Yoshitaro Nomura who'd just come up, Japan's greatest assistant director.

Mr. Kurosawa coldly ignored the producer, Mr. Kido's proxy, refusing even to look at him, but broke into a smile for Mr. Nomura.

Yoshitaro Nomura (1919-2005)

He immediately introduced us. "Hashimoto, this is Yoshitaro Nomura, an assistant director for Shochiku. Nomura, this is the scenario writer who wrote *Rashomon* with me, Shinobu Hashimoto."

After Mr. Nomura and I bowed our heads and exchanged greetings, Mr. Kurosawa asked, "Hashimoto, you're Taisho what?"

"Huh?"

"The year you were born."

"Seven."

"What about you, Nomura?"

"Taisho eight [1919]."

"So you're pretty much the same age... Your time is certainly coming. You guys better get along and work together."

I worked with Mr. Nomura six years later. The film was an adaptation of Ashihei Hino's Akutagawa Prize-winning story, *Tales of Excrement and Urine*.

I did the majority of my work with Toho as a screenwriter. A big gun at Toei, Mitsuo Makino, favored me too, and I was also tight with producers and planners at Nikkatsu and Daiei, so there was no room left for Shochiku jobs. Their Ofuna studio felt like a film company in some distant foreign country, and if not for our chance encounter at Mr. Kurosawa's home and his introducing us, Mr. Nomura and I may have never met or worked together, unconnected in this world.

That said, our first work together, *Tales of Excrement and Urine*, wasn't all that good. The reason was the director tweaking the screenplay on his own. They weren't big changes but more like a mouse running around nibbling here and there. Normally, I never work again with a director who alters my screenplay. Top-of-the-line directors don't tamper with screenplays. The need to do so is rooted in the narrow opinions and whims of second- and third-rate directors. They only ever make the screenplay worse, and we call directors who regularly revise without permission "changers"; however, for these "changers" it's second nature, and they won't stop with their alterations no matter who the scenarist is or what the work. So when I learn that I'm dealing with a "changer" I studiously avoid working with him again.

Yet, in the case of Mr. Nomura, perhaps Kurosawa magic—our encounter at his residence, the strong karma of him bringing us together, had me besotted. I didn't abhor or avoid another go all that much and wrote *The Chase*, an adaptation of a Seicho Matsumoto story, to be the next work.

I was surprised when I saw the finished film. No, at first I couldn't believe it. From the first scene to the last, *The Chase* contained all of the screenplay's strengths and weaknesses as-is, with not a word or line altered.

His revising the screenplay on his own was the reason why *Tales of Excrement and Urine* hadn't come out as well as expected. He acutely discerned this, responded accordingly for the next work, and revised nothing whatsoever. I had to remove my hat and salute him.

Duly impressed... Mr. Kurosawa was damn right.

True to Mr. Kurosawa's endorsement, Mr. Nomura possessed a keen intellect and combined exemplary judgment with adaptability. He was shrewd beyond measure.

Yes, there are bits that a scenario writer skimps on. Then you see it filmed exactly as you wrote it, word for word. Treated to such a job on the director's part, you can't cut yourself any slack, to lose focus or to take it easy or to fudge it. After that, we made *Grave Tells All*, *Zero Focus*, *The Shadow Within*, *Castle of Sand*, and *The Village of Eight Graves*, said to be Shochiku's biggest hit since its inception, which means Mr. Nomura filmed more of my solo screenplays than any other director, a whopping seven.

Within my range of associations, in the film world as I've known it, no one was as clear-headed or as prescient as Mr. Nomura.

One day, he and I went together to the Yamaha Hall in Ginza for a preview screening of Spielberg's *Jaws*. When it was over we went to a nearby coffee shop, but neither of us spoke a word for a time.

Eventually I said, "It's a well-done film."

Mr. Nomura gave a big nod. "It's made up entirely of good takes."

I nodded silently. He was right.

I'm nothing more than a very ordinary fan when I watch a movie, but perhaps due to a lingering professional awareness, I catch occasional uses of bad takes on the screen. Almost no film is an entire string of good takes. Actors have their limits and there are budget and time constraints, so there is no helping it, cuts that ought to be retaken end up being green-lighted and make their way in.

With *Jaws*, however, I didn't catch a single bad take. For example, there is a memorable scene where a pier, pulled into the water by the shark, disappears. These weren't first tries, they'd rebuilt the pier five or six times, changed the speed, chosen a take they deemed good, and used it.

"It really was good takes from beginning to end, wasn't it?"

"Mr. Hashimoto... There's no need to watch any Spielberg films from here on out."

"Wha-"

Mr. Nomura looked at me, his eyes turned slightly upward and glinting behind his glasses, his demeanor malicious and a bit cold-blooded. "You could be a film director your whole life and just maybe make one film like that. So *Jaws* will be his best... No matter what he goes on to shoot, he won't make anything better."

Sensing a certain ring of truth in his words, I've passed on Spielberg films since then. Every time a Spielberg film opens though, Mr. Nomura's prediction nags at me and I check with people who've seen it. Taking their opinions as a whole, the prediction, marvelously, appears to have hit the bull's-eye.

His prescience was almost dreadful, as if he'd somehow overcome time and space.

Thanks to Mr. Nomura, however, I was once called to Shochiku head-quarters and given a dressing-down by Mr. Kido, who had returned as president.

Having gotten a phone call from Mr. Kido I went out to Tsukiji and faced him in the president's office at the company headquarters, where he showed me Shochiku's docket of films and asked my honest opinion about them. When I gave my two cents, he indicated some project parameters and asked my frank opinion on director and writer pairings and even how they squared with actors. Mr. Kido was famous for being one of the film industry's most cold-blooded and autocratic company heads, on par with Daiei's past president Masaichi Nagata. Though I'd heard he'd lost some of his mojo, he was hale and spirited and paid serious attention to voices from outside, and I even sensed his passion and his breadth and depth as a business executive.

Our discussion was mostly done and I was about to stand up when Mr. Kido said, "Ah, Hashimoto…" as if he'd forgotten something. "When it comes to Nomura, you didn't do us any favors."

I made a puzzled face. I didn't know what he was talking about.

"I'm not saying this because Nomura is Hotei's son."

Hotei was Hotei Nomura, who had established and led the Kamata studio, the predecessor to Shochiku's Ofuna studio, as one of the company's distinguished names. Yoshitaro Nomura was his eldest son.

"I'd meant to pluck Nomura out of the studio in a year or two so he could lead the production department at headquarters."

Startled, I looked at Mr. Kido. Come to think of it, about three or four years back, I'd heard a fragment of a rumor from someone that Mr. Nomura would be heading production at headquarters in a few years. The head of the production department was the most important and central post at a film company.

Mr. Kido continued, "After three or four years at production headquarters, I'd have sent him to marketing, and once he'd studied the business side, I meant to tap him as senior managing director or vice president, as my successor in waiting… I believed no one but he could shoulder Shochiku."

I held my breath.

"And yet, you've had him shoot independent productions like *Castle of Sand*, giving him a percentage cut of the take to boot, and killed the manager in him, and now he's one of those lifelong directors."

"…"

"You're probably feeling good that *Castle of Sand* was a hit, but you could have just stayed out of the way, you know… Thanks to you, Shochiku has lost its future pillar."

On the subway home from Shochiku headquarters to Shibuya, I wound up folding my arms and getting lost in thought. It was as though a gaping hole had opened up at the bottom of my heart.

Encounters, that's what it comes down to… If I hadn't encountered him back then at Mr. Kurosawa's house, Mr. Nomura would now be…

The president of a major film company enjoys a much higher social status and greater general regard than a film director. As to whether president of Shochiku was better than lifelong director for Mr. Nomura himself, I could neither wrap my head around nor judge… It seemed to fall out of the scope of some third party's will or thinking and to border, in fact, on destiny or fate.

But even so, for Mr. Nomura, what was I… What was I to him?

Perhaps because these thoughts about Mr. Nomura lurked in my mind, one day I carelessly let something slip out of my mouth.

Mr. Kurosawa trusted and expected much of both assistant directors, but perhaps because he had such strong likes and dislikes, he showed entirely different sides of himself to them. He was cold and cruel to Moritani, but to Mr. Nomura he was warm and kind.

Moritani lived in Hiyoshi on the Toyoko Line, and his commute into the city took him through Shibuya Station, which was close to Hashimoto Pro's office in Sakuragaoka, so he often stopped by. No matter how many hours we talked, however, he never said a word about Mr. Kurosawa, and for my part I also never mentioned Mr. Kurosawa.

Meanwhile, when Mr. Nomura did drop by, in contrast with Moritani he often brought up Mr. Kurosawa's films and person as we chatted. That was why I ended up blurting out, "So, for Mr. Kurosawa, what was I… What was Shinobu Hashimoto to him?"

Mr. Nomura's eyes glinted behind his glasses and his eyebrows twitched. In an instant, something cold ran down my spine. I'd said something I shouldn't have, beyond the pale. That was my premonition.

"For Mr. Kurosawa, Shinobu Hashimoto was a man he should never have encountered."

"Wha-"

"Because he met such a man he made a film like *Rashomon*, and because it won a prize overseas for the first time since the war… Things that have nothing to do with cinema, ideas and philosophy and even social relevance, became a part of his works, and every one of them ended up strangely defensive and heavy and tiresome."

My nerves rubbed the wrong way, I felt indignant. I regretted my careless words, but it seemed to me as though Mr. Nomura's way of putting it was rather overbearing and hyperbolic. I lost sight of things and became emotional.

"But, Mr. Nomura, that would remove *Rashomon*, *Ikiru*, and *Seven Samurai* from Mr. Kurosawa's repertoire, wouldn't it?"

"He would have been better off without them."

"What?!" I raised my voice reflexively.

"Even without them, Mr. Kurosawa would have become the world's Kurosawa…a more down-to-earth and real grandmaster, as opposed to the name-only 'Kurosawa' we have now."

Mr. Nomura had his face lowered; his eyes, turned upwards towards me, glinted through his glasses; his demeanor was rather cold-blooded, cutting, mean-spirited. I froze, because I'd seen that face before…on Mr. Nomura himself, when he'd predicted that we would never need to see another Spielberg film.

"I assisted Mr. Kurosawa on two films, so I know how much directing ability…that's to say, ability, he has. His sense for images clears the world standard, and on top of that he's brimming with energy, some endlessly strong thing that makes his films soar even higher. So if it weren't for the impurities… Are you with me, if it weren't for the needless impurities, if he purely…I mean, purely pursued cinematic interest and nothing else, he could have been a cross between Billy Wilder and William Wyler."

I remained silent.

Billy Wilder was a master who elicited deep hums of approval with films like *Sunset Boulevard*, *Some Like It Hot*, and *The Apartment*, while William Wyler was celebrated around the world as a great director of big pictures like *Roman Holiday* and *Ben Hur*.

"A filmmaker with more finesse than Billy Wilder, and, for big pictures, a sturdier gait and sharper, cleaner images than Wyler. What sort of movies mightn't such a director make… I think you get the idea, Mr. Hashimoto. He'd make many fun movies, delivering to us, and fans around the world, thrills, excitement, and no-nonsense entertainment… and literally, without asterisks, be the king of world cinema… Don't you think so, Mr. Hashimoto?"

I felt dizzy. There was a kernel of truth to what he was saying, but it was sophistic in some way and fundamentally mistaken. I tried to say something. The words wouldn't come.

It was—a day towards the end of 1977…the year when *Mt. Hakkoda*, completed after three years of chasing after blizzards in the extreme cold of northern Japan's Hakkoda range, saw its release on the Toho circuit to record-breaking success.

Kagemusha

It was early summer in 1978, about half a year after Mr. Nomura's comments about the director, that Mr. Kurosawa came to the Hashimoto Pro office.

Teruyo Nogami came with him. Ever since *Rashomon* at Daiei, and with the exception of two Shochiku films (*Scandal* and *The Idiot*), she had been in charge of continuity for all Kurosawa works and was effectively the producer for works he directed at Kurosawa Pro.

I hadn't seen Mr. Kurosawa in about ten years, since *Dodes'ka-den*, and he seemed to have gained a lot of weight indeed. Perhaps thanks to having struggled up the Sakuragaoka slope that ran out front, his face was covered with sweat, and he was still panting heavily even after we sat down.

"Hashimoto, that's a steep slope."

"Yes, true… Once you're used to it, it's not so bad."

"I've come today to ask a bit of a favor."

Nogami took a screenplay out of a paper bag and handed it to Mr. Kurosawa, who placed it on the table. I glanced at the title: *Kagemusha*, or "The Body Double."

"I've done this script—could you read it and give me your opinion?" When I nodded he continued, "I'm in discussions right now with Toho about filming it, and I'd like to have your help on that front as well."

"I understand… I'll do what I can."

Mr. Kurosawa and Nogami finished their tea and left, and I immediately picked up the screenplay. In the screenwriter column were the names Akira Kurosawa and Masato Ide.

I was puzzled. While Mr. Kikushima's no-show couldn't be helped due to their falling out, Master Oguni's name wasn't there either. More than ten years after I'd split with Team Kurosawa, the "straight-to-final draft" system may have still been in place, but the roster of writers had changed… No, Masato Ide was someone whom Mr. Kikushima had discovered. I knew him well enough and seemed to recall his working on *Red Beard* with Team Kurosawa.

I finished the screenplay for *Kagemusha* in under an hour.

I felt beat, like all the energy had drained from my body. I let out a long sigh. *Yikes, it's hopeless…* It was poor, boring, and just very tiresome.

The story was simply that the Warring States-era warlord Shingen Takeda had had a body double.

The double's curious fate and exploits didn't amount to much, and it wasn't as though Shingen Takeda's own greatness was depicted. In particular, what gives the double away is the scar Shingen Takeda receives on his back when he trades blows with Kenshin Uesugi at the Battle of Kawanaka Island. There was no custom of daily bathing in those times, but people washed their bodies every day with cold or hot water. The double's identity coming to light because his back lacks that scar is just puerile.

At the beginning of Norio Nanjo's novel *The Third Kagemusha*, a warrior wails in agony as they gouge out his right eye with an arrowhead. The keep-lord protagonist's right eye has been pierced with an arrow in battle and crushed, so they're doing the same to his double's right eye. Compared with the intensity of this, it's a joke.

At any rate, the collaborative screenplay *Kagemusha* is a botched work.

Collaborative screenplays don't easily produce classics or masterpieces, but characteristically avoid turning out poor or botched works. Thanks to passing under multiple pairs of eyes, holes don't go unnoticed. Up to that point, Team Kurosawa's screenplays may have varied in quality, but not one of them was clearly poor or botched. If this was the result, however, the upshot was the end of the collaborative screenplay—the point of having more than one writer work on the same scene lost, the system itself came tumbling down.

I felt rather mournful about this.

Memories from long ago came to mind.

The flash of inspiration that was *Rashomon*, the near-perfectionist approach to story, theme, and characterization that was *Ikiru*, the astounding meticulousness and perspicacity for character settings that was *Seven Samurai*, where had it all gone?

Well, it was a fact that ever since *I Live in Fear*, which followed up on *Seven Samurai*, Team Kurosawa went about screenplay writing in a wholly different manner. Still, even though the "straight-to-final draft" was a method that led to various weaknesses, I had a hard time believing it could produce something this inferior in quality.

Why? How?

No, this was no time to be poking around or ruminating. The question at hand was what to do with this *Kagemusha*. It would be best not to film it, but shelving it was impossible. Mr. Kurosawa's real work on *Dersu Uzala* in the Soviet Union had taken place four years earlier. Partly because of the Soviet Union's foreign reserve situation, I'd heard, his director's compensation had come in lower than expected. That meant he'd gone without any income for the last few years... Since there was no way he had a substitute project in the wings, this *Kagemusha* some-how had to be forced onto a studio and placed on a production line by hook or by crook... The work's quality, whether it was a hit or a miss, was irrelevant.

Four or five days after they'd stopped by, I received a call from Nogami, and we went together to Toho headquarters. Our counterpart in negoti-ating the film's production was Mr. Tomoyuki Tanaka, the president of Toho Pictures.

Since producing films with independent productions was the coordi-nation department's job, Mr. Tomoyuki Tanaka of Toho Pictures wasn't whom we'd expected.

Toho headquarters had spun off its studio, which was perpetual-ly in the red, and set it up as a separate company with its own balance sheet, Toho Pictures. Perhaps Toho proper wanted to get a sense of Kurosawa Pro and Hashimoto Pro's plans and intentions ahead of time and put Toho Pictures in the middle to avoid direct contact with either of us.

Nogami took out some documents and proposed Shintaro Katsu for the lead role and a budget of one billion yen. Mr. Tomoyuki Tanaka seemed half-hearted and didn't make it clear whether or not Toho would pick up the film for production. We were told that he would give us an answer later, so, with nothing left to do, the two of us returned empty-handed.

After three or four days, Mr. Tanaka called Hashimoto Pro to say, "I'm at headquarters and about to head out to the studio, but could I stop by on the way?"

"Yes, please," I replied, "I'll be waiting."

Mr. Tanaka arrived about forty or fifty minutes later, and I met with him in my office.

"Hashimoto, about *Kagemusha*," he said, looking at me straight on. "Today, I want to put a direct question to you...the scenario writer I trust and respect most, Shinobu Hashimoto. All right?"

I was rather alarmed.

"The screenplay for *Kagemusha* that Kurosawa and Masato Ide wrote together... In your eyes, having read it, is it a good script, or a bad script?"

I twitched, as though an electric current had zipped through me. My breath caught deep in my throat, and I couldn't breathe. Never had I felt so desperate, like a man standing on a gallows with a noose wrapped around his neck. To call a screenplay that I was doing my utmost

198

to sell "a bad script"…yet I'd rather have my mouth rot than call it "a good script."

I swallowed once, twice, and gasped out, "Tomoyuki-san… That script is no good, it's poor."

Mr. Tanaka stared at me without saying a word.

"But Tomoyuki-san, think back to *Yojimbo*."

At the start of *Yojimbo*, the boss of production at Toho, Mr. Iwao Mori, read the screenplay and ordered it canceled even though shooting had already begun. "This screenplay isn't good, not something Kurosawa ought to be filming. If we quit now, the company will suffer a huge loss. But that's nothing compared to Kurosawa's honor. We need to cancel at once." And the one who bore Mr. Mori's intent and served as the messenger was Producer Tomoyuki Tanaka.

When Mr. Tanaka spoke to him, Mr. Kurosawa's face flushed bright red and he exploded in anger. Refusing to quit no matter what, he adamantly continued shooting and completed the film, and *Yojimbo* became an unexpectedly huge hit.

"There's that precedent, Tomoyuki-san… Since Mr. Kurosawa's mise-en-scène isn't something to gloss over, we can't tell just from reading the script. The *Kagemusha* screenplay has boring elements, but Mr. Kurosawa may have reckoned with them in his own way, and this could be another *Yojimbo*."

Yojimbo's audience accepted that it was make-believe from the start and went along with any bluffing and fanciness; in such cases people stayed with it as long as the mise-en-scène was solid. *Kagemusha*, on the contrary, somehow needed to convey truth and necessity but lacked them, so the story awkwardly stood out, and it was tedious in a way that no mise-en-scène could cover up. Although both screenplays were "straight-to-final drafts," *Yojimbo* and *Kagemusha* were essentially different, as chalk from cheese.

But I couldn't say so.

Mr. Tomoyuki Tanaka fell into silence, plunged into thought, but eventually nodded once, twice, and said, "Understood. Then I'm not asking Shinobu Hashimoto the scenario writer, but Shinobu Hashimoto the manager of Hashimoto Pro."

Once again I was shocked. Today's Tomoyuki-san, not the usual Tomoyuki-san, came equipped with a deep resolve.

"If Toho turns down *Kagemusha*, what will you do?"

After drawing a blank for a moment, I answered. My delivery was surprisingly natural and smooth: "If Toho turns it down, it'll be a co-production between Kurosawa Pro and Hashimoto Pro that I'll take to Shochiku and Toei's foreign-film circuit."

"Shochiku and Toei's foreign-film circuit, huh?"

The distributor of *Castle of Sand*, the foreign-film circuit sponsored by Shochiku and Toei was in no way inferior to Toho's foreign-film circuit and one of Japan's largest movie theater chains. "You bet. But given that Kurosawa Pro's production capability is an unknown quantity, Hashimoto Pro will go all out. We won't just have A and B units, but a mobile C unit."

Mr. Tanaka didn't speak.

"Listen, Tomoyuki-san, I'm standing with Mr. Kurosawa, side by side, with that main A unit... For the B unit, Shiro Moritani from Hashimoto Pro, and for the C unit...for the special mobile C unit, also from Hashimoto Pro, the Shochiku director Yoshitaro Nomura!"

Mr. Tanaka held his breath, not uttering a word.

"Tomoyuki-san, let alone Mr. Nomura, Moritani too is now a top-of-the-line director. You might think it's a bit too much and gross to rope in two top-of-the-line directors, but if we explain what's what then everyone will understand... They're the two assistant directors that Mr. Kurosawa trusted the most over his long directorial career. Of course those two assistant directors would repay their director and support him."

"..."

"Tomoyuki-san, these B and C units are strong. They'll show initiative, they'll challenge and goad on the main A unit. We're talking the largest-scale and liveliest sets in the history of Japanese cinema... Mr. Kurosawa came to me with his head bowed asking for help, and having accepted, I have to... So if I'm doing it, win or lose, my only possible move would be to go all in."

Later, I was relieved to hear that thanks to Nogami and other people related to the project, Toho had picked up *Kagemusha*. It was to be produced by Kurosawa Pro and Toho Pictures and distributed by Toho, with Tomoyuki Tanaka as the producer on the Toho side.

If Toho didn't make it into a film, I was ready to do just as I had told Mr. Tanaka. Deep down, however, I didn't want to. The MG (the minimum guarantee or advances on distribution revenue) for releasing *Kagemusha* on Shochiku and Toei's foreign-film circuit was estimated at around 800 million yen, but since the production would cost 1 billion yen, in the event that it failed Hashimoto Pro would need to shoulder the difference of 200 million yen. That would certainly hurt. What I feared most, however, was what might happen if Mr. Kurosawa and

I didn't agree on set. Mr. Kurosawa wouldn't budge an inch; I would also obstinately not give in. The set would spin completely out of control and collapse into extraordinary chaos. No matter what, I wanted to be excused from that kind of battle with Mr. Kurosawa.

That being the case, I was truly grateful that Toho had assumed production and absolved me of involvement in *Kagemusha*—but the finale wasn't inspired.

One day, nearly a year after shooting started on *Kagemusha*, I was chatting with the salespeople at Toho headquarters' marketing department when a member of the publicity staff for *Kagemusha* passed by.

"Ah, sensei, we didn't see you the other day at the screening."

"Yeah, I had other business to attend to."

"Do you have any plans after this?"

"Nope, nothing in particular."

"Then the third floor screening room is empty, so I'll get it set up."

Oops, I thought to myself, but it was already too late. The publicity staffer called the screening room right away to get it ready. I'd avoided the screening because I didn't want to see the film, and now I'd allowed myself to be caught in this of all places... My own social incompetence grated on me. I could have said "I have other plans," but because I had been careless enough to answer truthfully, I was going to end up watching *Kagemusha*.

The third floor screening room at Toho headquarters is small and narrow.

Watching a film alone in that screening room for my reference wasn't all that rare an occurrence. But today the circumstances were completely different.

Seated in the very middle of the room, I watched *Kagemusha* all alone. The technician would know at a glance if I nodded off or looked away. No matter how much I didn't want to see, there was nothing I could do but straighten my back and stare at the screen. It was a kind of torture.

It was tiring. I was in pain. The most painful thing about *Kagemusha* was its never-ending length of 16,201 feet and running time of 180 minutes and six seconds, which I absorbed alone—along with the awfully solemn and hollow conviction that the collaborative screenplay had come tumbling down.

"Ah, sensei, I've run into you at a good time."

I was at the coordination department at Toho headquarters when I crossed paths with their president, Mr. Matsuoka (Isao Matsuoka).

"I'd like to ask you a favor, sensei."

"*Nandessharo* (what might it be)?" Whenever I heard Mr. Matsuoka's broad Kansai accent, I immediately slipped into Kansai dialect myself.

"There's a film treatment I'd like you to read."

"Whose is it?"

"It's called *Ran*, and Kurosawa-sensei and the others wrote it."

"Huh, Team Kurosawa? What's it about?"

"It's Shakespeare's *King Lear*."

"Shakespeare's *King Lear*?" I immediately and instinctively began waving my hand to say no. "Uh-uh, there's no way I'd understand such a difficult thing."

I don't know what path the screenplay took after that, but it was decided that foreign-film distributor Herald would finance the film, and its production was announced with great fanfare.

When Toho's Mr. Matsuoka had asked me to read the screenplay, I'd turned him down, fearing a repeat of *Kagemusha*, but deep down I looked forward to the film getting produced and finished.

Mr. Kurosawa knew better than anyone that the *Kagemusha* screenplay had been a failure, so with this *Ran*, he'd be pulling all stops to regain his footing. Master Oguni was listed as one of the writers. There were three names altogether: Akira Kurosawa, Hideo Oguni, and Masato Ide. I had thought that with *Kagemusha* the collaborative screenplays had come to an end…so its resurrection depended on this Hail Mary pass of a work.

The thing is, I happened to travel to Kansai on business and to drop by Master Oguni's home. Since he worked a lot in Kyoto, he'd moved from Tokyo to near the eastern shore of Lake Biwa and taken up residence in a village below the famous Hyakusai Temple.

"Mr. Oguni, Herald is going to be doing *Ran*, aren't they."

"It's a big world out there, if someone's willing to film a script like that."

"What?"

"Hashimoto, the story of *King Lear* is told in first person by King Lear, so to speak. In which case, if you can't figure out Lear's all-important feelings, it's hopeless."

"Can't figure out Lear's feelings?"

"The characterization is shoddy."

Master Oguni had disagreed and clashed with Mr. Kurosawa during the writing process and quit after a huge fight, going home in the middle of the job. According to Master Oguni, as far as Shakespeare was concerned, the moment he wrote "King Lear" King Lear's presence and emotions were clear enough to anyone—the English royal family, the throne, the king's authority, the customs, the manners, the political structure, the aristocracy, the commoners, their relationship.

However, it wasn't so easy to translate that to our country.

In particular, if you set it in the Warring States era, you first needed to determine whether a keep lord had inherited his place or was an upstart. Then you had to think through his upbringing, from childhood to youth, and his years from the prime of life until old age, going through each important point up to the start of the drama, fleshing out how the lord appears to his retainers and subjects. Setting down his thinking, dreams, aims, and how he's lived was absolutely crucial, and if you started writing without all that, the man's all-important state of mind remained obscure, and the story became nothing more than the tale of a feudal lord in his dotage going back and forth between his children for no good reason.

I looked down and away, concerned. I'd been reminded of *Kagemusha*. In *Kagemusha*, too, the characterizations of both the double and the real Shingen were thin and barely realized. It was an odd convergence.

The Tokyo-bound bullet train that I boarded at Maibara was the last of the day—and there in the hushed car, with few passengers around me, I fell into thought.

I had only meant to make sure that Master Oguni was doing well when I stopped by his home at Hyakusai Temple; however, his wife had sent out for an extravagant bento, and Master had started drinking sake in good spirits. I couldn't possibly leave, and we'd ended up talking at length.

Whatever the circumstances, abandoning a project partway through wasn't something Master Oguni did casually. At the same time, he did have a stubborn and mulish side himself, and once he made up his mind, he wasn't above turning a deaf ear to no matter whom. Maybe Mr. Kurosawa had his reasons…other ideas that he was counting on. After the failure of *Kagemusha*, Mr. Kurosawa had his back against the wall. I couldn't imagine that he'd commit the same blunder, an absent or thin characterization, nor was I convinced that the screenplay was so poor as to deserve Master Oguni's indignation. I wondered if Mr. Kurosawa hadn't some plan or design for the mise-en-scène...something no one else could predict. In the past, he'd pulled a quick one and morphed from Monzaemon Chikamatsu into Namboku Tsuruya, and there was that formidable luck of his. When he was made to step down from directing *Tora! Tora! Tora!*, no Japanese film studios would have anything to do with him, he was cornered and out of options, but the Soviet Union had extended a hand to him out of nowhere. For the production of *Dersu Uzala*.

He had strong luck, and maybe he was wagering on something in particular with *Ran*.

The private screening of the finished *Ran* was held at a Toho theater in Yurakucho.

I attended with a light heart. I have a habit of leaving the theater immediately if a film isn't interesting. Whether it's three or five minutes in, the time doesn't matter. I avoid private screenings as much as possible because it's rude to leave once the film has started, and I only go if I'm reasonably sure or certain that it'll bear watcing from beginning to end. Today, however, I felt none of that fear or anxiety.

The theater was completely full. I don't know who hosted that screening, Herald or Toho's publicity, but with all the seats filled but no standees or auxiliary seats in use, it was quite the pro job, an impressively efficient turnout of invited viewers.

Ran began in the best mood possible amid high expectations.

As soon as it began, however, I cocked my head.

The opening was a short scene of beaters hunting down a wild boar; a feast at the end of the hunt followed. I thought it would be a scene of them roasting the various game they'd caught, a gorgeous, free and easy gathering fueled with sake, but it wasn't. Rather, their clothes tidy, with the grace and poise of Noh performers everyone piously lent their ears to the words of the feudal lord (King Lear).

All too explicitly, formalist beauty was taking priority over cinema's own realist visual aesthetic. I felt a strange discomfort, and amidst my slowly mounting anxiety that this film wasn't going to be fun, the story began in earnest.

At the hunting feast, King Lear cedes leadership of the clan to his eldest son. The king, however, is greeted with the strong words of his third son, whom he angrily disowns and banishes. The eldest son, who has become the fief-lord, acts cold and distant toward his father, and the irate King Lear tells the new lord that he isn't his only child. He takes his retainers and concubines from the first castle to go to his middle son at the second castle.

But the second son, who has heard from his brother, informs King Lear that the castle can take him in but not all the others, knowing perfectly well that his father would find this unacceptable. With no other option, still dragging his entourage with him, King Lear begins to wander the fiefdom.

Visually, Tatsuya Nakadai's King Lear is sharp and leaves a strong impression. His speech and action are crisp. But because the all-important point, how he's perceiving things, isn't as clear as it should be, there's an overbearing sense that the story is being foisted or forced on you—it feels strangely phony.

I already wanted to leave. Coming in, however, I'd seen and greeted many people in the lobby and the main hall. Herald people, Toho people, many friends and critics… Standing up and leaving the theater would be the shameless act of a heretic, simply off limits.

My gaze began to drift from the screen to fall on the backs of the audience. My seat was a little behind the center so I could see the viewers in front of me well. I usually stand right in the middle of the aisle behind the seats—in order to judge if the moviegoers are feeling entertained, or listless, or bored from how their heads and backs move.

People's response to *Ran* was clear to me then and there, to a painful degree. They were clearly perplexed. They were still giving the screen their full attention but didn't seem to know how to view this film.

I crossed my arms.

It was just as Master Oguni had fumed. The characterization was lacking at the script level; it was a clear mistake in the screenplay. No, I sensed something even more fatal than deficient characterization, and on top of that, the story structure seemed *ad hoc*.

As King Lear wanders the fiefdom with all his retainers and concubines in tow, the matter of where such a large group of people is staying every night or having their meals every day defies depiction, and the story sticks out like a sore thumb.

The audience was somehow still concentrating their attention on the screen, but there were limits to people's patience. Soon they would be unable to bear the tension, and the rest would be just tiresome.

Like *Kagemusha*, *Ran* lacked the compound eyes (objectivity) of having multiple writers working on the same scene and was a botched screenplay riddled with all the deficiencies of a one-sided subjectivity.

The Oguni residence below Hyakusai Temple on Lake Biwa's eastern shore, Master Oguni having drinks he poured himself—superimposed on the screen they floated before my eyes.

"So with *King Lear*, it's hard-going because of the material itself?"

"No, not really… It all comes down to arrangements and procedures, but *Ran* has none of that."

"Wasn't there a past Shakespeare? *Macbeth*, no? For *Hidden Fortress*? Or rather *Throne of Blood*."

"This is different from that. For *Throne of Blood*, the rooks were on board."

"The rooks?"

"You and Kikushima, Shinobu Hashimoto and Ryuzo Kikushima… The troop strength isn't what it was then."

"Now that you mention it, it felt like an all-star team of writers with so many faces lined up. Those Imaihama days were fun."

"Yeah, it's just too much of a difference compared to that era. Plus, it would be one thing if I were there but with just Kurosawa and Ide… No, for Ide, Kurosawa is too…"

Master Oguni suddenly disappeared and, surprised, I stared at the screen.

Suddenly a massive war was beginning.

With a large army the eldest and middle sons besiege King Lear at the front and rear gates of the third castle, that of the disinherited third son who has left the keep and relocated to the neighboring fiefdom. There the third son has taken fief-lord Fujimaki's daughter as his wife—in his and his troops' absence, and in spite of a contingent from the first castle, King Lear was allowed unimpeded entry into the third castle.

This, however, is by the eldest and middle sons' design. Neighboring Fujimaki has taken their brother as a son-in-law and gained his troops; King Lear occupies the castle that has been left empty. No doubt, Fujimaki will raise a large army and enter the third castle soon in order to prop up King Lear and to attack the first and second castles. Before Fujimaki can embark on an attempt to control their whole fiefdom, and to stamp out the root evil, King Lear must be taken out. While there's some logic to it, what a scheming path to parricide this is.

Yet the battle scenes are terribly intense.

King Lear's retainers are slaughtered one after the other, the castle is set on fire, and white smoke and flames begin to spread. His sword broken in the melee, King Lear no longer even has a blade with which to commit seppuku.

A long shot of the burning castle—an old man wanders out of

the inflamed keep on unsteady feet. In a white kimono, his white hair standing on end, it's the wraithlike King Lear, who has lost his mind.

"Ah!" I nearly cried in spite of myself. Against the backdrop of the burning castle, the wraithlike King Lear looked—for a moment, like Akira Kurosawa.

But it was just a momentary illusion, and in the next scene, a full shot with the army in the foreground, it was clearly Tatsuya Nakadai's King Lear.

The story not coming to a pause even when the third castle burns to the ground, ups and downs follow.

In the confusion of the castle attack, a subordinate of the second son kills the eldest son (the fief-lord) with a firearm, and the second son takes over the first castle as the lord of the realm. There he's ensnared by the passionate wiles of the eldest son's wife. She hails from the clan that once resided in the castle. Her relatives all killed by King Lear, forced to marry the eldest son, she bears a ceaseless and venomous grudge for King Lear and his clan.

Meanwhile, wandering insane, King Lear stays the night at the home of the son of a clan he has slaughtered, a young man whom he spared but blinded in exchange, and there hears the sound of a flute that transcends vengeance, etc… The film has all the engrossing ingredients of a period piece: the intense strife and massacre of battle scenes; the fateful affairs of men and women; the pathos of a ghastly King Lear alternating between mad exuberance and sanity; a lamenting tale of karma that transcends debts and grudges. Even so, it's curiously uninteresting. The high style and formal beauty of the marvelous mise-en-scène notwithstanding, no necessity binds the scenes together, and it's hard not to feel that disparate things are being lined up: here's this, and there's that.

I understood by now.

Excessive identification… No, it's beyond excessive.

It's true that characters in a drama don't come alive unless their creator has identified with them to a certain extent. However, there are limits.

The moment the insane King Lear staggering out of a roaring castle of flames looked like Mr. Kurosawa—I'd known it since then.

The screenplay of the film Ran *is by King Lear himself…or rather, by Mr. Kurosawa writing as if he were King Lear himself.*

Mr. Kurosawa's straightforward aim came across well. If that was the case, there was no need for a theme, a story, or any characterization. It all simply needed to proceed as the character intended and wished. The author and a character appearing in his work aren't identical, though.

They are distinct individuals with their own personalities, and even the author, barred from stepping right in, is limited to guessing or imagining a character's state of mind.

Going ahead even so and assuming those feelings clearly surpasses the limits of identification, so you lose objectivity and end up with something self-satisfied and self-righteous that merely asserts the character's ego.

A screenplay written solely from a character's subjective viewpoint, from which all objectivity has fallen away, tends to strike others as stuck up and awfully pushy.

I felt rather suffocated and couldn't stand to watch the film anymore.

On screen, insane King Lear wears a crown of grass, happy to think it a helm. He comes to his senses now and again when it's convenient. The fairly phony picture suddenly faded out, disappeared—and turned into the Oguni residence below Hyakusai Temple, on Lake Biwa's east shore. Master Oguni was pouring his own drinks with curious feeling.

"Kurosawa was a lucky director, yeah."

" … "

"I've worked with all the famous directors. Every one of them struggled…agonized over screenplays. Because a film depends on it. And in that, Kurosawa was blessed. Because he had what you might call an exclusive writing team."

" … "

"The Kurosawa picture. Whatever material that happened to get picked up and the total skill of the writers at that point in time, directly reflected, there's your Kurosawa picture."

The conversation paused.

"But Master, didn't Mr. Kurosawa go through a lot as the leader too?"

"Oh sure, he must have, but that doesn't add up to much."

"No, that's not true."

"Why not?"

"Mr. Kurosawa told me something once. Suspecting that one day I might turn my hand to directing he said, 'Hashimoto, do you even know what the most crucial thing is when you direct? If you're writing the screenplay alone, then fine, but if you're teaming up with other writers, the most important thing is not the to-do on the set. How you handle the other writers, first and foremost, is what'll make or break it.'"

Master Oguni stared silently at me.

"'The staff and actors on the set you can just yell at. But not so with writers. If you yell at them, they yell right back, and if you don't, they take it easy and cut corners. No bunch is harder to handle or to stomach. If you want them to do their job, every so often you need to crank out stuff that they can't match. Then they get serious and rouse themselves and give you more than anyone knew they had in them.'"

"…"

"As far as Mr. Kurosawa was concerned, he was furiously trying to get that kind of effort out of you, Master, and me, and others, as if his life depended on it. And…" I took a breath. "I've done eight Kurosawa films, but haven't you and Mr. Kikushima done even more?"

"Yeah, maybe ten? About the same for Kikushima."

"You, Mr. Kikushima, me… Gathering a quirky, hard-to-tether bunch like us and having us work on a string of jobs, together… Do you think anyone else could have done it?"

Master Oguni was silent.

It was still early evening in the village on the eastern shore of Lake Biwa, but there was not a sound.

"I'm afraid only Mr. Kurosawa could pull it off… And on that point, I think there never was, nor will there ever be, another Kurosawa… Going forward, I don't think we'll ever see a filmmaker build a formidable team of writers and lead it himself the way Mr. Kurosawa did."

Master Oguni poured himself another, drank, and said, "It's certainly as you say." He had yet another, filling his own glass again. "But that's all over now."

With that, he lit a cigarette and inhaled, his eyes narrowing.

"See, the people really were all there. For the first half, you, Shinobu Hashimoto, were the ace pitcher, and for the latter half it was Ryuzo Kikushima…Japanese cinema's peerless stars. But first Hashimoto leaves, followed by Kikushima…then on top of that, even me, the reliever, quits… With just him and Ide it can't be done. The collaborative writing of Team Kurosawa that produced many a masterpiece and critical success for Japanese cinema has collapsed with *Ran*… It's over."

The film *Ran*, however, was not over yet. A terrible battle has begun—with a hail of bullets. In order to rescue his father, King Lear, the third son leads his troops from Fujimaki's neighboring realm and fights the army of the second son, the fief-lord. The third son routs the second son's army and discovers and rescues King Lear, who has collapsed while wandering the plains.

The battle scenes, far more dynamic than that of the previous film, *Kagemusha*, are fun to watch. Once the drama returns, however, the screenplay's shortcomings come to the fore, and the sense of solidity dissipates. King Lear regains his sanity and hugs close his third son. So it is that only his third son truly loves him as family. Yet, the feature's most moving scene is somehow bland, as though it's not the viewer's concern, and the movingness is lost on us strangers to an almost curious degree.

The third son puts King Lear over the back of his horse and begins to ride home. Yet, ambushed at a seemingly safe location, the third son is shot and killed. A crazed King Lear clings to his son, and from the extreme shock, he expires while clutching his child in his arms.

Meanwhile, the neighboring Ayabe army has assaulted the first castle, and death nears for the second son and his wife as well. Thus, King Lear's progeny all perish, and with the ruling Ichimonji family no more—*Ran* (the "revolt" or "disturbance") ends.

Kagemusha was released in 1980, and *Ran* in 1985, so five years stood in between them. I assumed that the screenplay for *Kagemusha* had been written before *Ran*.

As I discovered many years later, however, the screenplay for *Ran* had been written before *Kagemusha*. Because *Ran* would cost so much to produce, no company was willing to pick it up. The impasse necessitated writing *Kagemusha*, which became a film first.

Ran was an earlier screenplay than *Kagemusha*, so sequentially it's *Ran* and then *Kagemusha*.

Ran as an earlier screenplay than *Kagemusha*—for me, as a scenario writer, this fact taught me that a certain order and progression underlay even the succession of failed works and collapse of the collaborative screenplay.

The collaborative screenplay's collapse evidently began with *Ran*. *Ran* was the harbinger, and it manifested as a decisive failure in the form of *Kagemusha*. The collaborative screenplay, which had given the world of cinema twenty-three ambitious Kurosawa works over the course of thirty-nine years since the year after the end of the war, lost its raison d'être with the hypertrophy of accumulated and layered errors in the last two works and came to a full stop—ending for eternity, never to be resurrected.

CHAPTER FIVE:
WHAT FOLLOWED FOR MR. KUROSAWA

Among the things that Mr. Kurosawa said to me, one made a lasting impression.

"Hashimoto, writers have autobiographies, right?"

"Yes, they do."

"All of them are interesting to read. Because a lot of things happen in a person's life. But my own autobiography won't happen until I've run out of works to write... That is, I think it'll be the very last thing I write."

I also had that impression, so I nodded.

He continued, "That's why I think of an autobiography as a person's last testament."

I don't know when Mr. Kurosawa began writing *Dreams*. But when nearly forty years of collaborative screenplay writing had ended with *Ran*—no, *Kagemusha*—and he began writing by himself, I think this was the first thing he began work on.

Dreams is an omnibus film of eight dreams that Mr. Kurosawa had experienced since childhood, his autobiography so to speak.

Film directing is physically intensive work, and Mr. Kurosawa was seventy-nine years old, nearly eighty. Therefore, it might be his final film. It wouldn't be odd if he wrote the screenplay, went to the set, and finished it with such a sense and preparedness in mind.

The screening of *Dreams* took place at the Toho Theater in Ginza of all places, the same venue as *Ran*. Five years had passed since *Ran*.

If I've read a screenplay, I don't see the film. Reading a screenplay is the same as seeing the film, and there's no reason to see the same film twice. Yet, though I had read the screenplay for *Dreams*, I went to the screening. *Dreams* was Mr. Kurosawa's autobiography, in other words, his last work. For me, it was also his last will and testament.

Yet, when the viewing started, as if to duck my investment and mindset the film on screen was gentle, lighthearted, and enjoyable.

Dreams is comprised of eight episodes, the first of which is "Sunshine Through the Rain" (the Fox Takes a Bride). There was a nameplate on the upper right-hand side of the black post of the main gate reading "Kurosawa" that hadn't been in the screenplay. Seeing it, I could almost sense some of the emotion that Mr. Kurosawa had poured into this film.

Both the first story and the second, "The Peach Orchard" (The Peach Festival of the Hina Dolls), made me recall my own childhood, and my heart ached with sweet reminiscences. Mr. Kurosawa was eight years older than me, but our generational sensibility was probably the same.

The third story, "The Blizzard," was too much. A frightening snow woman kept attacking on and on, and it was tiresome.

I wondered if *Dreams* would show Mr. Kurosawa's best and worst as they were. Each story was independent of the others, however, so it wasn't as though they were linked. As such, the weaknesses would be contained within a story and not carry over, so you could watch the next story with a fresh mind. I was grateful for the omnibus format.

The fourth story was "The Tunnel."

A heavily armed troop emerges from the darkness of a tunnel.

I held my breath in intense shock and reflexively let out a muffled cry. *Yes! This, this is it!* It was what I had long awaited, the first beautiful image of color film that I had seen.

"Nice, nice. This is good! Mr. Kurosawa!"

When movies were made in black and white, images were made of light and shadow, and many films emerged that foregrounded the aesthetic of black and white interweaving—precious, but not so rare. Meanwhile, for color films, which weren't a contrast between light and shadow as color entered everything, achieving what might be called filmic beauty was beyond difficult, a nearly impossible feat. Hence, in its use of darkness and light, this scene in the fourth story of *Dreams* might be considered a precious monument that achieved, by Mr. Kurosawa's hand and probably for the first time in the world for color film, a cinematic aesthetics.

I was delighted, and my entire body was jiggling with joy.

The fifth story was "Crows."

When I read the scenario, this short entry, 37 or 38 half-sheets long, was the one I liked the most. It was a lovely and at the same time somehow profoundly sad story.

But when I saw it filmed, and parts of paintings, a covered wagon on the drawbridge, women doing laundry, started moving, and people in motion entered into paintings, the fun of it made me gasp and sucked me into the screen.

The story itself, though, is unbearably sad. The painter Van Gogh's head is wrapped in bandages so a young Mr. Kurosawa asks him, "Are you all right? You seem to be injured."

"Ah, this… Yesterday I was painting a self-portrait, but I couldn't get the ear right…so I cut it off."

Is there a sadder story in the world?

At the same time, with Van Gogh's sliced-off ear, what I had imagined to be ninety-nine percent certain but had no proof for and couldn't conclude seemed to take on clear contours. That is, what I yearned to know most about Mr. Kurosawa concerned the creative method that affected the quality of screenplays: namely, why he had shifted from the "writer leading off" approach, which had a relatively high success rate, to the flawed "straight-to-final draft" style...and Mr. Kurosawa himself was hinting at his motivations here in this fifth story of *Dreams*.

When I finished reading the screenplay for *Kagemusha* and was astonished by its unanticipated poorness, I was stunned by how far the road had diverged and grown apart between us two as scenario writers. We had once walked the same path, but at some point we'd gone our different ways...and I could only think that it had happened with *Seven Samurai*.

When we finished *Seven Samurai*, as a craftsman who wrote scenarios I'd gained my compass and ruler (the criterion, the motions, and something like know-how), but I couldn't help but feel that Mr. Kurosawa, on the contrary, had thrown away all the unique and unmatched tools of the trade he'd already acquired, the rules of sequence, the leaps, the cheerful abandon.

Well, why? How come? The reasons remained a vast, deep, and murky puzzle, but now it's clear to me. In the same way that Van Gogh had cut off his own ear, through which noise entered, Mr. Kurosawa had thrown away as nuisances the whole gamut of knacks and tricks (his ruler and compass) that came in the handiest during advance preparation.

Mr. Kurosawa hated, was exceedingly put off by, anticipation.

"Unless you're a genius, you can't see the end from the starting point."

During the writing process that equaled a marathon, his scenario philosophy, not keeping your chin tucked in corresponded to reading ahead and fixating on some far point when the going got tough. Since you couldn't see the bend after the next one, you ended up short of breath in no time, and your legs stopped pumping.

The premise of his scenario philosophy, "You can't stop working even for a day," was this strict ban on looking ahead.

Since we weren't geniuses, we might try to read ahead but simply couldn't. If we attempted foresight and did see, then having seen something we shouldn't be able to see meant that it might be an illusion... Proceeding on the basis of an illusion was the most dangerous thing of all, so every attempt to read ahead was admonished.

Mr. Kurosawa must have plunged into thought when *Seven Samurai* was finished.

Derived from *A Samurai's Day*, which never saw the light of day, and *The Lives of Japanese Swordsmen*, a fey child begat by chance, *Seven Samurai* was sudden mutation as success case... After that, no matter how strenuously he pushed the "writer leading off" approach, he couldn't count on chance byproducts and sudden mutations, and as a result, there was no hope of measuring up to *Seven Samurai*, let alone exceeding it (put differently, it could be said that *Seven Samurai* was the ultimate endpoint of the "writer leading off" approach).

So, what to do now?

No, before that, it was necessary to rethink, from the ground up, the doctrine of a writer leading off.

No matter how efficiently he put his experience (his ruler and compass and such) to use, there seemed to be no way of making anything new of interest. That is, experience manifested its prowess and handiness most when it came to theme, story, characterization, composition, all those things that required foresight and reading ahead. If the framework relied on something as uncertain as foresight and reading ahead, then even before one bit of the work has come into being, you have formulated most of it via vague foresight. It gets cramped into that framework—becoming puny and deformed.

As long as the customary advance planning wasn't jettisoned whole, there was no potential for new work. It followed that a preparatory draft for the final draft, in the form of a writer leading off with a first draft after meetings, was out of the question. Henceforth, a "straight-to-final draft" would do, no theme, no story, no characterization, and no composition (I don't know what else to think but that Mr. Kurosawa doubled down and decided that it was ideal and only natural if all those things that belonged to advance preparation emerged of their own as the work progressed and took on a manifest form when the work was complete).

It was our crossroads—with *Seven Samurai* I finally acquired a compass and ruler and somehow managed to enter into the company of craftsmen, while in contrast Mr. Kurosawa underwent my speculated shift and threw away his ruler and compass. Then, if Mr. Kurosawa was no longer a craftsman, what exactly did he turn into? If it was the nature of the artist to cut off his own ear like Van Gogh, had Mr. Kurosawa, too, turned into an artist, as he seemed to be suggesting? Yes, indeed. Mr. Kurosawa ended up transforming from a great craftsman of the highest skill into an individual artist.

His way of writing screenplays changed completely from *I Live in Fear,* just after *Seven Samurai*—but I failed to notice that this followed from the difference between craftsman and artist. The invisible divide steadily widened, however, and from around the three great "straight-to-final draft" hits, *Yojimbo, Sanjuro,* and *High and Low,* it became a clearly visible and acute gap. Thinking on it now, the disgrace of *Tora! Tora! Tora!*

would never visit a craftsman in servitude to capital; it was a tragedy that occurred because he'd become nothing other than an artist who desired to shoot as he liked…no, who could only shoot as he liked.

During *Dodes'ka-den*, made at the nadir of his fortunes, I didn't discern any special artistic consciousness on Mr. Kurosawa's part, perhaps because the scale of the budget and everything else was extremely limited. But he came back like a phoenix and finished filming *Dersu Uzala* in a red state as a state guest of sorts, and after he returned to Japan, with *Ran* on which he wagered all, the consciousness soared and progressed into something decisive.

The Van Gogh story in "Crows," the fifth episode of *Dreams*, clearly indicates this.

Because the peaceful scenery around him doesn't lend itself to a painting, the young Mr. Kurosawa won't paint. Van Gogh chastises him for this.

"Why won't you paint? It's not that things that look like paintings become paintings. If you look closely at anything in nature, it becomes beautiful. Nature becomes a dream-like picture and leaps into me."

All you need to do is focus on whatever you're going to paint.

In film, too, all you need do is focus on the first scene.

That is, in film the first scene is the most important, and dearest, and as long as he renders that into image and focuses on it, thanks to his sensibility and talent the screenplay should emerge on its own. The first scenes of *Ran* and *Kagemusha* amply prove this.

Ran's opening scene is the hunt, but that's the prologue, and the next scene's heading is clearly given as "Jumonji" (meaning the character for the numeral ten, which looks like a cross or plus sign, while "Ichimonji" means the character for the numeral one, which looks like a bar or minus sign). In an enclosure made by the Jumonji banner draped in the mountains are all the key personages. King Lear (Hidetora Ichimonji) names his eldest son his heir and expels his third son after an emotional clash, and the stormy tale begins. The symbolic crest visible on the background banner, this could be termed a high-handed one-act play.

In *Kagemusha*, by way of a prologue, we read that there are three men with the same face at the Takeda manse in Tsutsujigasaki and begin with a mysterious, bizarre scene with all three of them, Shingen Takeda, Shingen's younger brother Nobukado, and the double.

Simply focusing on the opening scene without even determining the outline of the story (beginning, development, climax, ending), envisioning the next scene from there, then proceeding likewise—writing the whole scenario in such a manner falls outside of the realm of artisanal skill or work and can only be described as the doing of an artist.

Moreover, with *Ran*, Mr. Kurosawa was making an even bigger wager as an artist. By the time he finished filming *Dersu Uzala* in the Soviet Union and returned to Japan, he was already sixty-five years old, and he couldn't have expected to make many more films going forward. So, for the next "King Lear," he wanted to bet his winning chip no matter the outcome.

Yet, conflict broke out between him and Master Oguni when they got to work.

Although setting out without having decided the theme and story was customary after *I Live in Fear* and the shift to the "straight-to-final draft," because the story of King Lear was multifaceted, Master Oguni advocated for their importance. Mr. Kurosawa wouldn't hear of it, and as a result Master Oguni compromised on theme and story. The tale did have its flow, and if they followed it, things wouldn't get too far out of hand.

On the next issue of characterization, however, they clashed head-on.

Because Master Oguni thought that this related to the drama's foundations, he wouldn't give in. Master Oguni usually ignored trivial matters, but he always spoke up about crucial elements that had to do with a work's foundations, and Mr. Kurosawa, who knew this about him, valued and acceded to his views.

But not this time.

King Lear's personality and such were already clear from his speech and behavior in the first scene, a kind of one-act play, and it would suffice to extrapolate from there. Fleshing out his character from scratch, that is to say, advance preparation, was unnecessary. Mr. Kurosawa had made a certain decision in private.

In order to make the story interesting, and the character more profound and multifaceted, rather than the customary method he would take the purer, robust, and direct track of embodying King Lear's feelings... Having decided that writing while putting himself into King Lear's shoes would make the script new and interesting, he had bet on it. Hence he stubbornly refused to acquiesce, and Master Oguni, who scripted eleven of Mr. Kurosawa's films and served as navigator and command tower, quit writing and took the extraordinary step of withdrawing from the project and going home.

With Master Oguni gone and only Ide left, Mr. Kurosawa proceeded to write feeling himself as King Lear. Even if Ide thought that this was wrong, all alone, he couldn't deter Mr. Kurosawa.

Normally, in writing a scenario, if the writer doesn't identify with (insert his feelings into) the characters to some extent, the characters don't get going. But there's a limit to this identification, and if you go there you make sure through revision (objectification) that you haven't gone too far. If there's excessive identification, the characters become self-righteous, and the work self-satisfied and pushy.

Yet Mr. Kurosawa went beyond the frame of mere identification and felt as King Lear—in other words, since he was King Lear, and he understood himself perfectly fine, he pressed on with the drama. But because others didn't comprehend King Lear's feelings as well as King Lear did, they couldn't keep up with his tumultuous fate. When King Lear expressed surprise, anger, or grief, the audience watching him experienced a moment's delay. The pause was a moment of interpretation: since he was expressing surprise he must be surprised; since he seemed angry he must be angry; and since he was grieving he must be sad. In following a movie this is terribly tiring.

On top of that, because the story hadn't been assembled as a composition, the scenes seemed skewered together (one whole clump after the next). In the absence of organic connections from scene to scene and of a sense of speed that comes from the occasional leap, the story dragged.

The work failed as a result.

If *Ran* had been made into a film soon after the screenplay's completion, then the prudent Mr. Kurosawa would have recognized its folly, and the work called *Kagemusha* would not have been made. Unfortunately, because no backers were willing to put up the high cost of producing *Ran*, there was no other option but to precede it with *Kagemusha*. Since its screenplay was rushed, it committed the same errors as *Ran*, a lack of characterization and a faulty composition.

No, in *Ran*'s case it was just King Lear, but with *Kagemusha* Mr. Kurosawa put down his feelings as both the double and Shingen. Splitting into two and amplifying itself, the self-satisfied high-handedness surpassed *Ran*'s, yielding a woefully tiresome film.

Seen through a craftsman's eyes, the failures of *Ran* and *Kagemusha* simply expose a complete lack of advance planning in the writing and the "straight-to-final draft" system's inherent contradictions and irrationalities, which burgeoned with the months and years—and at the final stage erupted like a volcano.

Artists sometimes fail, and make big mistakes.

No, Mr. Kurosawa didn't become an artist by choice. I believe it was a step and a route he had to take to grope his way toward new works whether he liked it or not. Yet, because he took the path of an artist… While craftsmen rarely taste failure in exchange of being denied a resounding success, artists wager on an ever-fine line between success and failure, and it is their destiny to be hounded by the fateful outcome. It was because Akira Kurosawa had become an artist that he failed.

So then, did Akira Kurosawa return once more to the craftsman's road with *Dreams*?

No, once an artist's habits become second nature, it's your lifelong lot from which you cannot secede until the moment you stop drawing breath. For him, whether it was *Dreams* or something else, he could only engage with material as an artist. Only, in *Dreams*, he focused a cool, piercing gaze on the weaknesses of *Ran* and *Kagemusha*. He didn't repeat the same mistakes.

Even regarding the structure, as *Dreams* is the story of his own life, lining them up in order from childhood, adolescence, youth, middle age, and old age suffices. Moreover, the introduction and beginning of each episode progresses the story in the proper "kishotenketsu" narrative structure unlike the singular ones in *Ran* and *Kagemusha* that swing for the fences. As for characterization, although he himself is the main character he doesn't over-identify, and he lets others take on movement, speech, and action and resolutely stays on the receiving end for a balanced and stable character development.

In addition, while *Ran* and *Kagemusha* achieved a new filmic aesthetic through compilations of formal beauty and their taut, strong handling of battle scenes, in *Dreams* he marshals that experience to relentlessly pursue a color-film cinematic aesthetics through camerawork. Since some of the episodes fail or fall short it cannot be called a perfect work of art, but perhaps, for the first time in the world, color image and sound has engendered… placed a hand, a foot, on being an artwork.

(You could say that *Dreams'* success owes to reflecting on the failures of *Ran* and *Kagemusha* as well as to the two works' pursuit of formal beauty and tireless obsession for achieving an aesthetics for color films.)

"Mount Fuji in Red," the sixth story of *Dreams*, and "The Weeping Demon," the seventh, are bores. They're on the loquacious side, the stories drag, and it's rather tiresome.

However, the next story, the eighth "Village of the Watermills," is magnificent.

> The flow of a pretty brook... I've never seen such a beautiful shot of flowing water in any film.
>
> That clear, cool water continues to flow like a soft breeze over the algae on the waterbed.
>
> On the shore, wildflowers of many colors are blooming all around, and a water wheel turns slowly drumming a rhythm.
>
> The mysterious speech of the 103-year-old man (Chishu Ryu) from the watermill and the elegant funeral that follows—all of it is underlain by the beauty of this water.
>
> The funeral is just splendid, like a bustling festival.
>
> Various instruments ring out, like the trumpet and trombone, and the clothes of both the men and women are terribly idiosyncratic and gaudy but oddly suit them. The old man from the watermill takes the lead, ringing Shinto bells, and the elegant funeral procession marches in unison to the tune of an Oriental march.

It somehow feels good; with this kind of funeral, anyone might fly away without feeling death's sorrow. It seems like a paradise unseen in this world—no other images and sounds fit the title of "dream" so perfectly.

Wasn't *Dreams* a world of beauty the cinematic arts (film) had attained at long last?

I didn't stand when the screening finished, staying in my seat. It was really too bad. If I had been the producer, I would have proposed the following to Mr. Kurosawa.

Cut out the third story, "The Blizzard," the sixth story, "Mount Fuji in Red," and the seventh story, "The Weeping Demon." No, if you delelted all that the film will come out too short, so at least "The Blizzard." At any rate, scrap "The Blizzard."

Because "The Blizzard" is physically exhausting, when you reach the sixth, "Mount Fuji in Red," and the seventh, "The Weeping Demon," the fatigue surges back and exacerbates their actual congestion. My hunch as someone who has dealt with film for years is that as long as you get rid of "The Blizzard," the sixth and the seventh stories would feel less tiresome. So just by dropping "The Blizzard," the film would be cleaner and come together almost unrecognizably well.

But no, dropping "The Blizzard" would not be so easy.

It would shorten the length of the film, and that might have contractual issues on the business side, but first and foremost, there would be an immediate firestorm of moral accountability. It wouldn't be easy to apologize to the actors nor to acknowledge the work of the staff and obtain their understanding. "The Blizzard" was filmed on a set made of cotton and salt and Styrofoam. You'd be beaten black and blue by everyone involved. I can handle all that for you, though. So please, drop the third story.

What would Mr. Kurosawa say, I wondered.

"Ah, Hashimoto, it's been bothering me, too, I'll drop it then, sure… That would make it much tidier. Since each of the stories stands alone, doing so wouldn't change the tune of it."

This, however, was a too naive and self-serving fantasy, and the real Mr. Kurosawa would turn pale and unleash his wrath, his eyebrows standing on end. "How dare you?!"

Even so, I wouldn't give up. For the sake of this film, I'd fight to the bitter end. If I remained unusually persistent, perhaps Mr. Kurosawa might rethink it a little, endowed as he was with that filmic intuition and sensibility of his.

No, while we're at it, I'd rather cut the sixth and seventh stories as well. If you do that, then Van Gogh's flock of crows flying away in the fifth story, "Crows," connects to the shot of the beautiful flowing river in the eighth story, "Village of the Watermills." It's thrilling just to think about. Minus the parts that don't work, *Dreams* stands perfectly, on both feet and not just on one leg, as a work of art, as Akira Kurosawa's new representative work for all the world to see… But this was the screening of the finished film, the completion of which had long since transpired, and I was just a bystander with no connection to *Dreams*, so there was no point in my ambling about such a virtual world.

When I left the theater where the screening was held, I headed for the Tokyo Kaikan not far from the Imperial Palace moat. I was showing my face at an after-screening party for the first time since entering the industry—but I wanted to see Mr. Kurosawa.

The party at Tokyo Kaikan was packed with people, its atmosphere glittering. There were tables scattered here and there, but people stood around eating and drinking, and the conversations were lively.

I wove my way through the noisy crowd looking for Mr. Kurosawa, and I ran into the cameraman, Taka (Takao Saito).

"Taka, the scene where the soldiers come out of the tunnel was fantastic."

"Ah, that one, when I looked at it through a magnifying glass, the

222

Funeral scene in "Village of the Watermills," the eighth story of *Dreams*.
Chishu Ryu in the center.

image came on to me with a terrible intensity, so I thought...this is gonna be good."

"How did you film the water in the river at the watermill?"

Taka smiled broadly. "Dredging the bottom of the river, planting algae, the setup was a big hassle."

"Where's Mr. Kurosawa?"

"He's here, he's here. There!"

Looking in the direction that Taka was pointing, I recognized the tall Mr. Kurosawa at a glance. He was with an art guy, Muraki (Yoshiro Muraki), and another person who seemed to be an assistant director, and was weaving between tables and clusters of people to say hi to the guests.

I waited for Mr. Kurosawa to approach me, then stepped forward to greet him.

Mr. Kurosawa stopped and looked at me head-on. For a moment, he had a bewildered expression. For me to show my face at an after-party—for Mr. Kurosawa too, it was an unlikely encounter in an unanticipated place. In any case, it was the first time we had seen each other since the production of *Kagemusha* a decade ago.

"Mr. Kurosawa."

"…"

"Of all your films," I said, "I think today's is the best."

Mr. Kurosawa didn't reply but nodded once, twice. Then he broke out in a smile. He seemed honestly happy. It had been more than forty years since Mr. Kurosawa and I had met, but this was the first time I'd ever seen him with such an untroubled, happy smile.

That smiling face—was the last I ever saw of Mr. Kurosawa.

A film review or two that called *Dreams* a failure caught my attention. Different people experience movies differently, but something about them made me wonder.

What kinds of reviews had the people who considered *Dreams* a failure given *Kagemusha* and *Ran*?

The relationship between film journalists (the film reporters at newspapers and critics, etc.) and we on the production side is one of give-and-take. There was an incident once. In the evening edition of a newspaper, a film studio had taken out a huge advertisement announcing a film premiere; however, in the arts column in the same issue, a film reporter who had seen the film at a screening lambasted it as a failure, beating it black and blue. The studio's publicity department was furious and announced that they would no longer advertise in that newspaper in what became a huge dispute.

After the incident, studio publicity departments started to vilify film reporters and critics who gave bad reviews and stopped sending them screening invitations and tickets. Badmouthing a film was a form of obstructing business, and if it wasn't any good they shouldn't write anything and spare themselves some space. That was the argument of the film studios (the production side).

Not receiving those screening invitations and tickets was inconvenient, and so, in order not to antagonize publicity departments and be seen as adders, film reporters and critics ended up holding back on scathing reviews and negative reporting as long as the faults weren't egregious.

A much-awaited Kurosawa film is released after five years. You catch the screening, but it's boring and tiresome. But it's the first Kurosawa film in a while, and the newspapers and weeklies have to say something in their arts columns. At the same time, you can't say that it's boring or tiresome or a failure, so you force yourself to find, or make up, praiseworthy bits. For *Kagemusha*, seeing the film is fulfilling! I was shaken to the core of my soul! Living, breathing pictures of samurai, the epitome of formal and cinematic beauty! Et cetera, et cetera, a great storm of rave reviews. With *Ran*, there was an even louder chorus of unqualified praise in film reporting.

Even so, having to laud the tiresome *Kagemusha* and then to fanatically extoll the boring *Ran* didn't sit well with the film reporters and critics; they were ticked off and harbored a lot of pent-up resentment and stress. With *Dreams*, because some of the episodes failed, when one person took issue others immediately piled on, and together they declared the film a failure.

There are sayings like "taking Edo's revenge in Nagasaki" and "the sins of the father visited upon the son." It seemed as though the innocent *Dreams* was paying for the huge failures called *Kagemusha* and *Ran* being exalted and adorned with shiny phrases.

I have doubts about this sort of collusion and the give-and-take between the mass media and film producers, and I'd like to see critics be more trenchant with their yeas and nays.

For example, even if they ruled that *Ran* and *Kagemusha* were failures, since Mr. Kurosawa had made so many superior films and a failure or two were a matter of course, audiences would take it in stride and look forward to the next work.

On the contrary, when something that you didn't enjoy receives praise as being interesting, or as a masterpiece, you're left cold. You start to wonder if such critical praise isn't just flattery intended for Mr. Kurosawa, or worse, a form of recalcitrance and intimidation conducted on his behalf, and antipathy towards Mr. Kurosawa himself deepens. The mass media is influential when it comes to Mr. Kurosawa's films. How many huge fans of Kurosawa were pushed into becoming anti-Kurosawa by *Ran* and *Kagemusha* and the media's advocacy for them? In my own circle too there had been passionate Kurosawa fans, but the two films and the surrounding din ended up making them anti-Kurosawa. It's really a shame, regrettable.

When someone asks me which of Mr. Kurosawa's films I enjoyed the most, I answer without hesitation, "*Seven Samurai*." But if I'm asked which one I like best, I reply "*Dreams*" without hesitation and add, "As a filmmaker's last will and testament, there's no greater work."

When *Seven Samurai* premiered, it didn't come in at the top of the year's best ten. Yet, with the twentieth century over, when it comes to selecting the best hundred films of the last hundred years, its release-year ranking immaterial, *Seven Samurai* is number one.

Hence, with the passage of time, I wonder if the representative work of his early period will be *Seven Samurai*, and that of his later years, *Dreams*.

Mr. Kurosawa made two films following *Dreams*, *Rhapsody in August* and *Madadayo*, but since I'd already seen the autobiographical *Dreams*, which should be considered his testament, I never saw those other two.

It was at a lodge in Kita-Karuizawa, where my eldest daughter worked and where I'd gone to escape the Tokyo heat, on September 6, 1998, eight years after I'd seen his memorable smile at Tokyo Kaikan, that I learned of Mr. Kurosawa's passing.

After being interviewed by Kyodo News, which filed the first report, I absently did the math. I was eight years younger, so Mr. Kurosawa was— resting in peace after 88 years.

I wanted to try to attend the funeral, but illness forbade me, and so I sent the following condolence telegram to the farewell gathering.

> Goodbye, Mr. Kurosawa.
>
> Mr. Hisaita, Mr. Kikushima, Kei Uegusa, Ide, Master Oguni—and even Mr. Kurosawa have all departed from this world, and now the only screenplay writer left is me who, decrepit with age, going in and out of hospitals, cannot even attend the farewell gathering.
>
> I want to ask a favor of our leader, Mr. Kurosawa. Tell everyone, "Hashimoto'll be here soon." Leave some space for me to sit with my legs crossed.
>
> It will probably be only a little while, so until then, Mr. Kurosawa, from Kita-Karuizawa where it's sleeting, goodbye.

EPILOGUE

Ryuzo Kikushima

It happened shortly after Emperor Hirohito passed away and the era name changed to Heisei.

One day, I was told by one of the old-timers at the Japan Writers Guild, Mr. Toshio Yasumi, "Hashimoto, Kikushima's condition isn't very good."

"I heard it was bad, but is it really that bad?"

"Yeah...liver cancer. He was at a hospital in Isawa, near Kofu in Yamanashi Prefecture, but it wasn't looking good so he returned to Tokyo, and now he's at Toho University Hospital in Ohashi. It sounds like he doesn't have much longer."

"What?"

"You should go pay him a visit as soon as possible."

Toho University Hospital, in Ohashi, Meguro Ward, wasn't very far from my house. As I'd been admitted there before, I more or less knew my way around, and I went there right away. His private room in the inpatient ward was on the right-hand side of a long, narrow corridor.

I stood in front of a room that had "Ryuzo Kikushima" on the nameplate and knocked, but there was no answer. I waited a moment, then knocked again, but there was still no answer, so with trepidation I turned the knob and opened the door, and Mr. Kikushima was there lying on his back in bed. But I didn't see his wife, Mrs. Miyako Kikushima, anywhere. It seemed as though she had gone out shopping or something.

As I stood for a while at the entrance, Mr. Kikushima, barely conscious, dreamily twisted his head a bit.

"Mr. Kikushima! It's Hashimoto, Hashimoto! Can you tell?!"

"Ah...ah..." Mr. Kikushima's face was strained with pain. It wasn't clear if he knew who I was. I started to feel terribly sad.

"Mr. Kikushima, you have to get well!"

"Ah...ah..."

"Mr. Kikushima, you can't die—you have to get well... You and I are the rooks. Not just in the Japan Writers Guild, but for Team Kurosawa too, Mr. Kikushima, you and I were the rooks."

"Ah...ah..."

"But, Mr. Kikushima, why did you give up on Team Kurosawa? You really didn't have a choice up to around *Yojimbo* and *Sanjuro*. But with *High and Low*, when I thought you'd cut ties, you actually waded in deeper and even took a seat on Kurosawa Pro's board, so Mr. Yasumi and I couldn't ask you... I mean about that Agency for Cultural Affairs film theater and studio. With Mr. Yasumi as the king, and you and I as the rooks, there's nothing to fear in the world. But without you, we were short on pieces...one key piece short no matter how we looked at it."

Starting around 1968, the year the Agency for Cultural Affairs was established, Mr. Yasumi and I held meetings with the bureau to create a national film theater and a national film studio on the same schedule.

Mr. Toshio Yasumi and the first director of the Agency for Cultural Affairs, Mr. Hidemi Kon, enjoyed a close relationship, and they had discussed in absolute secrecy how the Japanese film industry (the conditions of film production), heading towards decay and collapse, might be developed in such a way as to lead it to prosperity. They reached the following agreement.

For the time being—before anything else, the most pressing issue was the construction of a national film theater and a modern national film studio outfitted with the newest equipment. Moreover, an accompanying film bank (investment banking for films) was also critical.

Mr. Kenji Adachi, the second agency director, took up this reform proposal overseeing the film industry's near future from Mr. Hidemi Kon, the first director, and affixed a budget to it, having already dispatched two delegates from the agency to Italy's Cinecittà national studio for a comprehensive tour. The rest, persuading industry managers and executives to accept and consent...fell to Mr. Yasumi and myself.

(From the directorial side, on the recommendation of Mr. Kurosawa and Mr. Keisuke Kinoshita, Masaki Kobayashi of the Four Horsemen Club joined us as a committee member, but partway through he stopped showing up, and so it was Mr. Yasumi and me who went around to each of the film company offices.)

The only one opposed to a national film theater was Chairman Kido of Shochiku, and the rest of the film companies were indifferent to the idea, neither for nor against it (because of our schedules, Toei was the only company we couldn't visit). Mr. Kido's objection was that, with the establishment of a national live performance theater, kabuki actors' schedules had become tight and that it was a major hassle for Shochiku. We didn't need a national theater for cinema too; his opposition was merely emotional. As for the executives at the other companies, they had no opinions beyond the fact that since we already had a national live performance theater, it made sense to have one for cinema too, and none of them opposed the establishment of a national film theater.

The responses to a national film studio, however, were complicated. Each company had its own production policies and studio philosophies, and it was anyone's guess how they might be affected by the existence of a national studio. Nikkatsu wanted their studio bought whole if the government was going to create one.

It was at this point that Toho's Iwao Mori told us he wanted to speak with us directly, so Mr. Yasumi and I went to Toho's headquarters.

"This is the response from Toho on the issue of the Agency for Cultural Affairs' national studio."

As Mr. Yasumi and I remained silent, Mr. Mori barged ahead.

"If such a studio would benefit the future of Japanese cinema, it would be a fine thing, and Yasumi-sensei and Mr. Hashimoto would have accomplished something good. However, Toho has opinions, or rather conditions, concerning the studio."

Mr. Yasumi and I sat unspeaking and unmoving.

"If a strike breaks out at Toho's Kinuta studio thanks to the construction of this national studio, Yasumi-sensei and Mr. Hashimoto, the two of you will deal with it and attend to all the consequences… Are we agreed?"

Startled, I looked at Mr. Yasumi, whose cheek was twitching.

"Are we agreed?" Toho's Iwao Mori insisted. "If the two of you will assume responsibility, Toho is in favor of a national film studio. However, if you will not, Toho is opposed to its establishment."

When Mr. Yasumi and I left Toho headquarters, we headed to the coffee shop directly ahead. We were both sunk in silence, our spirits terribly heavy.

"Hashimoto, what should we do?"

"This has become a bit difficult."

Mr. Yasumi had a leaden expression on his face. I had only ever heard about strikes, so I didn't know much about them, but Mr. Yasumi and Mr. Mori had experienced the Toho Dispute. The occupying American forces' tanks had surrounded the Kinuta studio, and the Great Toho Strike, disquieting, simmering with violence, was considered the largest one since the war. The memory of it still too fresh for the participants, just hearing the word "strike" brought forth a visceral distaste and anxiety that made them skittish and drained all ambition.

Well, it wasn't as though I didn't feel a touch of anxiety myself. Our country's film companies were entertainment businesses with many theatrical holdings, and they had their choice of films from around the world to screen in them. There was no need to gamble on risky films made at their own studios, shrinking production departments was an unavoidable prospect, and there were even rumors that these might be cut loose. A national studio coming into existence might be taken as a good opportunity for layoffs. Not only Toho's Kinuta studio, but Shochiku's Ofuna and Toei's Oizumi studios feared the possibility of strikes.

Moreover, given that Toho's Mr. Mori was mouthing such words, Eiren (the Motion Picture Producers Association of Japan) would follow his clarion call, adopt opposition as its unified stance, and pit the film industry's entire might in an unbending front against the establishment of a national film studio.

"It's probably going to be difficult to get a studio," I sounded out Mr. Yasumi.

"All right, Hashimoto... I guess we go for just the national film theater."

"But if we create only a film theater, it's like plowing the field and forgetting the seeds."

"Too bad... I guess we'll have to forget about the film theater, too."

I came to a realization inside my spinning head. Had Mr. Kikushima been with us... The gung-ho, never-give-up Mr. Kikushima would have calmly spouted, "Toho's Iwao Mori mooning us is no reason to back down. What does a strike at a film company have to do with a national studio? In general, the problem with film companies is that they think only of their own convenience. If flies swarm around them, they need to wave them away with their own hands. So what if Eiren rallies and builds a united front? We have the backing of the government of Japan... With sensei (Mr. Yasumi) at the head and Hashimoto on our side, we can hang in there to the bitter end and bring about both the theater and the studio and make those film company guys cry."

In fact, had Mr. Kikushima shouldered some of the weight from the beginning, Mr. Yasumi would not have lost his fight. For a man who'd long since abandoned selfish desires, and who wished only for the prosperity of the film industry and slaved to that end, there was no reason to back down now. But with just the two of us—I had some confidence that with Mr. Kikushima we could have overcome the situation.

Mr. Kikushima and I were a tight, harsh tag team, one playing the good cop and the other the bad cop, roles we got used to during organizational negotiations with Eiren and Minporen (the National Association of Commercial Broadcasters in Japan) until we were experts at concluding most any deal on desirable terms. Yet, alone, without a partner, I couldn't dance the dance, and this was the limit—there was nothing more to be done.

"Mr. Yasumi, maybe we have no choice but to let it go."

"Then I'll take care of things with the Agency of Cultural Affairs, so there's nothing in particular you need to do."

"Yup...there's nothing."

"How much have you told Mr. Kurosawa?"

"I told him about the film theater. But I didn't mention the studio."

"What did he say?"

"He said we absolutely need a national film theater, that without one we cannot hold an authoritative, formal international film festival in To-kyo, so do whatever you can to get it built. As for the studio...he has too many dreams. L-shaped stages, high stages for angled shots, stages with sets like drawers. I worried that if I told him, he'd get all serious and take point and fall prey to the mass media...so I didn't share the studio idea."

"Hmph."

"But Mr. Yasumi, it really is too bad, isn't it... I'd meant to ask Mr. Kurosawa to lead the national film studio."

"Huh? Kurosawa? Kurosawa would never agree to that."

"Actually, it would work out fine. Like I said, he has too many dreams about studios. Well...at first he might say, 'Me, lead a studio? You must be joking.' But soon it will be, 'Shinobu Hashimoto, head of planning... Ryuzo Kikushima, head of production... I have no choice but to lead that studio, eh?'"

Mr. Yasumi afforded a smile. It was the sour smile of someone track-ing a large fish that's slipped out of his hands, a stupefied and resigned sourness. Shooting stars have long tails. "Japan's national film studio, led by Akira Kurosawa... That would have worked."

There at Toho University Hospital—there at the bedside of the critically ill Mr. Kikushima, I sat muttering to myself. As before, Mr. Kikushima was breathing in short, rapid gasps.

"Mr. Kikushima...if only you hadn't gotten so involved with Team Kurosawa, a national film theater and studio wouldn't have stayed just a dream."

"Ah...ah..."

My mutterings, sometimes audible and sometimes unvoiced, were in-stinctual ruminations, a throbbing of the heart, a gnashing of teeth—they had no meaning to others and could only be uttered to Mr. Kikushima. I had always wanted, no matter what, to tell Mr. Kikushima.

It was all rather confused and incoherent though, my accusations and complaints falling into a long monologue, only to return to accusations and complaints again.

"If we had created a national studio... I would have been the head of planning, and you, Mr. Kikushima, would have overseen producers as the head of production, and Mr. Kurosawa would have been our superior, the studio chief, overseeing directors... From this studio might have come writers surpassing you and me, and second and third Akira Kurosawas surpassing Mr. Kurosawa as a director...yet it doesn't necessarily follow that Japanese cinema would improve or prosper."

Mr. Kikushima, I was betting something different on this studio. My goal was cinematic freedom, liberalization... Mr. Kikushima, is cinema truly a liberalized product? I don't think so. It's a kind of controlled merchandise. Why, you ask? Aren't all movie tickets the same price? The contents and scale of each film are different. Would it be so strange to have 300-yen [three-dollar] films, 500-yen films, 1,000-yen films, and others you pay two, three, or five thousand yen to watch?

Moreover, there are time constraints on these equally priced movies, a timeframe of between one and a half and two hours into which the structure of every story must fit.

In the period when the five film studios had weekly double features and produced innumerable films, the planning department gasped for air saying there weren't enough projects. But even today, here at the nadir when the number of films produced has fallen dramatically compared to the peak, producers and planning supervisors continually bemoan the lack of projects. In any period, we're chronically starved of plans for films.

Why is that? Because we've standardized their length. With fiction, you have three different modes: the short story, the novella, and the novel. But there are no short stories or novels for cinema, which is fixed and limited constantly to that medium length. Yet, it's not as if film works can't stand unless they're novellas.

A taut film filled with content, only 30 or 40 minutes to an hour long, would maintain its tension far better than your average slack-paced film. The sense of release after watching it would be pleasant and enjoyable and have strengths at the box-office level.

Because admission prices are uniform, the industry considers it a matter of service to have long films and outright rejects shorter ones, not even glancing in their direction. As such, if we were to abolish the uniform pricing system and set ticket prices appropriate to the films, it would be completely possible, on the business level, to make short works, and the brief screening time and quick turnaround might provide better returns.

At the same time, lifting the ban on short films would bring fresh energy and liveliness to the production side. The number of projects would increase dramatically. There are huge numbers of prose short stories that sit waiting, untouched.

(Since I happened to debut with *Rashomon*, I at least skimmed over Ryunosuke Akutagawa's oeuvre. If short stories could be made into films, then even Akutagawa, who wasn't prolific, provides material for a couple of dozen works, and with other writers added to the mix, the number of plans seems astronomical.)

If there's one thing you can say with certainty about short works, as stocks of past writing to be adapted are depleted, original screenplays will proliferate at a rapid rate. A different beast dramatically and compositionally, they need none of that bothersome "*kishotenketsu*" four-box structure that's so indispensable for novella-length works. They can be told in three movements, intro, event, go, a one-two-three! pattern.

Through this kind of revolution in scenario writing, it would become easy to extract the drama concealed within various social phenomena. Thanks to the speed with which an idea is implemented, dramas that had been difficult to concretize would issue one after another, and cinema would enter into an entirely new era of activity.

This new system of abolishing timeframes and uniform ticket pricing wouldn't just give birth to newfangled, appealing short forms but also fundamentally change and transform long-form film production.

An author's best fiction often tend to be novels, but there are hardly any examples of proper adaptations. The vast majority of them are limited to one film so they're little more than massively truncated digests of the original. In some cases it's done in two parts, but even if a novel is extended over two films, it's the same difference, and the fact remains that the story is altered as a result of eliminating large amounts of it.

For example, *Gone With the Wind* is considered a classic among films.

"But Mr. Kikushima, that's a lie… In truth, it's a big insipid blob, isn't it?"

People who have read the original and are familiar with its content know the characters' roles and how the story unfolds, and the point is not enjoying cinema itself; rather, seeing the film is just somewhat useful in recalling the original's appeal.

If you hadn't read the original and didn't know its content at all, would it really be interesting as a movie? The only way to make a novel's adaptation interesting is to avoid cutting the story and to put the particulars on screen, and in the case of *Gone With the Wind*, you'd need six to eight two-hour films. Only if it's made in such a way, without omissions, can the moving line at the end, "After all, tomorrow is another day," leap out to the audience's hearts with an impact that fiction could not match.

You can't abridge novels… Based on the original's full girth and sense of weight, you'd calculate how many two-hour films would be appropriate and systematically produce them. That's how you'd make a long work if uniform ticket pricing and time constraints were eliminated… Mr. Kikushima, I know you can tell. The question with this kind of screenplay would be how many films it would take, and if you could just get that out of the way, the drama would be quite easy to adapt. The work would be pleasant, and the writing fun. At the same time, if this process and direction were to become established, there would be an almost inexhaustible supply of long-term projects.

If we stopped charging a flat fee for movie tickets, and at the same time the timeframe ceased to exist, films would diversify and liberalize, and there would be short stories, novellas, and novels, and no way of running out of projects. A whole host of ambitious and challenging works would stand a chance of going into circulation, and we'd witness unprecedented energy in the world of cinema.

But this is—nothing more than the naïve fantasy of one scenario writer, and in fact it's not so simple.

The film companies of our country have production departments, but these are humble enclaves that you could easily miss, and the reality is that the companies have extensive movie-house holdings that they operate as a firm—they're theater bosses.

It was the custom for theater operators to charge a flat admission rate since the beginning of cinema, and far from being contradictory or irrational, the practice poses no obstacles or inconveniences on the business side. Charging different prices according to the film is too out there to be taken seriously given the instability and fresh risks. Such a proposal, pearl for swine, a dialogue with extra-terrestrials, would fall on deaf ears…and in the end they would treat you like an idiot and shoo you away.

Before my eyes arose a towering barrier, a giant, precipitous mountain range.

"But…if we had a national film studio and a national film theater, Mr. Kikushima…the view would change considerably. Ambitious short and long films would be planned and produced, one after the other, at the national studio, completely independent of the film companies… That's to say, we wouldn't use their theaters at all, but directly screen all the finished works at the national film theater."

"Ah…ah…"

Mr. Kikushima twisted his neck left and right, continuing to breathe in gasps. I didn't know if he was aware of me at all, only that there seemed to be a sudden flicker of strength in his pupils when he sometimes looked at me.

"This national film theater, Mr. Kikushima, it would be a huge theater with medium- and small-sized auditoriums and the latest equipment, a new hall of fame of Japanese cinema bathing in the limelight. Ambitious short and long films would be priced according to each film and released there… The impact would be enormous, and with the right box-office clout and resulting influence, it would diversify and liberalize the film world, o-or serve as the bridgehead… In this way, ahead of the rest of the world's film industries, a cinematic revolution…the diversification and liberalization of cinema kicks off at Japan's national film studio, with you, me, and Mr. Kurosawa presiding."

Mr. Kikushima turned his head slightly with a pained look, scrunching his face, clenching his teeth, and closing his eyes, and tears glistened at the corners of his eyes. My heart flared with emotion. Mr. Kikushima knew who I was, and he had understood most of what I had said.

I wiped my tears with a fist.

"But it was…it was all a dream." I continued to wipe my tears. "The Agency for Cultural Affairs…had already procured land for the film theater, so they didn't accept the news easily. Though they tabled the national film studio, they didn't want to give up on the national film theater. Mr. Yasumi had to keep telling them no, that he couldn't obtain industry consent, until the agency eventually gave up. An opera organization had been campaigning for the establishment of an opera house…so it will become one (today a part of Tokyo's Opera City in Nishi-Shinjuku, in Shinjuku Ward)… I-It was all…"

I still had so many things I wanted to say, but due to my overflowing tears no more words would come.

Mr. Kikushima left this world—on March 18, 1989, six days after I visited the hospital.

Hideo Oguni

Master Oguni departed from this world seven years after Mr. Kikushima, on February 5, 1996. He was ninety-one years old at the time of his death.

Master had been a member of novelist Saneatsu Mushanokoji's utopian New Village, so his ashes were interred in a mausoleum in the southeast part of the village, in Moroyama Town, Iruma County, Saitama Prefecture, alongside Mushanokoji and others.

I'm an infirm, senile old man, but I can more or less drive a car, so at the beginning of spring I go to Ogose in Saitama to see the plum blossoms, and since Moroyama is only a short detour from there, I sometimes enter New Village and find myself standing in front of the mausoleum in the southeast.

There's something I recall every time I stand in front of Master Oguni's ashes.

This was during *Seven Samurai.* One evening after we'd finished work, Master Oguni, his cup of whisky and water sitting on the table, suddenly said, "Hashimoto... I'm going to say this to you in place of the late Mansaku (Mansaku Itami)."

I sat up straight, surprised. Something like electricity shot through my body at the mention of my master.

"Are you listening? There are three kinds of scenario writers. Those who hold their pencil by their fingertips and write smoothly with just their fingers, and those who hold their pencil by their fingertips and write not just with their fingers but with the strength of their palm. Most are either of those two kinds...but you write with your elbow, with the strength of your arm."

"..."

"There's no one in Japan who can rival you in arm strength. But thanks to that brawn, you create impossible or unnatural situations. When you succeed you get cheers and applause, but there's a much greater possibility of failure." Master Oguni's dentures rattled against his lower jaw as he concluded, "In scenarios, there's winter, then spring, then summer,

239

Hideo Oguni (left, 1904-96) and Ryuzo Kikushima (1914-89)

and autumn comes... That's the way to write."

I looked at Mr. Kurosawa, startled. His whiskey glass in hand, Mr. Kurosawa was holding his breath and staring at Master. Even more than me, the recipient of this advice, Mr. Kurosawa was gazing steadily, short of breath, at Master Oguni.

It's possible that Master Oguni's words weren't directed just at me, but at Mr. Kurosawa as well.

There was an occurrence thanks to which Master Oguni's words made my heart ache with regret.

The first film produced by Hashimoto Pro, *Castle of Sand*, was a hit, as was the second film, *Mt. Hakkoda*. But the third film, *Lake of Illusions*, was a failure.

The motive behind the plan for *Lake of Illusions* was simple. *Castle of Sand* features a parent and child's journey, the pair walking, and *Mt. Hakkoda* has the Aomori regiment and the Hirosaki regiment walking in the snow—two films back to back with people walking. So next, I wanted to make a film with someone running in it.

Make the runner a girl, that would be cool. Make her a prostitute on the shore of Lake Biwa (at a soapland in Ogoto), that would be cool too. Have her run along the shore with a dog, visually cool. But that dog

240

gets killed and, of all things, the man who kills it comes to her as a client. Enraged, she tries to stab him with the large kitchen knife that he used to kill her dog, and when he flees in a panic, she chases after him.

A girl chases a fleeing man along the Biwa lakeside.

The man has been training so he's a confident runner, and though the girl pursues him desperately, she can't overtake him. But at last, when the man reaches Lake Biwa Bridge, he's unable to continue, and the pursuing girl catches up with him and kills him with one thrust of the knife, avenging her dog—but committing murder, notwithstanding the dramatic flow and momentum, oversteps the limits of the theme, running, and is clearly absurd. Moreover, in addition to her having an actual lover, she's also strongly attracted to another man, an astronaut, and their stories are linked up in a fateful historical tale from the Warring States era. In the last scene, in outer space some 85 km above Earth, the astronaut flies over Lake Biwa Bridge, off which the girl, who murdered the man who slew her dog, seems to have jumped to drown herself. He lays down a flute that has connected them since the Warring States era, and it intersects with the crescent shape of Lake Biwa to form a crucifix. As timeless as the planet's rotation, the flute in the sky above Lake Biwa has a piece of Mino paper attached to it with the girl's name (her nom de guerre) written on it in ink. For Oichi of Ogota—

It's forcibly brought together as a story but is too absurd, and the situations are unnnaturalness plastered on implausibility.

I didn't have any faith in my screenplay, so I had Yoshitaro Nomura read it for me. If Mr. Nomura said it was okay, we'd start filming it, and if he said it was too implausible and likely to fail, I was ready to think better of it and cancel. Mr. Nomura's opinion, however, was that "The brand-new and unprecedented dramatic quality exceeds the scope of customary film sensibilities and theories, so to be honest, I can't really say. I don't think anyone can determine if this script is good or not without seeing the film."

I was at a loss. Master Oguni's words came back to me.

No matter how implausible or unnatural the situation, I could finish the script with sheer brawn, and it would also pass muster on set. But at the final stage, during the film editing, some huge fundamental defect and error would inevitably come to the fore. There were a few intertwined, overlapping layers of them in this particular screenplay.

"Maybe I should have Master Oguni read it."

But I imagined that Master Oguni would immediately and vehemently oppose production of the film. While I fretted, preparations for production proceeded, and unable to back out, we began shooting. The result, a mediocre film haunted by the screenplay's implausibilities, a box-office bomb, was painful defeat.

I always apologized to Master Oguni in front of the mausoleum at New Village, where his ashes rested in peace. "I'm sorry, Master. It was as you said. I ignored your advice and messed up big time…when you went to the trouble of warning me in Itami-sensei's place."

But I always—and at that precise moment, imagined a strange scene.

If Mr. Kurosawa stood where I stood in front of the mausoleum and faced Master Oguni, what might he say? Actually, chances were that he'd mumble words similar to mine.

"Oguni… I'm sorry… *Ran* and *Kagemusha* were both a bit implausible. You know, their situations too forced."

Akira Kurosawa

In March 1995, Mr. Kurosawa collapsed at an inn in Kyoto while he was writing the screenplay for the film *After the Rain*, and he passed away on September 6, 1998.

Collapsing in the middle of writing is the most an artist can wish for, and it was indeed a grand end.

Mr. Kurosawa passed away in the early autumn, two years after Master Oguni departed, so you might say he followed Master into the next world.

So, what exactly was Mr. Kurosawa to me?

Before I try to summarize that, I'd like to line up the films that comprise his fifty-year legacy.

Title	Year	Production Studio	Producer (Planning)	Screenwriter (in credits' order)	Cinematographer (Cooperation)	Assistant Director	Cast
Sanshiro Sugata	1943	Toho	(Keiji Matsuzaki)	Akira Kurosawa	Akira Mimura	Hitoshi Usami, Toshio Sugie, Seki Nakamura	Susumu Fujita, Denjiro Okochi, Ryunosuke Tsukigata, Yukiko Todoroki, Ranko Hanai
The Most Beautiful	1944	Toho	Hitoshi Usami (Motohiko Ito)	Akira Kurosawa	Jyoji Obara	Hitoshi Usami, Hiromichi Horikawa	Yoko Yaguchi, Takashi Shimura, Takako Irie, Ichiro Sugai
Sanshiro Sugata Part II	1945	Toho	Motohiko Ito	Akira Kurosawa	Takeo Ito	Takehiro Aoki, Hitoshi Usami, Hiromichi Horikawa	Susumu Fujita, Denjiro Okochi, Ryunosuke Tsukigata, Yukiko Todoroki, Akitake Kono
The Men Who Tread on the Tiger's Tail	1945	Toho	Motohiko Ito	Akira Kurosawa	Takeo Ito	Hitoshi Usami	Denjiro Okochi, Susumu Fujita, Kenichi Enomoto, Tadayoshi Nishina, Masayuki Mori, Takashi Shimura
No Regrets for Our Youth	1946	Toho	Keiji Matsuzaki	Eijiro Hisaita	Asakazu Nakai	Hiromichi Horikawa, Akitoshi Maeda, Masaru Horiuchi	Setsuko Hara, Denjiro Okochi, Susumu Fujita, Akitake Kono
One Wonderful Sunday	1947	Toho	Sojiro Motoki	Keinosuke Uekusa	Asakazu Nakai	Tsuneo Kobayashi, Zenju Imaizumi	Isao Numasaki, Chieko Nakakita
Drunken Angel	1948	Toho	Sojiro Motoki	Keinosuke Uekusa, Akira Kurosawa	Takeo Ito	Tsuneo Kobayashi	Takashi Shimura, Toshiro Mifune, Reizaburo Yamamoto, Yoshiko Kuga
The Quiet Duel	1949	Daiei	(Hisao Ichikawa, Sojiro Motoki)	Akira Kurosawa, Senkichi Taniguchi	Soichi Aisaka	Baiya Nakamura, Takumi Furukawa, Fumiki Saijo	Toshiro Mifune, Takashi Shimura, Miki Sanjo, Noriko Sengoku
Stray Dog	1949	Film Art Association = Shin-Toho	Sojiro Motoki	Akira Kurosawa, Ryuzo Kikushima	Asakazu Nakai	Ishiro Honda, Zenju Imaizumi	Toshiro Mifune, Takashi Shimura, Keiko Awaji, Isao Kimura
Scandal	1950	Shochiku	Takashi Koide (Sojiro Motoki)	Akira Kurosawa, Ryuzo Kikushima	Toshio Ubukata	Teruo Hagiyama, Keizaburo Kobayashi, Yoshitaro Nomura	Toshiro Mifune, Yoshiko Yamaguchi, Takashi Shimura, Yoko Katsuragi
Rashomon	1950	Daiei	Jingo Minoura (Sojiro Motoki)	Akira Kurosawa, Shinobu Hashimoto	Kazuo Miyagawa	Yasushi Kato, Mitsuo Wakasugi, Tokuzo Tanaka	Toshiro Mifune, Machiko Kyo, Masayuki Mori, Takashi Shimura

Title	Year	Production Studio	Producer (Planning)	Screenwriter (in credits' order)	Cinematographer (Cooperation)	Assistant Director	Cast
The Idiot	1951	Shochiku	Takashi Koide (Sojiro Motoki)	Eijiro Hisaita, Akira Kurosawa	Toshio Ubukata	Teruo Hagiyama, Keizaburo Kobayashi, Yoshitaro Nomura	Masayuki Mori, Toshiro Mifune, Setsuko Hara, Yoshiko Kuga
Ikiru	1952	Toho	Sojiro Motoki	Akira Kurosawa, Shinobu Hashimoto, Hideo Oguni	Asakazu Nakai	Hisanobu Marubayashi, Hiromichi Horikawa, Teruo Maru	Takashi Shimura, Miki Odagiri, Yunosuke Ito, Nobuo Kaneko
Seven Samurai	1954	Toho	Sojiro Motoki	Akira Kurosawa, Shinobu Hashimoto, Hideo Oguni	Asakazu Nakai	Hiromichi Horikawa, Katsuya Shimizu, Sakae Hirosawa	Takashi Shimura, Toshiro Mifune, Isao Kimura, Keiko Tsushima
I Live in Fear	1955	Toho	Sojiro Motoki	Shinobu Hashimoto, Hideo Oguni, Akira Kurosawa	Asakazu Nakai	Hisanobu Marubayashi, Samaji Nonagase, Yasuyoshi Tajitsu	Toshiro Mifune, Eiko Miyoshi, Takashi Shimura, Akemi Negishi
Throne of Blood	1957	Toho	Akira Kurosawa, Sojiro Motoki	Hideo Oguni, Shinobu Hashimoto, Ryuzo Kikushima, Akira Kurosawa	Asakazu Nakai	Samaji Nonagase, Katsuya Shimizu, Yasuyoshi Tajitsu	Toshiro Mifune, Isuzu Yamada, Minoru Chiaki, Chieko Naniwa, Takamaru Sasaki
The Lower Depths	1957	Toho	Akira Kurosawa	Akira Kurosawa, Hideo Oguni	Ichio Yamasaki	Samaji Nonagase, Yasuyoshi Tajitsu, Yoshimitsu Banno	Toshiro Mifune, Isuzu Yamada, Kyoko Kagawa, Ganjiro Nakamura, Koji Mitsui
The Hidden Fortress	1958	Toho	Masumi Fujimoto, Akira Kurosawa	Ryuzo Kikushima, Hideo Oguni, Shinobu Hashimoto, Akira Kurosawa	Ichio Yamasaki	Samaji Nonagase, Yasuyoshi Tajitsu, Yoshimitsu Banno	Toshiro Mifune, Misa Uehara, Minoru Chiaki, Kamatari Fujiwara
The Bad Sleep Well	1960	Kurosawa Production = Toho	Tomoyuki Tanaka, Akira Kurosawa	Hideo Oguni, Eijiro Hisaita, Akira Kurosawa, Ryuzo Kikushima, Shinobu Hashimoto	Yuzuru Aizawa	Shiro Moritani, Yoshimitsu Banno, Kiyoshi Nishimura	Toshiro Mifune, Kyoko Kagawa, Masayuki Mori, Tatsuya Mihashi
Yojimbo	1961	Kurosawa Production = Toho	Tomoyuki Tanaka, Ryuzo Kikushima	Ryuzo Kikushima, Akira Kurosawa	Kazuo Miyagawa	Shiro Moritani, Masanobu Deme, Yasuhiro Yoshimatsu	Toshiro Mifune, Tatsuya Nakadai, Eijiro Tono, Isuzu Yamada, Yoko Tsukasa, Daisuke Kato

Title	Year	Production Studio	Producer (Planning)	Screenwriter (in credits' order)	Cinematographer (Cooperation)	Assistant Director	Cast
Sanjuro	1962	Kurosawa Production = Toho	Tomoyuki Tanaka, Ryuzo Kikushima	Ryuzo Kikushima, Hideo Oguni, Akira Kurosawa	Fukuzo Koizumi, Takao Saito	Shiro Moritani, Yoichi Matsue, Masanobu Deme	Toshiro Mifune, Tatsuya Nakadai, Yuzo Kayama, Takako Irie
High and Low	1963	Kurosawa Production = Toho	Tomoyuki Tanaka, Ryuzo Kikushima	Hideo Oguni, Ryuzo Kikushima, Eijiro Hisaita, Akira Kurosawa	Asakazu Nakai, Takao Saito	Shiro Moritani, Yoichi Matsue, Masanobu Deme	Toshiro Mifune, Tatsuya Nakadai, Tsutomu Yamazaki, Kyoko Kagawa
Red Beard	1965	Kurosawa Production = Toho	Tomoyuki Tanaka, Ryuzo Kikushima	Masato Ide, Hideo Oguni, Ryuzo Kikushima, Akira Kurosawa	Asakazu Nakai, Takao Saito	Shiro Moritani, Yoichi Matsue, Masanobu Deme	Toshiro Mifune, Yuzo Kayama, Kyoko Kagawa, Terumi Niki
Dodes'ka-den	1970	Shiki no Kai = Toho	Akira Kurosawa, Yoichi Matsue (Shiki no Kai)	Akira Kurosawa, Hideo Oguni, Shinobu Hashimoto	Takao Saito, Yasumichi Fukuzawa	Kenjiro Omori, Yoshisuke Kawasaki, Koji Hashimoto	Yoshitaka Zushi, Junzaburo Ban, Tatsuo Matsumura, Atsushi Watanabe
Dersu Uzala	1975	Mosfilm	Nikolay Sizovb, Yoichi Matsue	Akira Kurosawa, Yuriy Nagibin	Asakazu Nakai, Yuriy Gantman, Fyodor Dobronravov	Vladimir Vasilev, Norio Minoshima	Yuriy Solomin, Maksim Munzuk
Kagemusha	1980	Kurosawa Production = Toho Pictures	Akira Kurosawa, Tomoyuki Tanaka	Akira Kurosawa, Masato Ide	Takao Saito, Shoji Ueda (Kazuo Miyagawa, Asakazu Nakai)	Fumisuke Okada, Hideyuki Inoue, Takao Okawara	Tatsuya Nakadai, Kenichi Hagiwara, Jinpachi Nezu, Tsutomu Yamazaki
Ran	1985	Herald Ace = Greenwich Film Productions	Katsumi Furukawa, Serge Silberman, Masato Hara	Akira Kurosawa, Hideo Oguni, Masato Ide	Takao Saito, Shoji Ueda (Asakazu Nakai)	Fumisuke Okada, Takashi Koizumi, Ichiro Yamamoto	Tatsuya Nakadai, Hisashi Igawa, Peter, Mieko Harada, Daisuke Ryu, Hitoshi Ueki
Dreams	1990	Kurosawa Production	Hisao Kurosawa, Yoshio Inoue	Akira Kurosawa	Takao Saito, Shoji Ueda (Kazumi Hara)	Takashi Koizumi, Okihiro Yoneda, Naohito Sakai	Akira Terao, Hisashi Igawa, Chishu Ryu, Mieko Harada
Rhapsody in August	1991	Kurosawa Production	Toru Okuyama, Hisao Kurosawa	Akira Kurosawa	Takao Saito, Shoji Ueda	Takashi Koizumi, Okihiro Yoneda, Naohito Sakai	Sachiko Murase, Hidetaka Yoshioka, Richard Gere
Madadayo	1993	Daiei = Dentsu = Kurosawa Production	Yasuyoshi Tokuma, Gohei Kogure, Hisao Kurosawa	Akira Kurosawa	Takao Saito, Shoji Ueda	Takashi Koizumi, Okihiro Yoneda, Naohito Sakai	Tatsuo Matsumura, Kyoko Kagawa, Hisashi Igawa, George Tokoro, Hidetaka Yoshioka

He made thirty films in all, and with the exception of the early *Sanshiro Sugata* and its sequel *Sanshiro Sugata Part II*, each was completely different, and there's not one film that's like any of the others. There's so much variation you're almost appalled, each film different in hue, form, and even scent, and taken together they're like a beautiful kaleidoscope.

(Mr. Kurosawa's name isn't listed in the screenplays for *No Regrets for Our Youth* and *One Beautiful Sunday*, but as I noted in the beginning, Mr. Kurosawa just removed his name out of politeness when the screenplays were finished, and the truth is that they were substantially collaborative screenplays. Also, the writers' names weren't listed (ordered) according to their level of contribution to the film, but rather reflected the feelings of the person who wrote the names on the top sheet when the screenplay was finished. If Mr. Kurosawa wrote it, he would either leave out his own name or put it at the very end, and if someone else wrote it, Mr. Kurosawa's name came at the top...the point being that the level of contribution and order of names weren't interrelated. It was nothing more than an indication that all of the writers had equal rights and responsibilities concerning the work.)

To judge from the variety of Mr. Kurosawa's films, from their utter lack of similarity or resemblance to one another, I think we can say that in a nutshell he was a filmmaker and a writer who went all out in pushing himself to diversify his output.

He absolutely would not make a film that was similar to or resembled another one. In order to pursue this kind of diversity, he needed a roster of many dissimilar writers, and all in all it could be said that his methodology, from a writer leading off to the straight-to-final draft, as well as his transformation from craftsman to artist, came from a desire to make diverse films.

Thus making films that each differed in tone, gambling everything on his material and sparing no effort, his unflagging pursuit of diversity sedimenting—it was after nearly half a century of directorial history, at the age of eighty, that he finally arrived at the *Dreams* stage.

Furthermore, *Rashomon* was one hour and 28 minutes, while *Seven Samurai* was three hours and 27 minutes. *Rashomon* was a short story of not quite an hour and a half, and *Seven Samurai* was a novel of over three hours; Akira Kurosawa works not only aimed at diversity but also had liberalization in their sights, an escape from the novella (four-box structure). If his will to liberalize had been a little stronger and more concrete, and if the film world itself had acknowledged it—his oeuvre might have been a far more elegant mosaic, a three-dimensional mountain range.

The national film theater and national film studio of my dreams was for the express purpose of diversifying and liberalizing cinema—yet, while no doubt this was a notion and thirst arising from my own decade or two of studying the business, it's also true that Akira Kurosawa's person and films had an outsized influence.

But putting aside these problems inherent to cinema, for the most part his influence had a direct bearing on the particulars of writing scenarios, the how-to, in a way that opened my eyes to my own practical skills—immeasurably important treasures.

I had been an arrogant scenario writer.

Working with Mr. Kurosawa, I had my eyes on him but intended to overtake him soon enough, to leave him in my wake as a scenario writer. I didn't doubt even a bit that it was just a matter of time, that the day wasn't far away.

On the first day of *Seven Samurai*, however, I was stunned when I saw Mr. Kurosawa's thick college notebook. From the main character Kambei on down, he had written out the traits and behavior of each of the seven in detail, with illuminating drawings here and there, in an extraordinary effort, no, an obsession for fleshing out the characters.

At this rate, forget surpassing him, I'd have to try my hardest just to keep up.

In order to overtake him, I'd have to carve the characters out more meticulously and thoroughly than he did...but I couldn't draw, so how would I make up for that handicap? As long as I couldn't substitute something for it, there was no way I could do anything like surpass him.

In any case, I had to come up with some method...

When *Seven Samurai* was finished and I returned to Tokyo, I threw myself into the "Yamanote Line method."

When you get on the Yamanote Line and sit down, you see people lined up in the seats opposite or hanging on to straps around you. People's faces are interesting things... There are faces that are camera-worthy and faces that are pointless to frame. When I came across the sort of face that would breathe and light up in a camera's frame, I observed it thoroughly, committing to memory not just the person's facial features but body type as well. Then I imagined the person in a variety of situations, the full range of human emotions, and got off the train at the same station and followed him or her up to the ticket gate. I didn't exit myself though, instead sending the person off until I could no longer see his or her receding figure. Then I snapped a shutter deep in my bosom, connected the station to the person's profile, and packed it away in the storehouse of my brain.

Then, if it was the inner circle of the Yamanote Line, I got on the outer circle in search of that next person.

I repeated this at spare moments during work, continuing for about a year, and came up with a storehouse of about sixty or seventy male and female profiles, an average of three people each for twenty-three stops on the Yamanote Line (Tokyo, Ueno, Ikebukuro, Shinjuku, and Shibuya have a lot of transferring passengers and only a diluted sense of people's lives, so I excluded those five stations).

It took time and effort, but it was a convenient storehouse and a great treasure.

When I started on a work, I would look up a character by station name, selecting the perfect person and assigning the role to him or her (for example, if I needed a athletic male in his late twenties, then starting at Uguisudani and going around to Nippori, Tabata, Komagoe, Sugamo, I'd find the right person within five to ten stations, and the bulk of the characterization for a work took only a half-loop or one loop around the Yamanote Line). On top of that, since I'd already carved out the character with the real person and it came back to me, I didn't need to start from the ground up. In most cases the person obligingly stepped into the role, and for someone like me, who couldn't draw, relying on real images was a great boon.

The first film for which I used the "Yamanote Line method" was *Darkness at Noon*.

I was relieved when the film was completed. There was a sinking in, like a settling of my individuality…like I was building milestones by finishing, and stacking up one by one, my works as an individual.

At the same time it also had the thud of an anticlimax. It was as though the things I had clung to stubbornly, unable to let go, had suddenly come unstuck and fallen away. Catching up to Akira Kurosawa as a writer, overtaking him…how tedious…why hustle over such a foolish point? At any rate, I grasped that all of that was utterly pointless.

Our births and upbringings, our tastes and inclinations, and our outlooks on life differed, so there was no chance that we aimed for the same things. Mr. Kurosawa had his way, and I mine, and there was no such thing as surpassing or overtaking—just building up your own self, each work a signpost on your own path of milestones.

Milestones… Anyway, I'm truly grateful for that college notebook, so completely like a nuclear warhead to me. That was what gave birth to the Yamanote Line method, after all.

After that, I changed out the people in the Yamanote Line twice, but for many years the method formed the foundation of my individual works and served me, in my capacity as a craftsman, as one of two wheels, the other being the one-third system I devised (a method of not structuring the entire film but just the first third and starting on the scenario, then structuring the next third and continuing with the scenario, then completing the final third—in short, only vaguely working out the four-box structure in advance and parting the story into thirds).

Darkness at Noon, The Chase, The Great White Tower, Harakiri, I Want to Be a Shellfish, Samurai Banners, The Human Revolution, Japan's Longest Day, Tidal Wave, Castle of Sand, Mt. Hakkoda, etc... All of those nearly eighty film screenplays and a number of television dramas owe to the two systems' organic coupling.

I have an acquaintance (a writer who's my senior) who bluntly gives me his unvarnished opinions.

I've been told, "Maybe because you have twin roads side by side, the series of Kurosawa films and the series of works that are properly yours, your presence suffers from a split focus and is blurry...you lost out in a big way. If you hadn't done Kurosawa films, your own presence would be clearer, larger, no?"

But this is like counting the years of a child who has died. All of it is in the past, and as there are no ifs or but's in the path a person's life has taken, at this late date such a hypothetical perspective doesn't have much meaning for me.

Rather, to give my own unvarnished opinion, I was "born" as Mansaku Itami's only direct disciple and "raised" by Team Kurosawa and its harsh unrelenting discipline; is it right that the series of works by someone nurtured in such a way is merely what it is?

As someone aiming to become a scenario writer, I was fortunate in my circumstances, and there was no better environment or itinerary. Shouldn't the body of works of someone who followed the royal road, the elite course, have more of a bounce, more of a sense of force, a more uniform quality?

I sometimes have days when I feel rather guilty and apologetic towards Mansaku Itami-sensei and Mr. Kurosawa.

I wasn't in Tokyo, but in Kita-Karuizawa, at my eldest daughter's workplace (villa), when I heard to my great shock that Mr. Kurosawa had passed away.

Thanks to one telephone interview after another with newspapers and television programs beginning with the press agency Kyodo News, I was

250

worn out, exhausted. After they had all had a turn I relaxed a bit, went out into the garden, and sat in a chair where the leaves beyond the garden were beginning to turn, there at the foot of Mt. Asama.

Seated by the porch, I counted on my fingers facing a copse of larch trees.

I counted one by one on my fingers, like a vacant somnambulist, looking up at the coloring lacquer and wax trees between the proud branches.

Mr. Kikushima (Ryuzo Kikushima), Ide (Masato Ide), Master Oguni (Hideo Oguni), and before them Kei Uegusa (Keinosuke Uegusa), Mr. Hisaita (Eijiro Hisaita), and now the team leader, Mr. Kurosawa... Apart from me, every writer who had written screenplays for Team Kurosawa had departed for the next world, and not one remained.

I was abandoned, a lonely figure pierced through by the autumn wind.

(Senkichi Taniguchi, who had written *The Quiet Duel* with Mr. Kurosawa, passed away in 2007 after the publication of the hardcover edition of this book, but he had originally been a director and a friend of Mr. Kurosawa's since their assistant director days. Mr. Kurosawa, who had written a few screenplays for Mr. Taniguchi's films, casually asked for his help on *The Quiet Duel*, and given their relationship he couldn't be considered a Team Kurosawa writer.)

Irritated, I suddenly wanted to write and write and write.

But that was impossible. Ever since my right kidney had been removed ten years earlier, I had gone in and out of hospitals for gallstone removal, an inflamed spleen, pulmonary emphysema, chronic bronchitis, an enlarged prostate, etc., and I'd been forced to quit working—I hadn't written, no, since ten years before, couldn't write at all.

When my condition improved, couldn't I...just three twenty-minute sessions per day, for just an hour, sit at a word processor? While it would proceed slower than a snail's pace and, moreover, probably look like torn-up fragments, I'd write about Mr. Kurosawa.

The greatest characteristic of Kurosawa works was the collaborative screenplay, where Mr. Kurosawa didn't write alone but in collaboration with other writers. Since this was a singular work process that took place behind closed doors, its reality was totally opaque to an outsider, nor was it possible to fathom.

Without some degree of understanding of it, however, critiques of Kurosawa films could only ever be superficial and shallow, and further, many aspiring directors and writers dearly wanted its workings revealed.

No, not just for the handful of critics, or folks who aspire to enter the business, but also for the vast, overwhelming number of film fans who like, who love cinema, I wanted to write about the essence of cinema—that it's a show with a mechanism, and that the mechanism is the scenario, and that the scenario exists according to a mechanism of its own, and that what screenplays are meant to be and how they are made and their resulting quality affects and determines the film. No doubt, a direct treatment of how our country's greatest filmmaker, Akira Kurosawa, approached the screenplays of his own films would widen and deepen and give further inflection to people's interest in and enjoyment of films.

As things stood, the truth of the unique collaborative screenplay would forever be buried in darkness and remain unclear. Wasn't it the responsibility of Team Kurosawa's only surviving writer to leave at least an outline or, if not, a fragment?

But I didn't write. I couldn't write. Even though I was a craftsman who'd made my living penning words—no matter how hard I tried, I couldn't scribble a word.

Cabbage fields spread across the expansive highlands.

A rolling field of cabbages stretched beyond belief, and though at Agatsuma River far in the distance a precipice dropped off, to the left was the Azumaya mountain range, the border with Nagano Prefecture, directly ahead were the peaks of the Baragi Highlands, and on the right, above Kusatsu's Shirane mountain range, white clouds that seemed almost painted floated in the boundless sky.

The settlement of Tsumagoi and the streets of Nagano Haramachi lay along the Agatsuma River, at the bottom of the valley, so I couldn't see a single house.

When I got out of the car and stood by the side of the road, I saw nothing ahead but cabbage fields, and to the right and to the left, cabbage fields, and behind, the cabbage fields at the foot of the north slope of Mt. Asama. The only things these highlands had were blowing wind and cabbage, cabbage, nothing but cabbage—the cabbage fields, among the largest in our country, of Gunma Prefecture's Tsumagoi Village.

Past Onioshidashi and its hardened lava erupted from Mt. Asama, a left turn from the agricultural artery road towards the foot of the northern slope brought you to a hill, a little above the Yamanashi Cultivation on the map. It was about thirty minutes from my eldest daughter's workplace and my favorite place in all of Kita-Karuizawa.

I came here two or three times a year as I passed the summer in Kita-Karuizawa, and always before returning to Tokyo. There was no knowing if my condition wouldn't get worse the next year or if I'd still be able to drive somehow to Kita-Karuizawa. It could be my last look, and I wanted to feel the highland breeze and to take in the view just once more.

Throughout the huge cabbage fields were open structures, roofs and nothing more, where the picked cabbages were collected and loaded onto trucks. When the sun was strong, getting out of the car and standing in the shadow of one of those structures promised a cool breeze. The cool, refreshing highland breeze blowing across the foothills of Mt. Asama…an indescribable feeling, a true paradise on earth.

But really, I thought, *nothing is as unfathomable as a human being's lifespan.* I may part from these vast cabbage fields, but I somehow came back the next summer. It had been so for the past few years. Three had transpired since Mr. Kurosawa's passing, and this was the fourth. If my condition stabilized and even improved to a certain extent, it was my intention to write about him and me; my condition remained unstable and didn't improve, and there was no escaping my strength declining with every year I gained.

At this rate, putting together coherent clusters of words would become simply impossible.

I exhaled and looked out from my vantage point over the cabbage fields, to the left, right, and straight ahead. Then I looked up at the 360-degree panorama of sky. The cabbage fields spread far, but the sky was a different order of vast.

Heaven and earth are all too unending. Human beings are all too puny.

I was but a terribly microscopic black bug whose very existence was suspect.

Even if it was just a character or two, I'd put them down when I returned to Tokyo. Sit at my word processor for just three or five minutes. That's how bugs lived—writhing. I couldn't begin because I wanted to see it completed, to see it polished. But it didn't matter if I finished it or not, if I completed it or not. Just doing as much as I could was enough. If I was unable to continue, I'd just quit. If I happened to die in the middle… if I wrote up until the moment I died, as a bug's life goes there could be nothing more satisfying. Either way, just a character, or two, when I returned to Tokyo…

I breathed in a chestful of the refreshing highland breeze. The foothills of Mt. Asama's northern slope undulated endlessly, and the white clouds above Kusatsu's Shirane mountain range to the right stretched and tore as if swept across by a paintbrush—and transformed bit by bit into the cirro-cumulus clouds of autumn.

An army outfitted with breastplates and helms passes under a great gate.

The grand, formidable force kneels as one in the courtyard of a pal-ace, bends, and fires their crossbows.

The entire screen is filled with the sky, sparkling crossbow bolts cascading down like a late-afternoon shower.

I was watching a Chinese film at home on television when my elder daughter, who was visiting me from her own apartment, informed me, "Dad, the director of that film is called the Chinese Akira Kurosawa."

"Hunh, the Chinese Akira Kurosawa?"

My younger daughter, whose husband and kids I lived with, said from behind, "There's also a director in South Korea who's called the Korean Akira Kurosawa."

"Huh, in Korea, too? So there must be second and third Akira Kuro-sawas in Japan?"

My daughters looked at each other and tilted their heads. "In Japan? I feel like I've heard something... I can't quite remember, who was it? There was someone who was said to be the closest filmmaker to Kurosawa."

"Well, that's just dandy, to have Akira Kurosawas here and there and not just in Japan."

For an Akira Kurosawa to appear not just in Japan, but in China and South Korea, was a fine thing for the film world, but as someone who knew the real Akira Kurosawa, I'd like to give some advice and a warning to those promoting producers shrewdly perpetrating PR-jacks, to the peo-ple who are honored as "Kurosawas" themselves, and to their entourage.

Sharp scenes and precocious, affected images might attract people's attention, but that's also the cinematographer's skills, and one can't be called Akira Kurosawa on the basis of partial onscreen phenomena.

The condition for being Akira Kurosawa is, first, to have an excep-tional sensibility and talent and to be someone who can write a screenplay of the highest quality. At the same time, a basic requirement is having three or four writers of the same high level around you and culling a team from amongst them for each of your works; sitting at the same table with one or two of them and battling fiercely over who can write the better version of a scene; and bringing to the film set a collaborative screenplay, created through a unique writing method, and with a high degree of perfection, courtesy of a compound eye.

It's easy to say, but it's no simple thing to meet these standards. Yet, as long as there's a mutual trust and solidarity among the collaborating authors that is resilient enough to overcome difficulties and obstacles, it can be done. Even if you clear this basic hurdle though, there's still something missing.

That's whether or not you have your song.

The "repertoire song" is like a person's unique way of talking, the inflection of one's speech, and everyone has it as a sort of true nature they're born with. The question is whether that "repertoire song" can entice, fascinate, excite, and intoxicate people as much as Akira Kurosawa's did.

Akira Kursoawa had a song.

Straightening his back and sitting tight and proper on his knees on the tatami, he sang on with a faraway look in his eyes, unconsciously and lightly clapping to the beat. The lyrics, in strongly accented Akita dialect, were incomprehensible, but his voice had a luster and spring, it was crisp and dynamic—cheerful and hearty, yet for all of that, rather melancholy. His repertoire was the "Akita folksong."

What moulded each one of the thirty films he directed, from *Sanshiro Suguta* to *Madadayo*, into living, breathing things—it was his repertoire song.

(According to chronologies, he was born on March 23, 1910, at 1-1-50 Oi Town, Ebara County, Tokyo Prefecture near the present-day 3-25 Higashi Oi, Shinagawa Ward, but he definitely told Master Oguni, Mr. Kikushima, and myself that he had been born in Akita and come to Tokyo as a small child.)

There are no doubt many others in the world who can sing the "Akita folksong" better, more skillfully. But the "Akita folksong" he sang had a unique Kurosawa cadence that only he could deliver, skill be damned.

This "song" is a person's own that no one else can possibly imitate.

There will likely be many more exceptional filmmakers to come. Akira Kurosawa, however, was one for the ages, and second and third Kurosawas will never emerge for the rest of eternity.

But—even if there won't be a second or third Akira Kurosawa, there's something I want willing souls to inherit and attempt in future years. And that's the collaborative scripting that Akira Kurosawa practiced.

Kurosawa's films were literally the central pillar that supported Japanese cinema, and the vast majority of those screenplays were collaborative. The exact same thing can be said, however, about the different world of theater (including *bunraku* puppet shows), and not just about cinema.

There is a huge work, a landmark, that has supported Japanese theater from as far back as the Tokugawa period to this day with blockbuster hits. That would be *Chushingura*, the story of the forty-seven avenging ronin; the two works *Yoshitsune and the Thousand Cherry Trees* and *Sugawara and the Secrets of Calligraphy*, though inferior in quality, have enjoyed a comparable level of popularity and track record. These three works, considered the three great masterpieces of Japanese theater and boasting great audience attendance even today, were each collaboratively scripted by Izumo Takeda, Shoraku Miyoshi, and Senryu Namiki.

(One of the works, *Sugawara and the Secrets of Calligraphy*, has four authors due to the participation of Koizumo Takeda, as at that time the original Izumo Takeda was still of this world. When Izumo Takeda passed away, Koizumo or "Izumo the Younger" inherited the mantle, and it was after he became Izumo Takeda II that he wrote *Yoshitsune and the Thousand Cherry Trees* and *Chushingura* with Shoraku Miyoshi and Senryu Namiki.)

Izumo Takeda (father and son), Shoraku Miyoshi, and Senryu Namiki weren't great authors like Monzaemon Chikamatsu or Namboku Tsuruya. The collaborative script was undertaken by the leader of Osaka's Takemotoza, Izumo Takeda, in a desperate bid to save his troupe from dire financial straits after Monzaemon Chikamatsu's illness and death— but they unexpectedly scored a huge success.

Both Japanese film and theater rest on core works that were co-scripted.

Our sensibilities and talents only take us so far. But two heads are better than one, and the greatest feature of both cinema and theater is that you can pool your wisdom and abilities and collaborate on the script. Whether it's to be Team Kurosawa's aforementioned "writer leading off" approach or, depending on the material, a "straight-to-final draft"… No, rather than reinvent the wheel, an entirely new way of writing collaborative screenplays would be quite fine. At any rate, I hope writers pool their wisdom and abilities, backed by mutual trust and solidarity, in order to attempt new kinds of screenplays.

Japanese cinema and theater are both at a dead end, stuck.

In the case of film, the one and only way to reclaim prosperity is through the liberalization of cinema described in the "Ryuzo Kikushima" section, but it's not as though there are no provisional measures.

It's foolish to wait for a sudden mutation, for a genius writer to emerge. The solution must grapple with things as they stand, and for the current crop of writers (not just in Japan, but globally), solo screenplays don't offer a way forward.

A new collaborative screenplay, however, enfolds an unknown

potential for much interesting fare, and when these, overflowing with originality, issue forth—with the cry of a baby being born, directors too can come into the world and grow, and it is then that we will see a second or third Akira Kurosawa surpassing Akira Kurosawa.

Exceptional filmmakers are born only when they're led by exceptional scenarios.

Mr. Kurosawa never wrote New Year's postcards.

Yet, at Christmas he regularly sent Christmas cards to people. On his birthday he invited staff and others with whom he had ties to hold magnificent celebrations. He liked to eat meat far more than fish. These quotidian details suggest a preference for Western or European things over our musty native culture—but his works belied this to a surprising degree.

If you survey his thirty films, somehow they're awfully Japanese.

The long thin island nation of Japan, an archipelago in the vast Pacific Ocean, situated in the subtropics, nevertheless endowed with changes in temperature and humidity and four seasons. Those four seasons... Even though Mr. Kurosawa churned out his works as he pleased, arranged in order they line up curiously well to represent the four seasons and also seem to elucidate his life and career.

At the beginning and end are solo screenplays, but the vast majority of them are collaborative screenplays. The solo works are the buds of spring, the "writer-led-off" collaborations are summer, the "straight-to-final draft" collaborations are autumn, and the return to solo works is a winter of proud solitude.

Spring (buds)	*Sanshiro Sugata, The Most Beautiful, The Men Who Tread on the Tiger's Tail*
Summer (peak)	*One Wonderful Sunday, Drunken Angel Rashomon, Ikiru, Seven Samurai*
Autumn (harvest)	*Yojimbo, Sanjuro, High and Low*
Winter (solitude)	*Dreams, Rhapsody in August, Madadayo*

There's the simple overview, and glancing at it Mr. Kurosawa seems like the most typically Japanese person walking the royal road of cinema according to Japan's four seasons.

At the same time, when you take a step back for a broader view, you can say this as well: all thirty films are connected at a higher level and have a consistent theme.

There are no good people in this world. But there are no evil people either. Everyone lives burdened by good and evil.

Thirty years ago, Yoshitaro Nomura said to me, "For Mr. Kurosawa, Shinobu Hashimoto was a man he should never have encountered."

It flustered me, and losing no time, I panicked.

I had asked him, "For Mr. Kurosawa, what was I…what was Shinobu Hashimoto to him?" hoping for Mr. Nomura to sum up Mr. Kurosawa and myself. The response had been delivered in a sharp and reflexive tone.

I was astonished. If only because I had never even dreamed such a thing, I was dumbfounded. At the time, depending on Mr. Nomura's reply, I'd meant to follow up with another question: "In that case, what was Mr. Kurosawa…what was Akira Kurosawa to me?"

But I was in no shape to, unable to believe my ears at his shocking words. I could only listen in silence as Mr. Nomura gave his well-reasoned argument and panoramic vision of Mr. Kurosawa, how he'd have become a world-class grandmaster even if he hadn't met me, even without *Rashomon* and *Seven Samurai*—I could not get in a word or pose my next question.

As for me though, I've always felt that Mr. Kurosawa was someone I eventually had to encounter…and am glad to have encountered. No, I almost believe that I could not but encounter him and did so as a matter of course.

Mr. Kurosawa and I—our relationship was two people meant to meet indeed meeting and, with our respective eyes (our compound eye), seeing to and through the task at hand at any given moment. That's my only sentiment, but I can't help but feel that all of it was somehow predestined.

If your fate as a human being is about when and where you meet whom, and if it's predestined—then the desire, akin to a dream, to meet someone, the expectation, the throbbing of your heart, is humanity's eternal future-orientation. Sometimes, however, reminiscing and returning to what's been set in stone, to pinned-down fate, is sweeter, and boundless nostalgia achingly pulls at your heartstrings.

When Hashimoto Pro had its office in Shibuya's Sakuragaoka, I commuted every day on the Inokashira Line. Although I liquidated my office when my health declined and I could no longer work, I still go to Shibuya two or three times a week for hospital visits and to shop.

On my commute, and even now, perhaps out of habit, returning from Shibuya on the Inokashira Line I reflexively gaze out the window just

Akira Kurosawa (1910-98) during the filming of *Madadayo* in 1992.

before Shimokitazawa.

Whenever I see, from the Inokashira Line overhead, the top of an out-bound Odakyu train arriving, departing...or looming larger and crossing underneath, I remember the first time I rode the Odakyu train to Komae to meet Mr. Kurosawa.

I close my eyes when the train stops at Shimokitazawa.

In a few years, Shimokitazawa Station will be relocated underground, so Odakyu trains will be completely out of sight of the Inokashira Line. But that's still a few years from now, and I can't imagine I'll still be alive then. In which case, while I live...the Inokashira Line and the Odakyu will keep on intersecting, and that light melody will keep on playing.

Shin-Daita, where I get off, is only one station past Shimokitazawa, and with my eyes closed I hear deep down a faint sound that started upon crossing the Odakyu. That pleasant and rhythmical melody, springing casually on the Odakyu train I took to see Mr. Kurosawa for the first time, plays on today as well—a song that was popular more than seventy years ago, "Tokyo March":

> Shall we to the cinema? Shall we tea?
> Perhaps run away on the Odakyu?
> Changing Shinjuku, that Musashino
> moon shines over your department stores...

THE END

ABOUT THE AUTHOR

Shinobu Hashimoto (1918-2018) came down with consumption during his military training, and it was at the army sanatorium to which he was dispatched that he first became interested in writing movie scripts. While still working at a munitions firm's accounting department, he underwent a tutelage with Mansaku Itami, the leading prewar screenplay writer. Shortly after the war, inspired by his mentor's last words and passing, Hashimoto produced a treatment based on a short story by Ryunosuke Akutagawa, which rising star Akira Kurosawa turned into *Rashomon*. In addition to *Ikiru [To Live]* and *Seven Samurai*, Hashimoto's most intimate collaborations with the writer-director, he was also part of the scripting team for *Throne of Blood* and *The Hidden Fortress*.

His numerous solo screenplays for other directors, such as *Seppuku [Harakiri]* for Masaki Kobayashi, helped establish Hashimoto as Japan's foremost scenarist for the postwar period. In 1959 he made his directorial debut with *I Want To Be a Shellfish*, and in 1973 he set up his own production company and achieved major box-office and critical success with *Castle of Sand*. The many notable screenplays that he continued to pen include *Japan's Longest Day*, *Tidal Wave*, and *The Village of the Eight Graves*. Among his works on cinema, *Compound Cinematics: Akira Kurosawa and I*, a contemporary classic and scenarists' bible, is the first to become available in English.